SHAKESPEARE SURVEY

SHAKESPEARE SURVEY

AN ANNUAL SURVEY OF
SHAKESPEARIAN STUDY & PRODUCTION

5

EDITED BY
ALLARDYCE NICOLL

Issued under the Sponsorship of

THE UNIVERSITY OF BIRMINGHAM
THE UNIVERSITY OF MANCHESTER
THE SHAKESPEARE MEMORIAL THEATRE
THE SHAKESPEARE BIRTHPLACE TRUST

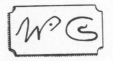

CAMBRIDGE
AT THE UNIVERSITY PRESS
1952

PUBLISHED BY

THE SYNDICS OF THE CAMBRIDGE UNIVERSITY PRESS

London Office: Bentley House, N.W.1
American Branch: New York

Agents for Canada, India, and Pakistan: Macmillan

Printed in Great Britain at the University Press, Cambridge
(Brooke Crutchley, University Printer)

PREFACE

No branch of twentieth-century scholarship has produced more significant results, alike for the student, for the actor and for the general reader, than the combined science and art of bibliography. Through the diverse studies carried out in this field, a surer approach is being made towards the preparation of a text which shall come as close as may be to what Shakespeare intended; and, at the same time, we are being brought considerably nearer to an intimate appreciation of the author's meaning.

To this subject of Shakespeare's text the present volume of *Shakespeare Survey* has been largely devoted. Peter Alexander discusses the editor's problems in general; Georges Bonnard makes a plea for still another edition, especially designed for continental readers; Alice Walker seeks to explain the puzzling relationship between the variant versions of *Othello* printed in quarto in 1622 and in the Folio of 1623; while the problem of *Pericles*, peculiarly complex and fascinating, is discussed by Philip Edwards.

Critical appreciation of Shakespeare's work is represented in this volume by three widely ranging contributions. Both S. L. Bethell and R. A. Foakes endeavour to track a fresh path through the rather perplexing and fashionable new field of 'imagery', each independently suggesting that before we proceed further in this territory we must pause to make sure of our orientation. Problems in the acting of Hamlet form the theme of a series of letters by Christopher Fry.

Special attention may be drawn to the article by Frank Simpson, in which are discussed two hitherto unreproduced drawings made in 1737 by George Vertue. One is a faithful delineation of the monuments in Stratford's church and the other presents the only view, made with any show of authority, of the poet's New Place.

Another library rich in sixteenth- and seventeenth-century literature is described in H. M. Adams's article on Trinity College, Cambridge; while the impact of Shakespeare's writings abroad finds further discussion in essays concerning the dramatist's influence on Pushkin and concerning the performance of his plays on the Flemish stage. For the English theatre Richard David has elected to review three recent productions at the Old Vic. The Shakespeare Memorial Library at Birmingham has provided a record of performances in the United Kingdom during 1950, while the reports of our correspondents collectively give a vivid picture of the widespread interest in his works in divers other countries.

In view of the fact that the Festival year, 1951, has seen numerous productions of Shakespeare's history plays, it is appropriate that the main theme of the next, the sixth, volume of *Shakespeare Survey* should be concerned with various problems relating to these dramas.

Contributions offered for publication in *Shakespeare Survey* should be addressed to:
The Editor, The Shakespeare Institute (University of Birmingham) Stratford-upon-Avon.

CONTENTS

Notes are placed at the end of each contribution

List of Plates . . . . *page* viii

Restoring Shakespeare: The Modern Editor's Task *by* PETER ALEXANDER 1

Suggestions Towards an Edition of Shakespeare for French, German and Other Continental Readers *by* GEORGES A. BONNARD 10

The 1622 Quarto and the First Folio Texts of *Othello by* ALICE WALKER . . . 16

An Approach to the Problem of *Pericles by* PHILIP EDWARDS 25

The Shakespeare Collection in the Library of Trinity College, Cambridge *by* H. M. ADAMS 50

New Place: The Only Representation of Shakespeare's House, from an Unpublished Manuscript *by* FRANK SIMPSON 55

Letters to an Actor Playing Hamlet *by* CHRISTOPHER FRY 58

Shakespeare's Imagery: The Diabolic Images in *Othello by* S. L. BETHELL . . . 62

Suggestions for a New Approach to Shakespeare's Imagery *by* R. A. FOAKES . . 81

Shakespeare's Influence on Pushkin's Dramatic Work *by* TATIANA A. WOLFF . . 93

Shakespeare on the Flemish Stage of Belgium, 1876–1951 *by* D. DE GRUYTER and WAYNE HAYWARD 106

International Notes 111

Shakespeare Productions in the United Kingdom: 1950 119

Shakespeare in the Waterloo Road *by* RICHARD DAVID 121

The Year's Contributions to Shakespearian Study

   1. Critical Studies *reviewed by* J. I. M. STEWART 129

   2. Shakespeare's Life, Times and Stage *reviewed by* CLIFFORD LEECH . . 137

   3. Textual Studies *reviewed by* JAMES G. MCMANAWAY 144

Books Received 153

Index 155

LIST OF PLATES

PLS. I AND II ARE BETWEEN PP. 54 AND 55

I. Vertue's sketches of the frontage and plan of New Place, Stratford-upon-Avon
(His Grace the Duke of Portland)

II. Vertue's sketch of Shakespeare's monument in Stratford Church
(His Grace the Duke of Portland)

PLS. III–VI ARE BETWEEN PP. 120 AND 121

III. A. *Twelfth Night*, Old Vic, 1950. Production by Hugh Hunt; costumes and settings by Roger Furse. The Opening Scene
(John Vickers)

B. *Twelfth Night*. Viola's Embassy to Olivia
(John Vickers)

IV. *Twelfth Night*. The Midnight Carousal
(John Vickers)

V. *The Merchant of Venice*, Young Vic, 1951. Production by Glen Byam Shaw; settings by Gay Dangerfield. Shylock Debates the Loan
(George Konig)

VI. A. *Henry V*, Old Vic, 1951. Production by Glen Byam Shaw; costumes and settings by Motley. "On this Unworthy Scaffold"
(John Vickers)

B. *Henry V*. The French Court
(John Vickers)

PLS. VII AND VIII ARE BETWEEN PP. 124 AND 125

VII. *Henry V*. Katharine's English Lesson
(John Vickers)

VIII. A. *Henry V*. The English Force Embarks
(John Vickers)

B. *Henry V*. "We Happy Few, We Band of Brothers"
(John Vickers)

PL. IX IS BETWEEN PP. 128 AND 129

IX. A. *Romeo and Juliet*, New York, March 1951. Sponsored by Dwight Deere Wiman; directed by Peter Glenville; costumes and settings by Oliver Messel
(John Seymour Irwin)

B. *Hamlet*, Royal Netherlands Theatre, Antwerp, 1945
(L. V. Cauwenbergh)

RESTORING SHAKESPEARE: THE MODERN EDITOR'S TASK

BY

PETER ALEXANDER

Abuse of the commentators and of the editors is a form of recreation with which many readers of Shakespeare have from time to time diverted themselves. Familiar, perhaps from their early years, with his plays in some well-known and standard text, they come in their maturer days upon remarks that disturb their repose in their long-cherished knowledge or on suggestions that offend their sense of propriety. Such reactions may be wise or unwise according to circumstances and the capacity of the reader; they are at least natural, but only some familiarity with the commentator's problem will enable even the judicious reader to pass a fair judgement on new suggestions and to reject them, if necessary, with the charitable allowance that the case usually deserves. For the commentator is doing his best to help in what is both a difficult and a delicate task, and only an arrogant assumption of omniscience on his part should call forth the reader's objurgation.

The offended, and often incensed, reader is of course in good company. The poets themselves have not hesitated to abuse the 'classical' editors whose monuments are now preserved in the particular Pantheon which their successors of to-day enter with reverence. The remarks which Keats made in his copy of Shakespeare have been preserved and edited for us, and they show how little compunction he felt in discharging on the eighteenth-century editors a fusillade of the most uncomplimentary comment. "Lo fool again!" after some weighty pronouncement by Dr Johnson himself is not uncharacteristic of the taxation, in the Shakespearian sense of that word, to which the learned editors are subjected. But Keats was a poet to the manner born and native to a domain which even Dr Johnson entered at his peril. The question whether Keats was always justified in his censure is not for the moment at issue; only those however, it is clear, who feel as free and sure in the element in which Keats soared should venture on the critical flights he naturally allowed himself.

There is too, the irate reader may plead, the example of the commentators themselves, for they have not spared one another. "Perhaps", as Dr Johnson observed, "the lightness of the matter may conduce to the vehemency of the agency; when the truth to be investigated is so near to inexistence, as to escape attention, its bulk is to be enlarged by rage and exclamation." The example set by the offenders themselves is not one that can be recommended as a model of general deportment, and their mutual censures often point the moral of the futility of such exasperation. To assess the relative merits of the editors would be an invidious and perhaps odious task; but whatever the judgement given after such a scrutiny, the claims of Theobald would have to be weighed with care. Yet Theobald is the first hero of the *Dunciad*, a poem by the poet who may be considered the outstanding man of genius who has given his time to editing Shakespeare. But in editing Shakespeare the race has not always been to the swift or the battle to the strong. Those who have done most to elucidate Shakespeare are not of the type of which Bentleys, Porsons and Housmans have been made; and Dr Johnson could describe Theobald as a man of narrow comprehension and small acquisitions, though there is no modern edition of Shakespeare that does not include many of the happy suggestions first proposed by Theobald.

Before condemning the commentators there is a story of W. G. Grace the reader would do well to remember. To a proud mother who introduced her son to Grace as a prodigy that had never dropped a catch, the Doctor replied: "He can't have played much cricket, Mam." The editor or commentator who has never made a bad shot is unlikely to have made any good ones. In the earlier days of editing the commentator was without the numerous aids that are now available in the shape of concordance and dictionary, and he laboured in the belief that the field needed a more thoroughgoing weeding than we now know was required. Those who fancied that Shakespeare's manuscripts had been left to the care of door-keepers and prompters were bolder in the exercise of conjecture than those can be who believe that in many instances the text they examine was printed from Shakespeare's own manuscript. The exuberance of conjecture in the earlier editors now that time has blown aside the froth, or filtered the body of their work from the lees, yields a lasting satisfaction to readers of Shakespeare. Beside the abandon of the early editors the circumspection that is required of their successors may seem unheroic, and modern corrections uninspired.

Most modern corrections are strictly speaking not emendations at all, but merely restorations of what was there already before the editorial process began. Compared with the *lucida tela diei*—the words of Lucretius that Housman so aptly used of those divinations that turn the obscurity of corruption to the sunshine of poetry—modern corrections seem matter-of-fact observations that afford merely a comfortable daylight. The reader confronted with the Folio text at *Timon of Athens*, IV, iii, 12,

> It is the Pastour Lards, the Brothers sides,
> The want that makes him leaue:

may fail to see what relevance such words have in Timon's fierce denunciation of his fellows and their society. But read

> It is the pasture lards the rother's sides
> The want that makes him lean

(where "rother" means "ox") and all is clear in sense and appropriate to the misanthrope's mood. This is a good instance of the contribution editors have made to the reader's ease and enjoyment. Those who are oblivious of their debts, and yet exclaim against their benefactors, should be condemned to read their Shakespeare only in the original texts. The modern editor despairs of achieving so startling a transformation in reading as Rowe and Collier effected in these two lines. He is working on a close glean'd field, and though there is sufficient left to satisfy the ambition of genius, the modern editor has usually to be content with a more modest return.

In the Globe text, prepared for Macmillan and Co. in 1864, the editors Clark and Wright marked with an obelus passages that seemed to them corrupt and to have defied emendation. Two of these passages have recently been corrected by Percy Simpson, with no or with so little change in the text that they may serve as typical instances of the kind of correction that is perhaps most characteristic of recent years. At *The Tempest*, III, i, 14–15, the Folio reads:

> But these sweet thoughts, doe euen refresh my labours,
> Most busie lest, when I doe it.

Ferdinand, in the midst of his log-carrying, is musing on Miranda. Many suggestions have been proposed to make sense of the second line; but, as Simpson observes, the comma after "lest", the stumbling-block in the expression, need be regarded not as a modern comma separating "lest" (=least) from what follows but as a mark of emphasis binding it to the final words. The sense is clear: Ferdinand is busiest when thinking of Miranda, and the text can stand when the dramatist's punctuation is translated into modern terms.

Simpson's correction illustrates what is now an important question for editors: the interpretation of the punctuation of the early copies. Before the work of the bibliographers—Pollard, McKerrow and Sir Walter Greg—few regarded that punctuation as of any significance. Simpson, however, converted many to a different view, and before him Alfred Thiselton had used it to advantage. Now that our ideas of the history of the text are so altered, much attention is necessarily given to such detail. Where doctors disagree the laymen may be permitted to suspend judgement, for the critics are not unanimous about the interpretation of the punctuation; but the main point is not in debate: the punctuation demands study and may prove significant. As an illustration of the possibilities in this field two further corrections may be cited. At *Merry Wives of Windsor*, III, iii, 69–70, the Folio reads:

> I see what thou wert if Fortune thy foe, were
> not Nature thy friend.

Clark and Wright do not obelize the passage, but their version:

> I see what thou wert, if Fortune thy foe were not,
> Nature thy friend.

is not satisfactory, and various emendations have been proposed. Here again the interpretation turns on the significance of the comma. Falstaff is trying to flatter Mistress Ford by admiring her parts—those that Nature gave her—and insisting how they would adorn a more exalted rank in society and the attire that is associated with such a station. But Fortune is her foe, since, as Rosalind reminds us, "Fortune reigns in gifts of the world, not in the lineaments of Nature": Mistress Ford is merely a citizen's wife. The comma therefore after "foe" is an emphatic one joining it to "were" and the passage should read:

> I see what thou wert if Fortune thy foe were
> —not Nature—thy Friend.

For if Fortune were her friend (not Nature, for Nature is that already) she would have the position in the world to match the lineaments that Nature has given her. Again at *All's Well that Ends Well*, IV, iii, 295, the Folio reads:

> A pox upon him for me, he's more and more a Cat.

Editors usually adopt the Folio punctuation, but the passage should stand in a modernized text as,

<blockquote>A pox upon him! For me he's more and more a Cat.</blockquote>

for the comma is again for emphasis.

These may seem slight and unimportant corrections, and so they are no doubt to the general reader. But they involve very important principles of interpretation that must eventually determine the correct reading at a number of places in the text of some of the best-known plays—places where the general reader, however indifferent to editorial principles, would at once be arrested by changes in the long-familiar wording.

Simpson's second correction requires no change whatever in the text. At *Love's Labour's Lost*, v, ii, 67–8, the Quarto reads:

<blockquote>So perttaunt like would I ore'sway his state,
That he should be my foole, and I his fate.</blockquote>

The Folio, which is more or less a reprint of the Quarto, reads similarly, with "pertaunt" for "perttaunt". This word is, of course, the crux of the matter, and many emendations have been proposed and some adopted in texts. But Simpson has shown why it must remain as it is in the early versions. He is able to cite the following passage, in support of his contention, from a treatise on certain terms used in card games: "A double Paire Royall, or a Paire-Taunt, is four cards of a sort." "Pertaunt" is therefore in all probability a winning holding or declaration at the obsolete game of 'Post and Pair'; and it would be in place in *Love's Labour's Lost* where the Queen and her three ladies may be said to be four of a sort about to win the hand from the love-lorn King and his gentlemen in the scene that immediately follows.

Dover Wilson has made another restoration to the text at *Titus Andronicus*, II, iii, 222, that seems as certain as Simpson's in *Love's Labour's Lost*. The readings in the First Quarto and the Folio are given in that order:

<blockquote>Lord *Bassianus* lies bereaud in blood,
Lord *Bassianus* lies embrewed heere,</blockquote>

The reading of the First Quarto (1594) was changed in the Second Quarto (1600) to what now stands in the Folio, and the Folio obtained this wording from the Third Quarto (1611), for the Folio is substantially a reprint of the edition of 1611, although there are certain additions from manuscript material. The changes made in the Second Quarto were in part due to the fact that the printer was working from a damaged copy of the First Quarto. The particular alteration now under consideration, however, seems to have been made because the word "bereaud" did not make sense. But Dover Wilson's suggestion that "bereaud" is a misprint for "beray'd" ("bereied") seems as certain as such suggestions can be; for the word is certainly used by the dramatists in the sense required here, e.g. Beaumont and Fletcher's *Knight of the Burning Pestle*, II, iv, 20:

<blockquote>Unless it were by chance I did beray me—</blockquote>

where "beray" means "befoul".

Dover Wilson's correction here illustrates a principle he has been at some pains to emphasize, particularly in his work on the text of *Hamlet*. The words, in the Folio text, "embrewed heere" do make sense of a sort; the First Quarto reading does not, at least at first sight. But here as in *Hamlet* Dover Wilson insists that where we may suspect the later reading of being itself an attempt to restore the sense to a passage that is obscured in an earlier version, we must address ourselves to the original obscurity for the correct interpretation and not be content with words that may indeed make sense, but not perhaps the precise sense intended by the author.

This correction also illustrates another aspect of emendation to which Dover Wilson has given much attention. It is not an exact restoration of the word of the text; there is a slight alteration, but of nothing more than a letter. This kind of correction in which the editor tries to restore the original by some trifling adjustment of the letters is, if Housman is to be believed, a favourite resource of Scots editors, for these cautious souls seemed to him to trust overmuch to this apparently conservative expedient. Dover Wilson has, however, made a special study of the handwriting used by Shakespeare, and a comparison of certain quarto and folio texts does bear out his contention that certain letters in that script do lend themselves to confusion one with another. Perhaps in his pleasure at finding a new key to certain difficulties he has overstressed its importance, but the next correction shows a very neat and certain use of the *ductus litterarum* by two American scholars.

At *Merchant of Venice*, III, i, 111–12, the Folio reads:

> I thanke thee good *Tuball*, good newes, good newes:
> ha, ha, here in Genowa.

The puzzling word is "here", for the speakers are in Venice; and "where" or some other word disposing of the confusion is usually substituted. But the American editors Neilson and Hill have by the simplest of devices made all clear. The letters most regularly confused by the compositors working from a script such as Shakespeare's are final *e* and *d*. Good instances of such a confusion in the printing of Shakespeare's text are so numerous that illustration is unnecessary, especially as it can be seen so clearly here. If the final *e* in "here" should be *d*, we have "herd", a spelling of "heard", and what Shylock says, as one can see from Tubal's earlier remark ("as I heard in Genowa"), is

> ha, ha, heard in Genowa.

This type of correction which not only restores a sense required by the context, but which also provides, as it were, its own justification on transcriptional grounds is naturally felt to be specially satisfactory; but many good corrections do not carry with them an explanation of the confusion that has given rise to them, and we can see from a comparison of versions that may be independent of each other (e.g. the First Quarto and the Folio texts of *Othello*) that confusions or alterations do occur that no tracing or readjustment of the letters could unravel or explain.

It is often possible, however, especially where we have for a particular play two versions that are printed from different manuscripts and we can obtain a more stereoscopic view, as it were, of the text than one version would afford us, to offer some justification based on transcriptional grounds for the proposed correction. At *Troilus and Cressida*, v, vii, 11–12, the readings of the First Quarto and the Folio are in that order as follows:

> now my double hen'd spartan,....lowe the
> bull has the game, ware hornes ho?

> now my double hen'd sparrow...lowe; the
> bull has the game: ware hornes ho?

The "doubled hen'd spartan" or "double hen'd sparrow" has naturally been found perplexing; but Leon Kellner (in his *Restoring Shakespeare*, p. 55) proposes to read "double horn'd Spartan". This fits the context admirably. Menelaus the Spartan is fighting with Paris, and, as Paris has seduced Helen, her first husband is given the cuckold's horns by that scurvy commentator Thersites. Here we have to suppose that the Quarto compositor misread "horned" as "hen'd" and that the editor or corrector who was preparing a copy of the printed Quarto, to give to the printer for use as his copy in printing the Folio, failed to make the necessary correction. The corrector had before him not only the First Quarto but a manuscript, perhaps in Shakespeare's own hand and not too clear in places, and, puzzled by the Quarto reading and finding his manuscript difficult to decipher, made a shot at the meaning and hit on the wrong word. The strength of Kellner's correction, however, does not depend on any guess we may make as to the origin and history of the corruption but almost solely on its fitness to the immediate context and propriety in the light of the larger context of Shakespeare's style and manner.

Very few of Shakespeare's plays have come down to us in two texts, each printed from a manuscript of a different kind from the other, and where the Quarto text has not been used in some form as copy for the Folio. *Othello* perhaps provides one of these exceptional opportunities for a comparison of two such texts. Neither the Quarto nor the Folio text is free from corruption, but so well do they supplement each other that the evidence we have for *Othello* is unusually good. Two recent corrections in this text may illustrate some of the considerations arising from a study of this evidence. At v, ii, 68–70 the Quarto and Folio read:

FOLIO	QUARTO
Oth. He hath confest.	He has confest.
Des. What, my Lord?	What, my Lord?
Oth. That he hath us'd thee.	That he hath...uds death.

The readings "us'd thee" and "uds death" have been regarded as variants; but a consideration of the nature of the texts suggests that they are each a part and a different part of the original, and that only when they are both included do we get what Shakespeare intended Othello to say. In a modernized text the passage should stand:

> *Des.* What, my Lord?
> *Oth.*   That he hath—ud's death!—us'd thee.

The explanation of the difference between the Folio and Quarto texts presents in this instance no difficulty. The Quarto compositor fell into the well-known type of trap set by similar beginnings to adjacent phrases: the likeness of "uds" to "usd" leads to the omission of the second limb. The Folio compositor was working from a different manuscript, and this had been purged of the oaths and asseverations such as "uds death" that are so frequent a feature in the other text: "uds death" had been marked for omission and the Folio compositor accordingly omitted it; the conclusion that is essential to the thought of the passage was, however, naturally retained. From the context we see that Othello can hardly bring himself to utter the words that he feels of such terrible significance, and the Quarto phrase emphasizes the struggle with which he expresses himself.

In another place in *Othello* the restoration proposed by Richard Flatter seems as warranted. In the quarrel in the guard-room the wounded Montano, according to the Folio, II, iii, 64, exclaims:

> I bleed still, I am hurt to th' death. He dies.

while the Quarto reads:

> Zouns, I bleed still, I am hurt, to the death:

Editors have regarded the termination of the Folio line—"He dies"—as a stage direction, inserted in the Folio text by some confusion of mind on the part of the individual responsible for its preparation for the printer, and included by the printer, confused in his turn by the addition, as part of the dialogue. Montano does not die, nor does it seem probable that he faints, as some editors suggest, for he at once closes with the drunken Cassio, as the exclamations of Othello and Iago indicate. It is hard therefore to resist Flatter's conclusion that "He dies" is really, as the Folio indicates, a part of the dialogue and is the expression of Montano's determination to retaliate on the man who has wounded him so grievously. The Quarto printer may have omitted the phrase for the same reason that modern editors have rejected it. It seemed odd, and could not be a stage direction. The colon after "death" may suggest that the Quarto printer did at first intend to add something, though such evidence is not indeed conclusive.

One last example of the dovetailing of texts must suffice as illustration of that process. Here the second text is a bad quarto, put together by needy actors, and printed by an unscrupulous stationer. At 2 *Henry VI*, IV, i, 68–71, the Folio reads:

> *Lieu.* Conuey him hence, and on our long boats side
> Strike off his head.   *Suf.* Thou dar'st not for thy owne.
> *Lieu. Poole*, Sir *Poole*? Lord,
> I kennel, puddle, sinke, whose filth and dirt
> Troubles the siluer Spring, where England drinkes:

The Bad Quarto, changing the Lieutenant to a Captain, reports this passage as follows:

> *Suf.* Thou darste not for thine owne.
> *Cap.* Yes Poull.
> *Suffolke.* Poull.
> *Cap.* I Poull, puddle, kennell, sinke and durt,

Capell, making use of the Bad Quarto, reconstructed the text as we have it to-day:

> *Suf.* Thou darest not, for thy own.
> *Cap.* Yes, Pole.
> *Suf.* Pole!
> *Cap.* Pool! Sir Pool! lord!
> Ay, kennel, puddle, sink, *etc.*

Capell noted that the disrespectful form of address "Pole" draws from the Duke of Suffolk, whose name was William de la Pole, the outraged exclamation "Pole!". But the texts fit more neatly than Capell observed and the hardly intelligible "Pool! Sir Pool! lord!" can be eliminated. If the two versions are superimposed (the Quarto version modified for comparison):

Lieu. Poole, Sir *Poole?* Lord,
Cap. Poull. *Suffolke.* Poull. *Cap.*

We can see that the Folio printer, confused by his copy, should have read:

Lieu. Poole. *Suf.* Poole! *Lieu.*

—although he would put *Poole* in italic as a proper name. The passage as modernized should therefore stand:

Lieutenant. Poole.
Suffolk. Poole!
Lieutenant. Ay, kennel, puddle, sink, etc.

These illustrations of modern 'corrections' that improve the text by restoring it more or less to the condition in which it was first transmitted to us may conclude with two examples of the art of the late Alfred Thiselton. At times he stoutly defended what is undoubtedly corrupt and unacceptable but, though he may have dropped some catches, he did excellent work in the Shakespearian field. *Measure for Measure*, IV, i, 61–3, where the Duke somewhat suddenly muses on the slanders that assail the man in authority, reads in the Folio:

Volumes of report
Run with these false, and most contrarious Quest
Upon thy doings:

Editors usually read:

Run with these false and most contrarious quests

but there is no need to remove the comma or make "Quest" a plural noun. As Thiselton observes: "'Quest' is of course the verb—capitalized because it is a technical term of the chase and used metaphorically—which signifies the giving tongue of the dog on the scent of game. 'Most contrarious Quest' is best explained by the phrase 'hunt-counter'." Thiselton's explanation is as neat as it is conclusive. The second example, for there are others to choose from, may be taken from *Antony and Cleopatra*, V, ii, 93–100, where the Folio reads:

Cleo. Thinke you there was, or might be such a man
As this I dreampt of?
Dol. Gentle Madam, no.
Cleo. You Lye up to the hearing of the Gods:
But if there be, nor euer were one such
It's past the size of dreaming: Nature wants stuffe
To vie strange formes with fancie, yet t'imagine
An *Anthony* were Natures peece, 'gainst Fancie,
Condemning shadowes quite.

The "nor" in "if there be, nor euer were" is usually changed to "or", but this destroys the sense and continuity of Cleopatra's argument. She first asks:

Think you there was, or might be such a man?

And when the answer is No, she insists that there might be and was indeed one such by asking, How, if there neither is nor ever were a man like Antony, could we possibly imagine him? For his greatness exceeds our powers of imagination. The "nor ever" implies the negative in the first alternative. Though I am aware that there are good judges who still prefer the "or ever" of the Third Folio, I am persuaded that Thiselton is right and that the First Folio reading should stand.

This final 'correction', however doubtful, is submitted to the reader's judgement to suggest to him that the textual critic even when agonizing over the choice between 'or' and 'nor' may be making a genuine effort to interpret Shakespeare and that this critical task, however humble in comparison with the great work of the literary masters in exploring the profundities of Shakespeare's mind and art, is a useful contribution to the interpretation, criticism and enjoyment of Shakespeare.

SUGGESTIONS TOWARDS AN EDITION OF SHAKESPEARE FOR FRENCH, GERMAN AND OTHER CONTINENTAL READERS

BY

GEORGES A. BONNARD

Recently an American scholar, after discussing this century's work in the presentation of Shakespeare's text, has suggested that even now there is room for editions of Shakespeare different from those we have, editions which will serve some purposes better than the existing editions do.[1] Among such editions there is one which deserves special consideration—a text of the plays designed for those many French, German and other continental readers who are well acquainted with the English language but who are not concerned with the detailed apparatus proper and necessary for university students. Again and again readers of this kind, in their desire to enter into the spirit of Shakespeare's poetic achievement, have turned to the plays as they appear in current editions but, finding themselves confronted by all sorts of difficulties, have been forced to abandon the English text and to revert to those translations from which they had hoped to escape. For them, it would seem, something must be provided different from anything that at present exists, some edition that would help them to realize the power of the poetry, that would induce in them the imaginative excitement without which poetry cannot be appreciated.

If an edition were to be prepared for these general continental readers, it would have to be printed in a pleasing format. Bulky volumes, two-column pages, a type so small that it imposes a strain on the eye, have never been in favour on the Continent. Our readers are not likely to buy a one-volume Shakespeare. They would no doubt prefer a Shakespeare in as many volumes as he wrote plays, a 'one volume per play' edition. The size of those volumes would have to be such that all lines of verse could be printed without turn-overs, for turn-overs are generally disliked abroad. Their weight should be so light that one could hold them for two hours at least without a sense of fatigue. Each page should contain from twenty to twenty-five lines of text, leaving enough space—about a quarter of the page—for the notes. Wide margins and judicious spacing should contribute to that liberation of the reader's imagination which we regard as essential. Perhaps it would be advisable in this connexion to depart from the habit of placing the names of the characters in front of the first line they speak, and follow the practice, universal in France, usual in Germany and Italy, of placing those names on separate lines in between the speeches. There would then be a possibility of adopting the happy idea suggested to McKerrow[2] by his collaborator, Alice Walker, of adding to the name of a disguised character his feigned name.

Our readers have been brought up on Racine, Schiller, Alfieri. The plays they are accustomed to read have all been published with the author's consent and under his control. Their texts are on the whole definitely established; they contain no textual difficulties, no hopeless puzzles; there is no need to emend them. To start reading Shakespeare under the impression that his text is of the same kind is bound to lead to grave misconceptions. It is therefore important that the text offered our readers should not pretend to be what it cannot be, an absolutely definitive one. It is important that they should be told that Shakespeare's plays were published in circumstances entirely different from those with which they are familiar. Every volume of our edition would therefore contain an introduction giving in as few words as possible the necessary information as to the manner his plays got into print, and adding for the particular play in that volume a brief summing-up of the findings of modern scholarship concerning its text. After reading such an introduction, which would be quite short (since no discussion of the technical problems involved would find a place in it), it would no longer be possible to come to the play itself in the wrong mood. One of the main reasons why uninformed readers trying to read Shakespeare in an ordinary edition find him so disappointing would be eliminated. All feeling of irritation, so destructive to the proper attitude towards a poetic text, would be suppressed.

The text itself, by which we mean exclusively the words spoken by the characters, should be given in modern spelling, except in those few cases where an old form must be kept for the sake of rhyme; here the old form would be explained in a note. In modernizing the text, we should even go further than those editors who, to make sure that a line is read with what they regard as the appropriate rhythm, retain many of the elisions, the 'short spellings', as McKerrow calls them,[3] of the original texts. Apart from such elisions as *e'er, e'en, 'tis, 'twere, 'twill*, with which our readers will be familiar, the normal long spellings of the present day would alone be used. Modern pronunciation makes it certain that people with a good knowledge of spoken English will read such forms as *touched, looked, limped, knolled* as one syllable, *boldened, slippered* as two, *sequestered* as three, even if the *e* of the ending is not elided. And if they have the least sense of rhythm they will easily feel when that ending should be pronounced as an additional syllable, even if the *e* is not surmounted by any diacritical mark. Nor should it be necessary to elide the *e* in the definite article or the *n* in the preposition *in*, as the early editions often do, merely to ensure that the proper amount of slurring is observed. The occasional substitution of an anapaest for an iambus does not ruin the rhythm of a blank verse and we do not know enough of Shakespeare's metrical habits to be sure that he would have objected to a line in which contracted forms seem to indicate a regular iambic rhythm being spoken with an anapaest or two.

Modernized as to spelling, our text would also be modernized as regards punctuation, since we wish to offer our readers as easily readable a text as can be. But it should not be wantonly modernized in the belief that the punctuation of the early editions, because it follows on the whole habits different from our own, has no value for a modern reader. There are many passages where it brings out so clearly how the lines should be spoken, what pauses should be made, that it would be a pity to discard it altogether.[4] And occasionally it is of greater help towards the understanding of a sentence than the punctuation of modern editors.[5]

As we said above, for psychological reasons that are particularly strong in the case of readers accustomed to plays published by their own authors, our text should not pretend to be a perfect one. It should appear to be no more than what it is, an approximation, fairly close in some plays, more or less distant in others, to what it would have been if Shakespeare himself had supervised its printing. It should not be the result of a vain and ill-directed attempt at reconstructing Shakespeare's own text by making indiscriminate use of Quartos and Folios and liberally indulging in emendations. It should, on the contrary, reproduce, though in modern spelling and with its punctuation modernized, whatever early texts modern scholarship has come to recognize as those which possess most authority. For the plays with only one authoritative text, there would be no difficulty: the copy-text would simply be reproduced. But in the case of the plays for which there are two authoritative texts, true to our principle of dealing fairly with our readers, we would like the distinction between what is due to the Folio and what comes from the Quartos to be made perfectly clear. What comes from the secondary copy-text—whether Folio or Quarto—might be printed in a type slightly different from that used for what comes from the main one.

But if it is highly desirable that our readers should be offered a text that did not pretend to be better than it really is, there is no reason why they should be troubled by wrong line arrangement, ascription of speeches to the wrong speakers, words, phrases, lines of the copy-text that, yielding no possible meaning, have been corrected by some one or other to the satisfaction of most, if not all, subsequent editors. By not correcting all those errors of the copy-text we should give them a text that would be much worse than whatever text they had been using so far.

McKerrow's most judicious decisions concerning the various cases in which the lines should be rearranged either as prose or as verse should be adopted by our editor. Those decisions are so clearly set out and so excellently justified in the *Prolegomena*[6] that there is no need to repeat them here. But neither such corrections nor that of a clearly wrong ascription of a speech would be carried out silently. A brief note would warn the reader that a correction has been made.

As regards emendations properly speaking, those lines or sentences only should be emended that cannot be made to yield any satisfactory meaning. The copy-text being the only true authority, any correction to it is necessarily conjectural, and no conjecture should be accepted in preference to the reading in the copy-text, unless that reading is unquestionably corrupt. Our edition aiming at providing the general reader whose mother-tongue is not English with a pleasant and readable text, it would be rather foolish to load its pages with the collation of all, or even a selection of, the emendations that have been offered in the course of the last three and a half centuries. Nor would such a reader require to be told the reasons for which one particular emendation has been adopted, in preference to others. But he would rightly insist on knowing whether what he reads comes from the copy-text or is some conjectural correction. Satisfaction would be given him by printing all corrections in italics, the text, wherever it follows the copy-text, being in roman. As the editor responsible for our text would be (at least let us hope so) a competent textual critic, he would preferably adopt corrections that had received the assent of most editors since they had first been made. A note would record the reading of the copy-text and give the source of the correction eventually adopted.

As to those famous passages which no one yet has managed to correct to the satisfaction of at least the majority of editors, they should be left as they stand in the copy-text, an obelisk being added in the margin to signify that they are hopelessly corrupt. In a note, a few—no more than two or three—of the interpretations or corrections that have been proposed, carefully selected, would be given.

It may well appear paradoxical to assert that the division of Shakespeare's plays into acts should not be preserved in an edition destined for readers whose dramatic taste has been formed on the classical tradition. Was it not in obedience to that tradition that the editors of the First

Folio attempted, and their successors in the eighteenth century carried out, such a division? But our readers, seeing a play regularly divided into five acts, and the acts themselves into a varying number of scenes, could not but expect a dramatic structure that would remind them of the classical plays with which they are familiar. They would inevitably expect each of the five acts to have its own function in the development of the action, and the division of an act into scenes to be no more than a typographical device to mark exits and entrances. What they actually find is so radically different that they cannot help feeling, cheated perhaps, at any rate perplexed, even bewildered. What sort of scenes are those, they would ask, in the course of which characters come and go, what are those acts of very unequal length without any clear function in the general construction of the play? Such questions will keep haunting them and disturb their enjoyment, which is exactly what an edition specially prepared for them should not do.

They should therefore be told—and this can be done in the general introduction—that the plays of Shakespeare are made up of a series of many acts, called scenes, varying in length from a few to four or five hundred lines, each being, like the act of a classical play, a definite unit, with its own locality, its particular time, its theme and function in the progress of the action, and that those many acts, called scenes, are not divided into scenes by the exits and entrances of the characters. Further they should be told that in between two successive acts, called scenes, when for an instant the stage is empty, a certain time is supposed to elapse, but that, whereas in a classical play that time is always short, here it may be a matter, not merely of minutes or hours, but of days, weeks, months and even years. Thus duly warned, our readers would know what to expect; they would not be surprised to see the text of their play divided into scenes only, and to observe that each of those scenes is in fact an act.

Our text would thus be throughout divided into the scenes proper to a Shakespearian play,[7] even in the case of those plays for which the copy-text has no clearly visible division whatever, or one only into acts, since there is practically no difficulty in ascertaining where a scene ends and a new one begins. And the scenes would be numbered consecutively from the first to the last; *As You Like It*, for instance, would thus have twenty-two. There would be no division into acts, since in most cases that division, however respectable a long tradition has made it, only serves to hide the true structure of the plays.[8] For purposes of reference, a table of correspondence between the scenes in our text and the traditional division into acts and scenes might easily be added at the end of each volume.

Each scene should be headed by its number: *Scene I*, and followed by a blank space before the heading of the next so as to bring out clearly its character as a unit. Those blank spaces would stand for the intervals during which, in an Elizabethan theatre, the stage remained empty. Just underneath the heading, there would be, in a roman type smaller than that used for the text itself, the usual stage-directions. In determining what stage-directions are necessary and in what form they should be given, the convenience of the reader should alone be taken into account. Those at the beginning of a scene would tell, first of all, how long a time has elapsed since the previous scene or the scene it follows in the action; then in what place the coming scene is going to be enacted (with 'place indifferent' or 'undetermined' if the text does not allow us to assign it to one particular locality); lastly in what way the characters enter the stage, in conversation, for instance, or quarrelling, or coming from opposite sides and meeting unexpectedly, and so on. These indications would be given in a simple, matter-of-fact style, and as briefly as possible, their purpose being to help and guide the reader's imagination. Other stage-directions would be given, not merely whenever a character goes out or comes in, but for asides and whenever there must be some business that the text does not make at once evident. A reader whose mother-tongue is not English would certainly require more such helps to be able to visualize the action than one on whom the words can exert their full power of suggestion. Still, even so, our editor should be careful not to go too far in this direction. The Latin stage directions of tradition would be regularly translated into modern English.

This edition, designed for general readers, must be self-sufficient. It must make it possible to read Shakespeare in the original without turning to any special grammar or dictionary, or to any other edition. Further, its readers must not be required to consult notes or a glossary at the end of the volume. The necessity of looking up anything in another book or in another part of the book one is reading is apt to bring the reader's imaginative activity to a sudden stop which, even if it is only momentary, is prejudicial to one's enjoyment, and therefore to the full understanding, of what one is reading. Every page of our edition should therefore contain all the information a reader who had carefully read the introduction would require in order to understand its text. That information would be given in the footnotes. From a line, a sentence he does not at once understand, our reader would instinctively glance to the notes to see whether there is one that might help him over his difficulty. In so far as his difficulty is not due to insufficient knowledge of English, he would find one which would give him in condensed form just what information he requires and no more, so as not to keep his attention away from his text more than is strictly necessary, in most cases a fraction of a second only. The notes would therefore be rather dogmatic in form. The explanation given would not be accompanied by a discussion of the word or passage; it would be neither justified nor illustrated by adducing quotations from Shakespeare himself or other writers; it would not refer to any of the books in which the scholar delights to dip to enlarge his knowledge of Elizabethan and Jacobean manners, beliefs, ideas, of the world in which Shakespeare moved. Such severe curtailment of our notes would be necessary for other reasons than the desire not to distract the reader from the text. Even an educated reader, who might be supposed to be able to dispense with, say, notes bearing on classical mythology, if his mother-tongue is not English, will need more explanation than an Englishman. The number of our explanatory notes would be large, and if the space allotted to the notes is to be kept down to no more than a quarter of the page (which is highly desirable for the sort of reader we have in mind) they must necessarily be as short as the editor can make them.

It would be a good thing if the introduction gave a list of such words as *affect, censure, presently, still* that are constantly used by Shakespeare with meanings they no longer have. They need not then be explained every time they occur in the text. Likewise a page or so of the introduction listing most of the grammatical usages proper to Elizabethan English with which our reader is not likely to be acquainted, though he will very quickly grow used to them, would make many notes superfluous. But even so the number of difficulties that remained would be considerable: obsolete words, words whose sense has altered more or less; such peculiarities of style as anacoluthon, disruption of the logical order of words, hendiadys, ellipsis, the use of an adjective instead of a complement or of a complement instead of an adjective; obscurities due, not to any corruption of the text, but to confusion of ideas, to different grammatical constructions being mixed up, to extreme conciseness or the sudden passing from one idea to an apparently unrelated one; words used in a metaphorical sense owing to the presence in the background of an image that a reader whose mother-tongue is not English must be helped to see; lastly, allusions to all kinds of topics which our continental reader is not likely to know anything about.

An editor does not like to confess his ignorance. And yet how many words and phrases, how many passages the meaning of which is uncertain, are explained by one editor in one way, by another in another! As our notes would perforce be, as we said, rather dictatorial in form, they should only be so when it is really possible to be positive. When there is no general agreement as to what a word, a passage, really signifies, our notes would describe them as of doubtful sense, and add two or three of the most plausible interpretations. We would like our edition to obey the golden rule of perfect candour towards the reader. And that is why our notes would also draw his attention to those features in the text—contradictions, loose ends, probable cuts and such like—that cannot really be explained away since they are most probably due to the state of the manuscript from which, directly or indirectly, the original text was set.

All the notes, both textual and explanatory, would be printed in a small roman type, on two columns because with a small type short lines are easier to read. There would be but one note for each line in which there was something to be explained, but that note might contain more than one explanation. No references to the notes would be given in the text, but the lines of each scene would be numbered from one onward, the numbers being placed in the margin on the right, opposite every fifth line. Each note would be headed by the number of the line with the corrections and difficulties of which it deals.

A word may be added regarding the introductions which the various volumes would require. One thing is certain here: the usual discussions about the date of the particular play, its relationship to its sources, its characters, should find no place in an edition intended for general readers. These are things desirable where students are concerned, but for the readers we have in mind such information had much better be laid aside and the space given to the kind of material suggested above. Students may gain from being told what to think of the play they are going to read. The educated but non-scholarly public would certainly prefer to be left to exercise their own judgements.

NOTES

1. M. A. Shaaber, 'Problems in the Editing of Shakespeare: Text', *English Institute Essays*, 1947 (1948), p. 107.

2. R. B. McKerrow, *Prolegomena for the Oxford Shakespeare* (Oxford, 1939), p. 58.

3. *Ibid.* p. 24.

4. A good example is Phoebe's speech to Silvius at the end of *As You Like It*, III, v. In the Folio it reads far more dramatically than in any modern edition.

5. To give only one instance, in the same comedy, III, ii, the Folio prints Rosalind's words to Orlando "you are rather point deuice in your accoustrements, as louing your selfe, then seeming the Louer of any other" with two commas, which brings out the logical construction of the sentence; both the old and the new Cambridge editions suppress the second one.

6. R. B. McKerrow, *op. cit.* pp. 44–9.

7. Not those of course into which, true with a vengeance to the classical tradition, Pope divided his text.

8. The scenes form natural groups, and in some plays, some of the acts correspond to the natural groups. But the main fact is that the number of those natural groups within a play is not, as a rule, five. That is why to try and impose on the plays a uniform five act division is bound to conceal their real structure.

THE 1622 QUARTO AND THE FIRST FOLIO TEXTS OF *OTHELLO*

BY

ALICE WALKER

It is generally held that the 1622 Quarto and the Folio texts of *Othello* were printed from different manuscripts, that the manuscript used for the Quarto was a transcript, and that a transcript also possibly intervened between the foul papers and the Folio. But no one seems very happy about *Othello's* textual history and I suspect it was very different from what is generally believed.

Until the question of the relationship of the extant printed texts is settled we cannot begin to guess at the character of the manuscripts, no longer extant, which lay behind them. It is my main purpose in what follows to show that the Quarto and Folio texts were not independent prints but that the Folio was printed from a corrected copy of the Quarto. I have finally suggested that the well-recognized inferiority of the Quarto text was due not to scribal errors but to memorial contamination.

The general superiority of the Folio text has never been questioned and we can safely assume that the manuscript which lay behind it was of good authority. In most cases where the texts differ it is immediately apparent that the Folio readings are better than those of the Quarto. But it is as well to understand the cause of the Quarto's inferiority in cases where the Folio reading is preferable, and it is even more important to be in a position to assess how far Quarto readings can safely be substituted where the Folio variants are unsatisfactory.

A few examples will make the application of my conclusions clear. At I, iii, 330–5 the Quarto text reads as follows:

If the ballance of our liues had not one scale of reason, to poise another of sensuality; the blood and basenesse of our natures, would conduct vs to most preposterous conclusions.

The Folio substitutes "braine" for "ballance". If we believe the Quarto and Folio were independent texts, then we can accept the Quarto reading, which makes not only sense but good sense, whereas the Folio "braine" is nonsense. But if we believe that the Folio was printed from a corrected copy of the Quarto, then we must assume that the Quarto "ballance" was an error, deliberately struck out by the corrector, and that although "braine" is wrong it is a corruption of the word he sought to substitute. An emendation is therefore required and Theobald's "beam" (i.e. the transverse bar from the ends of which the scales of a balance are suspended, which was extended in meaning to cover the balance itself) clearly gives what is required. An editor who believes that a corrected Quarto was the basis of the Folio text must therefore reject the Quarto's "ballance" and substitute "beam".

In such a case the general sense of the passage is unaffected whether we read "ballance" or "beam", but all problems are not so speedily resolved and at times the changes an editor must make are more drastic. Thus at III, iii, 340 the Quarto reads

I slept the next night well, was free, and merry;

the Folio has

I slept the next night well, fed well, was free, and merrie.

Editors believing in the independence of the printed texts have exercised a free choice and have preferred (presumably for metrical reasons) the Quarto line. But if an editor believes that the Folio "fed well" was marked for insertion in the Quarto text, he must either print the line as it stands in the Folio or make the reasonable assumption that "fed well" was intended to replace a metrical equivalent in the Quarto which, through the negligence of either the collator or the Folio compositor, was not removed. He might, therefore, and with good reason, decide that the line should run

> I slept the next night well, fed well, was merrie.

Further, if he believes the Quarto was a memorially contaminated text, the source of the corruption can readily be found in Othello's lines about Desdemona earlier in the scene (ll. 183–5) where the Quarto reads

> tis not to make me iealous,
> To say my wife is faire, feedes well, loues company,
> Is free of speech, sings, playes, and dances well.

The Folio lines tally except for the omission of "well" in the last line. But this is not the end of the matter. In the second line of the passage just quoted there are two hypermetrical syllables and "feedes well" anticipates the Folio's insertion in l. 340. Should the Folio have deleted "feedes well" when it reprinted the above passage and does this explain its otherwise unaccountable and erroneous omission of "well" at the end of the third line above? That is, has the Quarto transferred, through memorial confusion (due to the association of both passages with Othello's jealousy), the "fed well" of l. 340 to l. 184 and substituted for it in l. 340 an echo of "free of speech" in l. 185? If so, then an editor must also emend the Folio in ll. 183–5 and read

> 'Tis not to make me Iealious,
> To say my wife is faire, loues company,
> Is free of Speech, Sings, Playes and Dances well.

Fortunately, the elimination of 'feeds well' from this passage has not only textual theory but common sense to recommend it, for it is much more reasonable to suppose that Othello fed well with an untroubled mind (l. 340) than that Desdemona's feeding well (l. 184) was a motive for jealousy.

This is the kind of problem my conclusions raise and the way in which they are likely to affect the text of *Othello*, for, if the Folio text was printed from the Quarto, readings in which the two texts agree (as in l. 184 above) are not necessarily correct, since errors in the Quarto may well have been left uncorrected. As a final illustration, mention should be made of lines in the Quarto text but absent from the Folio which have sometimes been omitted by editors and at other times conflated with the Folio readings. It seems to me of some importance that one should determine whether Desdemona's words in the Quarto ("O Lord, Lord, Lord.") omitted by the Folio at v, ii, 83 have any authority, and, if not, how they found their way into the Quarto text. Editors have, in general, rejected them, though in other cases what may well be actors' interpolations have readily been accepted in modern editions. In what follows I have endeavoured to demonstrate that the traditional assumptions about the early texts of *Othello* are untenable and if the very different conclusions I have reached are correct then plainly the text of *Othello* needs a very thorough reconsideration.

The Bibliographical Evidence

Though there is no decisive bibliographical evidence that the Folio *Othello* was printed from a 'cured' and 'perfected' Quarto, such evidence as there is merits more consideration than it has, I think, had. Printing from a Quarto would be in accordance with normal Folio practice and the convenience of working, where possible, from print must have had the same appeal in Jacobean days as now. In most cases where the possibility of the use of a Quarto arises it is fairly easy to determine whether it was used or not. *Othello* is a difficult problem, partly because we have only one Quarto prior to the Folio[1] and partly because there is, so far as I can see, no typographical slip on the part of the Folio compositor to indicate conclusively that he was working from an earlier print.

Thus, the change from the Folio's normal "*Æmilia*" to "*Emilia*" on vv 5ʳ is less likely to be due to the influence of the Quarto's "*Emillia*" than to the compositor's running out of the italic ligature. Shortage of type may similarly account for the Folio's change[2] from its normal "*Caſsio*" to "*Caſsio*" (the Quarto's norm) on tt 4, though it does not explain a "*Caſsio*" on vv 1ᵛ and another on vv 4ʳ; but these may be merely instances of negligence. There are some coincidences in the use of brackets (e.g. I, ii, 69; I, iii, 93; IV, i, 20–2), but these might be explained as derived from the original manuscript or a common ancestor. The Folio, like the Quarto, sets Iago's extempore couplets in II, i to the normal speech margin and, again like the Quarto, indents the rhymes in the drinking scene, II, iii; but this arrangement too could be explained as a legacy from a parent manuscript.

Similarly inconclusive are some coincidences in line division. A typographical feature of the Quarto is the printing of an occasional decasyllabic line as two lines of verse.[3] On four occasions (I, ii, 28; II, iii, 63; II, iii, 368; IV, ii, 110)[4] this was apparently to accommodate a stage direction since the Quarto printed shorter entrances (as well as directions for exits, noises off, action, etc.) towards the right margin. Thus we find in the Quarto (II, iii, 368):

> That shall enmesh em all: *Enter* Roderigo.
> How now *Roderigo*?

The Folio centres, as a separate line, directions for entry and had therefore no need for recourse to this kind of device. When therefore we find in the Folio:

> That shall en-mash them all.
> How now *Rodorigo*?
> *Enter Rodorigo.*

it looks as if the Folio here preserved,[5] through inadvertence, the split line that was a necessity in the Quarto. We find, however, on three occasions in the Quarto (I, iii, 170; II, i, 81; IV, i, 226) similarly split lines with centred stage directions. These split lines may therefore have been a feature of the manuscript from which the Quarto was printed and, if derived from a parent manuscript, might occasionally have found their way independently to the Folio.

The typographical evidence thus provides no certain indication that the Folio was printed from a corrected Quarto, though the printed texts have a number of features in common which suggest this may have been the case.

COMMON ERRORS

Of greater significance are the errors common to the two texts. In ten cases at least the Quarto and Folio agree in readings which seem to me pretty certainly wrong. These are as follows:

I, iii, 42:	And prayes you to *beleeue* him[6]	Quarto
	And prayes you to *beleeue* him	Folio

Singer's emendation[7] to "relieve" is in accordance with the action taken. The line is otherwise singularly pointless.

I, iii, 231:	the flinty and steele *Cooch* of warre	Quarto
	the flinty and Steele *Coach* of Warre	Folio

Pope's reading "Couch" is clearly what is meant and this is invariably spelt "couch" or "cowch" on the thirty or so occasions when it appears in the Folio (as verb or noun).

I, iii, 235:	*This* present *warres* against the *Ottamites*	Quarto
	This present *Warres* against the *Ottomites*	Folio

The concord is anomalous and so is the spelling of Ottomites. The Second Folio altered the former to the singular: Malone to the plural.

I, iii, 264–5:	Nor to comply with heate, the young affects	
	In *my defunct*, and proper satisfaction	Quarto
	Nor to comply with heat the yong affects	
	In *my defunct*, and proper satisfaction	Folio

It has been customary since Capell to emend to "me defunct" and to take "the young affects in me defunct" as an explanatory parenthesis, referring to "heat". Hart's defence of "my defunct" is unconvincing.

II, i, 50–1:	Therefore my *hope's* not surfeited to death,	
	Stand in bold cure	Quarto
	Therefore my *hope's* (not surfetted to death)	
	Stand in bold Cure	Folio

The apostrophe is wrong; as the text stands, the word in question can only be taken as a plural noun.

II, i, 229–33:

When the blood is made dull with the act of sport, there should be againe to inflame it, and giue saciety a fresh *appetite*. Loue lines in fauour, sympathy in yeares, manners and beauties   Quarto

When the Blood is made dull with the Act of Sport, there should be a game to enflame it, and to giue Satiety a fresh *appetite*. Louelinesse in fauour, simpathy in yeares, Manners, and Beauties   Folio

What is wanted is Theobald's comma, instead of the period, after "appetite". The Folio's attempt to improve the sense by reading "a game" for "againe" overlooked the real cause of the trouble.

II, iii, 218–20:

	If partiality affin'd, or *league* in office,	
	Thou doest deliuer, more or lesse then truth,	
	Thou art no souldier	Quarto
	If partially Affin'd, or *league* in office,	
	Thou dost deliuer more, or lesse then Truth	
	Thou art no Souldier	Folio

Pope's "leagu'd" is necessary.

II, iii, 320–3:

for that he has deuoted and giuen vp himselfe to the contemplation, marke and *deuotement* of her parts and graces   Quarto

for that he hath deuoted, and giuen vp himselfe to the Contemplation, marke: and *deuotement* of her parts and Graces   Folio

Theobald's emendation to "denotement" seems sound; "deuoted...to...deuotement" is tautological and the sequence 'contemplation, mark and denotement' would have had even greater cogency for an Elizabethan than it has now.

III, iii, 440–1:

	If it be that, or any, *it* was hers,	
	It speakes against her, with the other proofes	Quarto
	If it be that, or any, *it* was hers.	
	It speakes against her with the other proofes	Folio

In spite of Greg's defence of "it", this seems to me dramatically wrong and I would accept Malone's emendation to "that". Iago's argument is, surely, that if Cassio had the strawberry-spotted handkerchief, or any handkerchief *that* was Desdemona's, it proved her guilt. He cannot be arguing that if Cassio had this particular handkerchief, or any handkerchief, *it* was Desdemona's. Iago works on Othello's feelings by suggestion, not by statement, and "it was hers" is out of character. Editors before Malone followed the Second Folio's emendation to "if't was".

III, iii, 468–9:

	And to obey, *shall be remorce,*	
	What bloody worke so euer	Quarto
	And to obey *shall be in me remorse,*	
	What bloody businesse euer	Folio

I doubt if the Folio reading was more than a makeshift effort to fill out the Quarto's metrically defective line. Neither the expression nor the use of 'remorse' is natural. Pope and Theobald thought a negative was required and accordingly emended "And" to "Not" or "Nor". The *Oxford English Dictionary* and Onions got round the difficulty by glossing "remorse" as "solemn obligation", but there is seemingly no parallel nor is the semantic development likely.

20

Sense can be wrested from the lines by taking them to mean "however bloody the business my participation will be a sympathetic act", but this still leaves an unnaturalness of expression. The lines are, I think, corrupt.

IV, ii, 63–4:	Patience thy young and rose-lip'd Cherubin,	
	I *here* looke grim as Hell	Quarto
	Patience, thou young and Rose-lip'd Cherubin,	
	I *heere* looke grim as hell	Folio

The Folio's "thou" for "thy" improves matters and Theobald's emendation of "here" to "there", which has been generally accepted, has the merit of bringing the reading into line with "there" in ll. 57 and 62. Hart's defence of "here" as a reference to Othello's blackness seems strained.

These passages are the ones at which, as an editor, I should boggle. At one time or another one critic or another has defended one or more of these readings, but no one, I think, has championed them all.[8] Even the most conservative critic would therefore agree that there are some errors common to the two texts. If the Quarto and Folio were printed from different manuscripts, then such errors must have originated in a common ancestor. An alternative explanation is that they represent contaminations of the Folio text by the Quarto through their having escaped correction when a copy of the Quarto was 'cured' and 'perfected' for Jaggard. In the errors themselves there is nothing to show which supposition is the right one.

THE ORTHOGRAPHICAL EVIDENCE

What is immediately apparent from the short extracts given above is the very close orthographical connexion between the Quarto and Folio texts. This is true of common words and of rarer ones. There are at least three nonce words in the Quarto and Folio *Othello*: 'moraller' (II, iii, 301), 'probal' (II, iii, 344) and 'exsufflicate' (III, iii, 182), of which two ("proball" and "exufflicate") appear in identical spellings. It might be argued that their unfamiliarity encouraged copyists and compositors to preserve them as they found them, but this explanation will not account for the identical spelling of more common words which could be spelt in a number of ways. "Morties" (II, i, 9), i.e. 'mortise', is common to the Quarto and Folio, though half a dozen spellings were possible;[9] "lushious" (I, iii, 354), as against "luscious" in the Folio text of *A Midsummer Night's Dream*, is again common to the printed texts; so too is "Pyoners" (III, iii, 346), as against "Pioners" in the Folio text of *Henry V* and all three texts of *Hamlet*.

No one who has collated the Quarto and Folio texts can, I think, fail to have been struck by the way in which compositors in different printing houses, at a time when spelling was still fluid, none the less spelt in the same way word after word for which at least two spellings were still current. The following is a passage from the Quarto (IV, ii, 57–64); Folio spelling variants are italicized:

> But there: where I haue *garner'd* vp my heart,
> Where either I must liue, or beare no life,
> The fountaine, from the which my currant runnes,

Or else *dryes* vp, to be discarded thence,
Or keepe it as a Cesterne, for foule Toades
To knot and gender in: turne thy complexion there,
Patience *thy* young and rose-lip'd Cherubin,
I *here* looke grim as Hell.

The Folio reads "garnerd", "dries", "heere" and emends "thy" to "thou". We have, of course, to reckon with the fact that the *Othello* printed texts are contemporaries. The compositors of Okes (the Quarto printer) and Jaggard have certain spelling conventions in common, and "heart", "beare", "fountaine", "keepe", "Cesterne", "complexion", "looke", "grim" and "hell" are normal Folio spellings; but others are what may be described as Folio variables: "currant", "runnes", "foule", "Toades" and "young" might well have been otherwise spelt without infringing such rules as existed in Jaggard's printing-house.

We might, of course, suppose that all concerned in the transmission of the Quarto and Folio texts took peculiar pains to preserve the accidental features (spellings, anomalous concords, etc.), including even the errors, of their manuscripts. If the Quarto and Folio texts were independent prints, then three agents at least[10] must have operated with singular like-mindedness: the copyist responsible for the Quarto manuscript and the Quarto and Folio compositors. But a scrupulously accurate hand and eye is just what we cannot assume in the transmission of the Quarto manuscript since this is entirely at variance with other features of the Quarto text.

VARIANT READINGS

The Quarto, as is well known, differs from the Folio to a marked degree in its readings (both in the dialogue and the stage directions). These readings are in general inferior to the Folio's and many of them can by no stretch of the imagination be explained as due to mis-reading. The following are a sample:

	QUARTO	FOLIO
I, iii, 252	vtmost pleasure	very quality
I, iii, 358	shee must haue change, shee must	She must change for youth
II, i, 65	beare all excellency	tyre the Ingeniuer
II, i, 96	So speakes this voyce	See for the Newes
III, iii, 3	know	warrant
III, iii, 125	presume	be sworne
III, iii, 148	I intreate you then	that your wisedome
III, iii, 154	Zouns	What dost thou meane
III, iii, 277	*Desdemona* comes	Looke where she comes
III, iii, 282	Why is your speech so faint	Why do you speake so faintly
IV, ii, 139	outragious	most villanous

Among stage directions we find:

I, i, 160–1	*Enter* Barbantio *in his night gowne*	Quarto
	Enter Brabantio	Folio

II, ii	*Enter a Gentleman reading a Proclamation*	Quarto
	Enter Othello's Herald with a Proclamation	Folio
v, ii, 83–4	*he stiflles her.* Emillia *calls within*	Quarto
	Smothers her. Æmilia *at the doore*	Folio

It is impossible to reconcile such verbal divergencies with any textual theory that involves supposing even ordinary care in the transcription of the Quarto manuscript. Given this tendency towards verbal substitutions in the Quarto, it is very remarkable to find that it agrees with the Folio in readings such as "This present warres", "Toth' very moment" (I, iii, 133), "morties", "lushious", "my currant runnes", and so on. It is, in fact, only possible to reconcile the evidence of the verbal variants between the printed texts with their close orthographical connexion, common errors and common typographical features by supposing that the Folio text was printed (with correction and amplification) from a copy of the Quarto. Errors common to the Quarto and Folio would thus represent Quarto errors that escaped correction when a copy of the Quarto was 'cured' and 'perfected' for Jaggard and orthographical and typographical similarities are thus, naturally, legacies in the Folio from the earlier print. I cannot see any other way of reconciling the similarities and dissimilarities presented by these two texts.

It is even more difficult to explain how it is that the Quarto and Folio texts preserve so many common accidental features if we recognize the Quarto variants for what they are: namely, not errors of transcription but memorial perversions.[11] The mislineations of the *Othello* Quarto and general tendency towards metrical irregularity, its interpolations, vulgarizations, omissions, and divergences from the Folio in stage directions are more reminiscent of the 'bad' Quarto of *Richard III* than of anything found in 'good' quartos. They cannot represent in such numbers, and in their occasional quite shocking inferiority, variants originating in alternative readings in foul papers. A single instance puts the nature of the Quarto variants beyond doubt. It occurs at III, iii, 154. Iago has just begun to sow the seeds of suspicion about Cassio in Othello's mind. He is feeling his way carefully, and hypocritically discrediting his own suspicions as possibly the imaginings of a jealously fanciful mind:

> I do beseech you,
>   ...that your wisedome
> From one, that so imperfectly conceits,
> Would take no notice, nor build your selfe a trouble
> Out of his scattering, and vnsure obseruance:
> It were not for your quiet, nor your good,
> Nor for my Manhood, Honesty, and Wisedome,
> To let you know my thoughts.

> *Oth.* What dost thou meane? (l. 154)
> *Iago.* Good name in Man, & woman...

Iago's evasions have aroused Othello's suspicions, but no more. For his controlled (and even a little dangerous) inquiry "What dost thou meane?" the Quarto has "Zouns". It is impossible to regard this as even a first thought from Shakespeare's foul papers. Metrically, it is unfortunate and dramatically, lamentable. It cannot possibly be a misreading of "What dost thou meane?". It can only be a blundering attempt to cover up a lapse of memory.

I do not suggest that the manuscript from which the Quarto was printed was 'yarked up' by actors. It strikes me, rather, as the work of a book-keeper who relied on his knowledge of the play as acted and on his invention where memory failed. Greg thought the *Othello* texts too good for 'reporting' to explain their differences, but if the Folio was printed from the Quarto neither text may be as good as it seems. There are many more passages in the play where error has been suspected than have been customarily emended, partly because they had seemingly the authority of independently transmitted texts behind them and partly because sense (at least of a sort) could be made of them. And there are almost certainly other common errors that defy identification.[12]

NOTES

1. The greater the number of Quartos, the greater the number of errors that accumulated in the course of reprinting, and such errors can be more easily recognized for what they are than all but the most obvious ones of a single print. The Folio's frequent use of later Quartos as the basis of its texts often resulted in the perpetuation of errors traceable to Quarto reprints (e.g. *Richard III*).

2. The name, however, was far less of a strain on Jaggard's typographical resources than the *Merchant of Venice* (with Bassanio, Nerissa, and Jessica) or *Julius Caesar* (with Cassius and Messala). The convention was maintained in the former play but not in the latter, where it breaks down on the fourth leaf of a quire.

3. As is well known, this is common in some Folio plays, owing to the narrowness of the column.

4. There are many other occasions when a line is divided for less obvious reasons. Some seem the result of mislineation.

5. There is a corresponding division of the line in the Folio at IV, ii, 110, but the line could not in any case have been got into the Folio column. At I, ii, 28 and II, iii, 63 the Folio prints as one line.

6. The italics in this and the following extracts are mine.

7. I mention only the emendations that have enjoyed wide currency and the editor who first adopted them rather than the critic who first proposed them.

8. There are others (I, i, 21; II, iii, 167; II, iii, 391; III, iii, 65–6) where error has been suspected which, for one reason or another, trouble me far less.

9. The following occur in the *Oxford English Dictionary* as examples of the use of the noun between 1590 and 1631: "morteses", "mortescis", "mortaise", "mortuis", "mortis".

10. The agents can be limited to three on the assumption that the Quarto manuscript was a copy of that supplied for the Folio.

11. A memorially recorded text would differ to a marked extent in its accidental features from one transmitted in the orthodox way.

12. The evidence of *Richard III* is disquieting. There are a number of readings common to the Sixth Quarto and the Folio which we know to be wrong from a comparison with the readings of the First Quarto. In themselves they would escape suspicion.

AN APPROACH TO THE PROBLEM
OF *PERICLES*[1]

BY

PHILIP EDWARDS

The play of *Pericles, Prince of Tyre* bristles with problems, but the cardinal one, to which all others are subsidiary, is, of course, the puzzle of how far it is Shakespeare's work. The style of the play is very unequal and there is the additional complication that, although three times printed in Shakespeare's lifetime with his name on the title-page, it was excluded from the First Folio. Dryden thought to account for its unevenness by allotting the play to the earliest part of Shakespeare's career, but since Rowe in 1709 found (unspecified) "good Reason" for believing that "the greatest part" of the play was not Shakespeare's, the hypothesis of divided authorship has in general ruled. Many different theories have been advanced. We are told that Shakespeare collaborated with one or more named or unnamed fellow-dramatists, that he revised an old play, or that an old play of his was revised by another; his hand has been seen in one act only, or in two, three, four or even all five acts. But it is not too much to say that the weight of opinion regards the earlier part of the play as largely non-Shakespearian and the later largely Shakespeare's.

There is no doubt we should like to have the matter settled, and the play's problems assume rather more urgency in the light of the increased interest shown recently in Shakespeare's 'Romances', with which *Pericles* is obviously closely associated. It is, however, improbable that any real advances can be made in the question of authorship on the customary basis—that is, the basis of style. For there is only one text of *Pericles* (that published in 1609, from which the texts of the other Quartos derive) and this is acknowledged to be in many ways imperfect. The allocation of different parts of the play to different authors may then be a dangerous game when it is not known how far the original language has been distorted. This, of course, is no new caveat. Malone, in 1780, put down much of the play's awkwardness to the irresponsibility of the printers, and Collier and Mommsen held that the play we have is but a skeleton of the full work.[2] The Cambridge editors stated emphatically that "the text has come down to us in so maimed and imperfect a state that we can no more judge of what the play was when it left the master's hand than we should have been able to judge of *Romeo and Juliet* if we had only had the first Quarto as authority for the text".

Clearly we need to know more of how far the play was altered from what was originally written and spoken on the stage, and it is the purpose of the present article to try to show in some measure the nature and extent of the corruptions to be found in the Quarto. Although the Quarto has been classed as 'bad' by Pollard, Quincy Adams, Sir Edmund Chambers, Sir Walter Greg and Leo Kirschbaum[3] no views have been advanced on the *kind* of 'badness' it evinces. I hope to demonstrate that it is indeed a 'bad' Quarto, a 'bad' Quarto of a very strange kind. It is possible that when the distortions and perversions of the play as we have it are understood, a new examination of the authorship-problem could be made that did not mistake accidents for substance.

25

THE FACTS

The 'booke'—that is, presumably, the prompt copy—of a play called *Pericles Prynce of Tyre* was taken by Edward Blount to Stationers' Hall to be registered on 20 May 1608 (he also took *Anthony and Cleopatra*).[4] No edition by Blount followed this registration. In the same year appeared a prose-work by George Wilkins—*The Painfull Aduentures of Pericles Prince of Tyre*—which purported to give a "true History of the Play" which had been "by the Kings Maiesties Players excellently presented". In 1609 a Quarto was published by Henry Gosson, *The Late, And much admired Play, Called Pericles, Prince of Tyre* with "By William Shakespeare" on the title-page.[5] The text of this Quarto, which is the basis of every subsequent edition, is the object of the present analysis.

TOKENS OF CORRUPTION

Gosson's Quarto is clearly not in the same category as the miserable 'bad' Quartos of *Hamlet* or *Romeo and Juliet*; its length is normal and much of it reads well. Nevertheless, certain features of it demonstrate that the text cannot have come directly from the pen of an author or from the playhouse but must have been assembled without reference to an authorized manuscript.

There are several instances of confusion of the action within a scene that suggest awkward attempts to glue together fragments of an imperfectly remembered original. One such instance is I, ii.[6] Pericles, fleeing from the fury of Antiochus whose dreadful secret he has unriddled, has just arrived at Tyre. The scene opens with the direction *Enter Pericles with his Lords*, but at the very first words—Pericles's "Let none disturb vs"—the Lords are required to file out in silence as they came. After a soliloquy in which Pericles expatiates on his misery and his fear of an invasion by Antiochus, we find the Lords filing in once more—*Enter all the Lords to Pericles*. Their behaviour now is not a little strange: they wish their prince *bon voyage*:

> 1. *Lord.* Ioy and all comfort in your sacred brest.
> 2. *Lord.* And keepe your mind till you returne to vs peacefull and comfortable.

Now Pericles has only just returned home and is purposing no fresh journey. When, indeed, shortly after this, he does hurriedly decide to leave his country, all is done with extreme secrecy and the Lords are told nothing until he has gone. Their clairvoyance here, therefore, is remarkable, but stranger things follow when Helicanus interrupts the remarks just quoted (which, their irrelevance apart, are perfectly dutiful) with a tirade against flattery. This begins

> Peace, peace, and giue experience tongue,
> They doe abuse the King that flatter him,

and includes most unexpected and unwarranted observations on the duty of kings to suffer reproach. The answer of Pericles to all this is first to send the Lords out *again*—this time with an injunction to see what ships are in the harbour—and then to remonstrate with Helicanus for his daring to do what there is nothing in the text to show that he actually did, namely, chide his Prince for his faults. Pericles then pardons him with the words

> thou art no flatterer,
> I thanke thee fort, and heauen forbid
> That kings should let their eares heare their faults hid.
> Fit Counsellor, and seruant for a Prince,
> Who by thy wisdome makes a Prince thy seruant,
> What wouldst thou haue me doe?

This scene is peculiarly absurd in that it is easy to guess from the evidence in the text itself what order of events is here garbled into nonsense. We may suppose that Pericles enters with his Lords and that they make their respectful greetings on his return to his country ("Joy and all comfort in your sacred breast"). But Pericles, in his uneasiness and anxiety of mind, rather curtly dismisses them, urging them as they go to watch the harbour (for ships from Antioch, of course). Alone, he gives sorrow tongue as in the text, after which Helicanus enters, by himself, determined to fathom the cause of his prince's moodiness. He takes him to task for his retiredness, and concludes his speech with a defence of his own temerity on the lines that the real crime against royalty is flattery and not such candour and frankness as he has shown. Pericles then expostulates, pardons, and explains his disquiet as in the Quarto.

The confusions in the text explain their own origin. The lords have been brought in a second time and have been robbed of some of the remarks relevant to their first entry because someone assembling the text has only the latter part of Helicanus's speech. If it be someone relying on an imperfect memory, he recalls a second entry, and remarks from Helicanus on flattery. He has forgotten Helicanus's reproaching the king, and that the later remarks are only a personal apologia for *not* being a flatterer. Somehow the speech against flattery must be motivated, and so the lords are brought in and made to say something—never mind its incongruity—that may have a flavour of flattery. In the event, the words spoken by the lords make no sense, Helicanus's speech is meaningless, and Pericles's behaviour to Helicanus incomprehensible; in fact, nonsense is created. A not very difficult puzzle has been unintelligently solved.[7]

An example of a different sort of corruption is in the pageant of the Knights with their *imprese* in II, ii. Thaisa describes the second knight to her father:

> A Prince of *Macedon* (my royall father)
> And the deuice he beares vpon his Shield,
> Is an Armed Knight, that's conquered by a Lady:
> The motto thus in Spanish. *Pue Per doleera kee per forsa.*

The motto is of course not in Spanish or any other known language. Dyce emended it to the hybrid *Più por dulzura que por fuerza* and by exchanging Italian *Più* for Spanish *Mas* later editors justified more completely the word "Spanish" in the text, while departing further from the words printed. Others pointed out[8] that the motto as a whole was nearer to the Italian *Più per dolcezza che per forza* than the Spanish *Mas por dulzura que por fuerza*. It does indeed seem likely that the "in Spanish" of the text is wrong. The nearest analogue of this device that Green could find (*Shakespeare and the Emblem Writers*, 1870, pp. 156–86) was the French *Plus par doulceur que par force*, and it is not impossible that the Quarto motto is a garbling of this, especially since all the other devices of the Knights have sources which Green traced. But whether the motto is

Italian or French, what has happened is that someone has tried to render phonetically words in a foreign language not understood and has perhaps thought to cover up his ignorance by attributing the words to a language obscure enough to most readers of Jacobean books.

Another kind of confusion that betrays the origin of Gosson's Quarto as an attempted reconstruction of someone else's work is the frequent repetition of words and phrases. Repetitions of this kind have been shown time and again to be the stigmata of memorial reconstruction in the 'bad' Quartos. Here are three examples. At I, i, 30-1 we have

> Her face like *Heauen*, inticeth thee to *view*
> Her *countlesse* glory....

Forty lines later in the same scene we have

> But ô you powers!
> That giues *heauen countlesse* eyes to *view* mens actes....

At v, i, 107 there is that moving speech of Pericles which begins

> I am great with woe, and shall *deliuer weeping*....

Fifty lines later Marina echoes this:

> as my good Nurse
> Lycherida hath oft *deliuered weeping*....

In the two following passages there is a strange repetition of the words *man that can resolve you...* *reverend sir, the gods.*

1. *Say.* Sir, this is *the man that can* in ought you would *resolue you.*
Lys. Hayle *reuerent Syr, the Gods* preserue you. (v, i, 12–14)

Th. ...*this man* through whom the Gods haue showne their power, *that can* from first to last *resolue you.*
Per. *Reuerent Syr, the gods* can haue no mortall officer.... (v, iii, 59–62)

In each example it is easy to see which passage is the rightful owner of the words or phrases, and which has become contaminated. Certainly we seem to have here the tricks of memory rather than the workings of the law of association in a dramatist's mind.

VERSE AND PROSE IN THE PRINTING-HOUSE

We come now to the chief evidence for believing that the Quarto of *Pericles* was not printed directly from an author's manuscript or, indeed, from copy compiled with any reference to an authorized manuscript, namely, the quality of the verse, and an examination of this involves a bibliographical excursus into the bizarre printing of verse and prose in the Quarto.

Not counting the Gower prologues and links, there are about 1550 lines of verse in the play (uncertain prosody and uncertain printing make precision impossible). Of this verse 452 lines are printed as prose and 140 incorrectly divided—in all amounting to over a third of the total.

In addition, 51 lines in the play are printed as verse which are actually prose. By far the greater number of these irregularities occurs in the third, fourth and fifth acts of the play—from the renowned speech of Pericles "The God of this great Vast, rebuke these surges" to the end. The first two acts, which contain a little more than half the total verse, are printed with fair regularity, containing a faulty proportion of roughly 10 per cent. But in the last three acts, this element of irregular verse rises steeply to 70 per cent, with no less than 415 lines of verse printed as prose. This irregularity in the verse, and the disproportionate way it is shared between the two halves of the play, throw great light on the nature of the copy for the Quarto.

It cannot immediately be assumed, however, that what stands in the text is the equivalent of what stood in the manuscript and it must be kept in mind that the idiosyncrasies of compositors may be partly responsible for the appearance of the text. It is clear from an analysis of the features of the printed page throughout the Quarto that three compositors were at work on the play (see Appendix, p. 47); we may call them x, y and z. Their shares in the text can be set out as follows:

```
x   A2 2v3  3v4  4v  .   .   .   .   .   .   .   .   .   C1 iv2   2v3  3v4  4v  .   .
y   .   .   .   .   .   .   .   .  B1 iv2  2v  .   .   .   .   .   .   .   .   .   .
z   .   .   .   .   .   .   .   .   .   3  3v4  4v  .   .   .   .   .   .   .   .   .

x   D1 iv2  2v3  3v4  4v  .  E1 iv2  2v3  3v4  4v  .   .   .   .   .   .   .   .   .
y   .   .   .   .   .   .   .   .   .   .   .   .   .   .   F1 iv2  2v  .   .   .   .
z   .   .   .   .   .   .   .   .   .   .   3  3v4  4v

x   .   .   .   .   .   .   .   .   .   .   .
y   G1 iv2  2v  .   .   .   .   3  3v4  4v  .  I1 iv2  .   .
z   .   3  3v4  4v  H1 iv2  2v  .   .   2v3  3v  .   .
```

Each compositor has a share in the first two acts, and it will be convenient to begin with this early part of the play, which has few problems, and go on to the perplexing later acts with some knowledge of the compositors' capabilities.

Acts I and II contain comparatively regular verse and there is nothing to make us suppose that by and large the copy did not present verse in a normal regular manner. Taking first that part set by x, we find the lining of the verse even and orderly, with no suggestion that the manuscript was difficult to follow or presented grave problems to a compositor. There is not one instance of verse in prose form and only six short passages containing decidedly erroneous lineation: I, i, 3–5; I, i, 143–58; I, iv, 99–101; II, iii, 87–8; II, iv, 3–9; II, v, 50–4. The second and the fifth of these passages are composed of uncertain verse that it is difficult to scan successfully, and the irregular lineation presumably derived from the copy. The others, however, seem to derive from the compositor. Three of the passages have one thing in common—there is a half-line in them. There are many examples in other texts of mistakes in the printing arising from a half-line of verse in the manuscript being written out on the same line of the paper as the succeeding full line of verse.[9] These errors are certainly of the same breed. Here is one example:

> *Per.* Arise I pray you, rise; we do not looke for reuerence,
> But for loue, and harborage for our selfe, our ships, & men.   (I, iv, 99–101)

This should presumably stand as:

> *Per.* Arise I pray you, rise;
> We do not looke for reuerence, but for loue,
> And harborage for our selfe, our ships, & men.

But here is the important point. The manuscript would read at this point

> *Per.* Arise I pray you, rise; we do not look for reverence but for love,
> and harbourage for our self, our ships, and men.

The compositor has rearranged his copy: not tumbling to the reason for the extraordinarily long line in the copy, he has taken upon himself the task of redividing two and a half lines of verse in order to give a more balanced appearance to his page. Here is a strange spirit of enterprise, an understanding of which helps to clear up many difficulties in the text. A similar rearrangement—again awkward enough—may be seen at II, v, 51-4, where the apparently overloaded line in the copy

> By the Gods I haue not: neuer did thought of mine leuie offence

has been the signal for *x* to make a crude averaging-out of the length of three whole lines. At II, iii, 87 we have an example of the 'overloaded' line where the extra length is not particularly noticeable, and the compositor has printed it as it stands:

> A Gentleman of *Tyre*: who onely by misfortune of the seas

The only erroneous division in *x*'s stint in the first two acts that is unlikely to have come from the copy itself and that does not involve this disturbing half-line is in the opening lines of the first scene of the play, following the Gower prologue. If a facsimile is examined it will be seen to show the sort of uncertainty that might arise if the compositor, meeting blank verse in the copy for the first time, was dubious of the nature of what faced him.

Remarkable evidence of the willingness of compositor *x* to rearrange the lining of his copy through a misguided zeal for an appearance of regularity is to be found in the whole scene of II, i. Pericles, shipwrecked, is cast ashore and succoured by fishermen, who direct him to Pentapolis. The speeches of Pericles are in verse, those of the fishermen in prose; but although, throughout the scene, the verse is quite regularly-printed blank verse, the prose is most strangely fashioned. At the beginning it is ludicrously manhandled into slices and printed to look like verse; a little later the prose appears normally, then as 'verse' once more—but now in very long lines that on one occasion (ll. 123-4) become simply prose lines furnished with initial capital letters. After a return to prose as prose, the fishermen's speeches end with prose as verse once more. Here are two examples:

> Nay Maister, sayd not I as much,
> When I saw the Porpas how he bounst and tumbled?
> They say they're halfe fish, halfe flesh:
> A plague on them, they nere come but I looke to be washt.
> Maister, I maruell how the Fishes liue in the Sea? (ll. 25-30)

> Mary sir, halfe a dayes iourney: And Ile tell you,
> He hath a faire Daughter, and to morrow is her birth-day,
> And there are Princes and Knights come from all partes of
> the World, to Iust and Turney for her loue.   (ll. 112–15)

Prose printed as verse is common enough in 'bad' texts, and as the damage is extensive (the scene is one of 170 lines) we could willingly enough impute this particular absurdity to the copy. But whoever was responsible for preparing the manuscript of the first two acts had an entirely satisfactory knowledge of metrics and the difference between verse and prose—the general regularity of the lineation of the verse proves this. This unjustifiable splitting-up of the prose is an illiterate gaffe and its origin almost certainly the printing-house—and the mind of compositor x. First, the peculiarly spasmodic appearance of the lining points to a 'trial and error' process by a compositor, especially when the 'verse' becomes justified or near-justified lines of prose with initial capitals; the arbiter of division is the width of the compositor's composing measure, not the width of the paper of the copy. Secondly, nowhere in the play, save in passages set by x, does prose as 'verse' appear: the eccentricity betrays him.

And it is not improbable that, given a manuscript where a line of verse stretched out across the page, without the initial capitals to which we are accustomed, a man without a knowledge of scansion found it hard to distinguish prose lines from verse lines. It was seen above that the first lines of blank verse in the play upset x. And here is a scene where he meets prose for the first time in his copy—and cruelly enough, the prose is intermingled with verse speeches. His aim being as we have seen it, to preserve the balanced appearance of his page and possessing, as we have also seen, the courage to take lineation into his own hands, he may well be understood here to be groping in puzzled fashion with copy he does not understand. As he goes through the scene he sets an increasing amount of prose as prose; this indicates not understanding but surrender.

So much, then, for x's share of Acts I and II; he is an efficient enough workman, but he is disposed to take strange licences with the lineation where he supposes his copy to be irregular.

The fortunes of y and z in setting up their shares of the first two acts may be more briefly dealt with. y sets up verse straightforwardly as verse except for a few errors. His first ten lines (B1), which are in verse, he sets up as prose—an initial misunderstanding to be compared with x's mislineation of the first lines of the play. His other errors, apart from an immoral habit of adding the last word of a line to the beginning of the next rather than widen the measure of his composing stick, involve, as did x's, half-lines (I, ii, 35–6; I, ii, 65–6; I, ii, 101–10). His reaction, when faced with the inordinately long line of the manuscript containing the half-line plus full-line is to print what he can on one line and then stumble into prose for a line or two until, as it were, he regains his equilibrium.

Compositor z is the least efficient workman. His section of this first half of the play (B3–4v) begins with a prose passage, which he sets up as prose. It then takes him the remainder of a forty-line scene, all in verse, to wake up to the fact that not all his copy is in prose. Once verse is established, however, he shows himself quite able to set up verse as verse (except for an interruption by the inevitable half-line, which throws his page into prose for a line or two at I, iv, 76–80).

In the first two acts of the Quarto we have nothing to argue that the verse was not written as verse in the copy. The comparatively few disarranged passages may mostly be laid at the charge of the compositors. And as for the compositors, in spite of these blunders, they are not wreckers and perverters of their copy. Each is able to follow and set up verse as verse with fair success. *x* has his failing of wishing to 'correct' his copy; *y* and *z* are occasionally immoral enough to slip into a line or two of prose.

In the last three acts of the play there is a much greater proportion of misdivided verse. Compositor *x* sets one sheet only (E), which comprises almost the whole of Act III. For the first half of this stint, all goes well. The verse is printed correctly. We should notice signs of what there has been no evidence of before, an untidy copy. In Pericles's speech

> *Per.* As you thinke meet; for she must ouer board straight:
> Most wretched Queene.

The phrase "for she must ouer board straight" belongs to the previous speaker. But half-way through E3 (soon after the opening of the second scene of the act) a transformation comes over the text. There is nothing less than a complete breakdown in the printing of the verse. Occasional lines or pairs of lines are divided correctly, but generally speaking, incorrect and positively absurd division now rules for the remainder of *x*'s section. On one occasion (Cerimon's speech at III, ii, 65-7) three lines of verse are printed as prose, and this was a peculiarity never appearing in *x*'s work in the first two acts. An example of the verse as it is divided up at this stage is as follows:

	No. of syllables
Cery. I hold it euer Vertue and Cunning,	10
Were endowments greater, then Noblenesse & Riches;	13
Carelesse Heyres, may the two latter darken and expend;	13
But Immortalitie attendes the former,	11
Making a man a god:	6
T'is knowne, I euer haue studied Physicke:	10
Through which secret Art, by turning ore Authorities,	13
I haue togeather with my practize, made famyliar,	14
To me and to my ayde, the blest infusions that dwels	13
In Vegetiues, in Mettals, Stones: and can speake of the	13
Disturbances that Nature works, and of her cures;	12
which doth giue me a more content in course of true delight	14
Then to be thirsty after tottering honour, or	12
Tie my pleasure vp in silken Bagges,	9
To please the Foole and Death.	6 (III, ii, 26–42)

Compositor *y*, taking over from *x* at sheet F, has nine lines of verse to complete a scene. *x* has been printing this in irregular verse approaching correctness in the last speech. *y prints these remaining lines as prose.* The little scene of 18 lines (III, iv) that follows is a bewildering mixture of verse correctly lined (8 lines), verse misdivided (2 lines) and verse as prose (8 lines). And this is typical of the remainder of the verse in the play which it falls to *y* to set. Four-fifths of it he sets as unashamed prose. Half of the remaining fifth is wrongly divided. Time and again speeches change in mid-career from the verse or prose manner in which they began. Or, in a solid block of verse-as-prose appear a few lonely lines of misdivided verse. Here is a short example of γ's text:

> *Per.* O stop there a little, this is the rarest dreame
> That ere duld sleepe did mocke sad fooles withall,
> This cannot be my daughter, buried; well, where were you
> bred? Ile heare you more too' th bottome of your storie,
> and neuer interrupt you.   (v, i, 162–7)

and another that follows a few lines later:

> *Mar.* The King my father did in *Tharsus* leaue me,
> Till cruel *Cleon* with his wicked wife,
> Did seeke to murther me: and hauing wooed a villaine,
> To attempt it, who hauing drawne to doo't,
> A crew of Pirats came and rescued me,
> Brought me to *Metaline*,
> But good sir whither will you haue me? why doe you weep?
> It may be you thinke mee an imposture, no good fayth: I
> am the daughter to King *Pericles*, if good king *Pericles* be.

As in x's section of these latter acts, we have confusion that seems to betoken a crowded and untidy manuscript confronting the compositor:

> *Li.* May wee not see him?
> *Hell.* You may, but bootlesse. Is your sight, hee will not speake to any, yet let me obtaine my wish.
> *Lys.* Behold him, this was a goodly person.
> *Hell.* Till the disaster that one mortall wight droue him to this.   (v, i, 31–8)

This passage should almost certainly be assigned to the speakers as printed in the Globe Shakespeare:

> *Lys.* May we not see him?
> *Hel.* You may
> But bootless is your sight: he will not speak
> To any.
> *Lys.* Yet let me obtain my wish.
> *Hel.* Behold him. This was a goodly person,
> Till the disaster that, one mortal night,
> Drove him to this.

Turning now to compositor z's share of the last three acts, we find little to detain us. Again excepting the Gower choruses and the Epilogue, z has something under 200 lines of verse to print, and it is all printed as prose: there is no sign of division, regular or otherwise.

The manuscript for the Quarto of *Pericles* from that point in III, ii where the regularity of the verse breaks down up to the end of the play must have been quite different in character from that of the first two acts. But it is not enough to say, as it was suggested for those first two acts that, by and large, the copy must have resembled what is presented in the printed text. It would be a strange coincidence indeed were the sharp distinctions in the arrangement of the verse in the sections of the three compositors caused by variation in the copy—that is to say, that the part of the manuscript z had to deal with was in 'verse-as-prose', the part for y in a mixture of 'verse-as-prose', regular verse and irregular verse, and so on. Equally absurd would it be to say that in the copy the verse was regularly set out and that the irregularities which appear in the text are compositors' distortions; if that were so, the same distortion would be observable in the first two acts.

It seems inescapable that from sheet F onwards (the responsibility of y and z), at least the bulk of the verse in the copy was written as prose with just about as much abortive and incorrect attempts at division as we find in y's printed text (though, since we know from Acts I and II that y was capable of an occasional departure from his copy into prose, a little of the verse-as-prose may here be his responsibility). The tendency in z to print prose is enough to have erased from his text the desultory slicings of lines of verse that are retained in y—had there been more than desultory slicings in the copy some evidence at least of them would have appeared in z's text.

The more difficult problem is to decide if x's share of the copy was in this same state of verse-as-prose accompanied by occasional bungling efforts to divide into verse lengths. There is no doubt that the simplest explanation of the verse as set by x is that up to the 'breakdown' at III, ii, 15, x was following the copy's regular verse, and that after that point the verse in the copy sank to the level found in y's section, and x served it as he had served 'irregularities' in the early acts—he redivided it. If the pages of misdivided verse (E 3–4 v) are examined, it will be seen that the division of the verse cannot be said to follow any aesthetic principle at all. It is simply a matter of arrangement of words to give to the printed page an appearance of verse. x has a composing stick set to a certain width, and division is easy enough for him when no principles of prosody have to be observed. From what we have gathered of x's temperament, his reasons are not far to seek: Act III has started with correctly lined verse (no inhabitant of a printing-house could achieve such sensitivity to rhythm as to divide the verse as it is there set out); then comes copy the appearance of which is very similar to the Fisherman scene (II, ii) with a strange intermingling of verse and prose. This being too much for x's tidy spirit, he hews the prose until it looks a little like verse. At least we can say that his efforts here are a little less misplaced than in the earlier scene since the verse is indeed in need of being divided; what he produces, however, is no literary achievement.

An Hypothesis Concerning the Copy

From the evidence, then, of the manner in which the verse in the copy for *Pericles* must have been set out, we have some reason for thinking that the latter half of the manuscript was prepared by a different hand from that responsible for the first half. Up to the end of Act II we have verse regularly lined, but after that, following a good beginning, verse was written as prose, though the speeches are studded with short-lived and often inept attempts to divide the verse as verse should be divided; the great variety in the printing of the verse in the latter half of the Quarto is caused by x's struggle to 'regularize' his copy. That the change is not due to the capriciousness of a single person at work on the manuscript is clear from other evidences of a second hand. We have already noted tokens of a confused and crowded page in the later acts. There are such pointers as the number of omitted entries and exits, which greatly increases after the end of Act II,[10] and differences in technique in setting out the action of the dumb-shows.[11] A change in handwriting—and for the worse—would seem to be indicated by an increase in the number of misprints in the Quarto which probably arise from compositors' inability to read what is before them—misprints like *steare* for *sceane* (scene), *sterne* for *stem*, *easterne* for *custome*, and *in oare*, *learning*, *foriner* standing for unguessable words.[12]

Poets, Poetasters and Pirates

If the 1609 Quarto of *Pericles* is reconstructed, or 'reported', we should infer, from the suggestion that two hands are at work on the manuscript, that the text was compiled by two 'reporters'. The brief examination that follows of the *quality* of the verse in the play will, I believe, confirm this. I wish to show that the verse nowhere convinces us that it is the free creative work of an original dramatist, and that the manner of reporting changes so radically in the last three acts that there is proof on aesthetic grounds of what we have reason to suspect on bibliographical grounds—that a second 'reporter' took charge of reconstructing the play at the end of Act II.

The verse of the first act of the play is generally lame and flat with strained rhymes and uncertain rhythms, and the meaning is often very far from clear. Textual corruption cannot be blamed for producing verse that reads rather like an insipid translation from another language:

> Nor come we to adde sorrow to your teares,
> But to relieue them of their heauy loade,
> And these our Ships you happily may thinke,
> Are like the Troian Horse, was stuft within
> With bloody veines expecting ouerthrow,
> Are stor'd with Corne, to make your needie bread,
> And giue them life, whom hunger-staru'd halfe dead. (I, iv, 90–6)

This is a not untypical passage, where sense struggles uneasily with nonsense, and where uninspired verse is laboriously measured out, ten syllables to the line. A careful reading of the first act, preferably in a facsimile of the Quarto (for editors have done violent things to 'improve' the text), may well make one doubt that any Elizabethan or Jacobean dramatist could have composed such verse. Its vapidity and, much more, its awkwardness suggest the imperfect attempt of someone to rework the images and ideas of another writer. Here are two further passages:

> Before thee standes this faire *Hesperides*,
> With golden fruite, but dangerous to be toucht:
> For Death like Dragons heere affright thee hard:
> Her face like Heauen, inticeth thee to view
> Her countlesse glory; which desert must gaine:
> And which without desert, because thine eye

Presumes to reach, all the whole heape must die:
Yon sometimes famous Princes, like thy selfe,
Drawne by report, aduentrous by desire,
Tell thee with speachlesse tongues, and semblance pale,
That without couering, saue yon field of Starres,
Heere they stand Martyrs slaine in *Cupids* Warres:
And with dead cheekes, aduise thee to desist,
For going on deaths net, whom none resist.   (I, i, 27–40)

...bring in our daughter, clothed like a bride,
For embracements euen of *Ioue* himselfe;
At whose conception, till *Lucina* rained,
Nature this dowry gaue; to glad her presence,
The Seanate house of Planets all did sit,
To knit in her, their best perfections.   (I, i, 6–11)

In the last passage in particular, although the general drift is clear, not the most lavish of conjectural emendations can restore order and sense. I suggest that just as there are in whole scenes confusions of the action, so here in the smaller area of single speeches we have the ingredients of images, words and phrases similarly confused. The most attractive hypothesis to account for the jumble is that some pedestrian writer is attempting to cobble together into a metrical pattern the imperfectly remembered verse of another writer, and that the logic of what he writes is the last of his cares. Perhaps, here and there, he repeats a line or two of the original perfectly; perhaps he wholly rewrites much, preserving only the sense of the original; but generally there is the strong impression of the oaf stumbling in borrowed robes. Indeed, how otherwise except as vestiges of an earlier and better version showing through layers of rewriting are we to account for the occasional and striking passages of powerful verse in the early acts? There is the famous

...the blind Mole castes
Copt hilles towards heauen, to tell the earth is throng'd
By mans oppression, and the poore Worme doth die for't:

But there are many other brief moments in the first act when a phrase runs trippingly off the tongue or an image flickers for a moment and then is lost, that show that somewhere below there is a poet—almost but not quite buried. It may be the cadence of:

If further yet you will be satisfied
Why (as it were unlicens'd of your loves)
He would depart...   (Cf. I, iii, 16–18)

or the feeling that poetry could be made out of:

You are a faire Violl, and your sense, the stringes;
Who finger'd to make man his lawfull musicke,
Would draw Heauen downe, and all the Gods to harken: (I, i, 81–3)

In Act II there are far more of these fossils of verse of a higher quality, yet the faults characterizing the verse of the first act are still everywhere to be found. A speech that begins:

> Yet cease your ire you angry Starres of heauen,

degenerates into

> Alasse, the Seas hath cast me on the Rocks,
> Washt me from shore to shore, and left my breath
> Nothing to thinke on, but ensuing death:

One that begins

> What I haue been, I haue forgot to know;

ends when Pericles, asking for assistance, utters this lurching couplet:

> Which if you shall refuse, when I am dead,
> For that I am a man, pray you see me buried.

There are many pleasing snatches of verse in the second act—

> To begge of you (kind friends) this Coate of worth,
> For it was sometime Target to a King;
> I knowe it by this marke: (II, i, 142-4)

or:

> ...spight of all the rapture of the Sea,
> This Iewell holdes his buylding on my arme: (Cf. II, i, 161-2)[13]

But these passages are embedded in verse of hobbling rhythms and general crudity. Such inequality cannot be explained in terms of revision—of a master's hand alighting on passages of an inferior play and bestowing improvements—such revision would be altogether too arbitrary and inconsequential.

It is interesting to note that in the prose of Act II—the Fishermen's speeches in the second scene—where there has been no attempt to belabour the words into an awkward shape, the general literary standard is higher than that of the poetry. The prose, that is to say, probably presents a less impeded report than the verse, and is consequently better in style.

Acts I and II, then, seem to give us the attempt of some versifier, working from his memory or from notes, to rebuild a play by a more competent writer. Perhaps the man is such a poetaster as G. I. Duthie detected in the 'bad' Quarto of *Hamlet*.[14] The result is a sorry one—jog-trot, awkward, humdrum and occasionally nonsensical verse, interspersed with fragments of the original. The whole may be likened to a repaired vase: many of the original pieces are missing, and those that survive are clumsily glued into place and patched with rough clay.

The verse of Acts III–V is generally of a far higher character:

> And humming Water must orewelme thy corpes,
> Lying with simple shels: (III, i, 64-5)

> ... hie thee whiles I say
> A priestly farewell to her: sodainely, woman.   (III, i, 69-70)

37

Oh come hither,
thou that begetst him that did thee beget,
Thou that wast borne at sea, buried at *Tharsus*,
And found at sea agen. (v, i, 196–9)

But fine though the rhythms may be, a reader soon notices that metrical regularity, so evident in the earlier part of the play, receives scant attention here. Anyone who tries to restore the misdivided verse as it is printed into its proper order faces an impossible task: the verse will not divide smoothly. There is only one good reason for this: that the verse is not the original verse but a not quite exact report; words and phrases essential to complete the metrical pattern have been forgotten and little spurious additions have crept in. Shakespeare's licences with the structure of blank verse in his later career are one thing; the deficiency of the kind we have in *Pericles* is another. The majority of critics are surely right in saying that in these later acts we are listening to Shakespeare, but equally surely we listen to him through an intermediary—someone who cannot quite render again the whole of the original, though to make good his shortcomings he does not try to recreate a metrical regularity such as is found in the early acts. The report of Acts III–V is accurate enough for us to hear the rhythms and feel the power and eloquence of the original, but not so perfectly accurate that we feel confident that we have Shakespeare, line by line, before us.

Some of the smaller corruptions may be seen in the continually appearing otiose interjections, which may ruin metre. Here are examples of how an interjection will be repeated throughout single scenes:

ô How Lychorida; now *Lychorida*; How? how *Lychorida*;
ô *Lychorida*. (III, i)

Come giue me your flowers; Come *Leonine* take her by the arme; Come, come, I loue the king your father; Come, come, I know tis good for you; Come say your prayers; Come lets haue her aboord. (IV, i)

Quotations to illustrate the generally imperfect metrical structure of the verse might be taken anywhere from the last three acts. Editors have done their best to regularize it, but they generally have to help themselves with a plethora of short and hypermetrical lines; even where they succeed in fitting a speech into a structure of ten-syllable lines, the regularity so gained does not carry with it the reader's conviction that this is a poet's way of handling the rhythmic units of his verse. There is little purpose, indeed, in trying to 'restore' the correct line-divisions of the poetry—for we have in these later acts only the *disjecta membra* of once powerful verse. It may indeed be suggested that a new 'reporter' takes over the task of reconstructing *Pericles* from Act III onwards. He knows the text better than his predecessor, and he sets about his work in a style that, had it been maintained beyond the first 90 lines, would have given us very little indeed to grumble at. But his eagerness to get all right flags, and he writes down what he recalls partly in verse, partly in prose and so we lose sight, presumably for ever, of the genuine version of the last three acts, from the opening of III, ii.

The Usefulness of Wilkins

A most important witness to testify to the 'badness' of the Quarto of *Pericles* is George Wilkins's prose redaction, published in 1608, *The Painfull Aduentures of Pericles Prince of Tyre*.[15] Unfortunately, Wilkins is a slippery customer and the relation of the novel to the Quarto is not a simple one. But the matter is not so complicated as the writings on the subject since Delius first put Wilkins forward as a man of mystery would seem to suggest. It is not possible within the limits of this article to discuss in detail the extraordinary subtle and ingenious arguments that have been put forward to show, for example, that the novel is the source of the play or that the novel is based upon the play at an earlier stage of its history—before it had received the revision which is found in the Quarto.[16] Those who wish to believe the relationship between novel and play a complex one will no doubt always be able to find evidence for their theories, but there is really nothing in Wilkins that prevents our believing that he was writing up, in a free and casual manner, the play of which the Quarto of *Pericles* is a report. The reasons for the divergencies between the two works are not difficult to find. They are explained partly by the corruptness of the Quarto, which falsifies or omits incidents and passages included in Wilkins, and partly by Wilkins's laziness and carelessness. Everyone knows that Wilkins's work is fraudulent, because so much of it is calmly copied from Laurence Twine's *The Patterne of Painefull Aduentures* (a recension of the *Gesta Romanorum* version of the Apollonius-Pericles story). His riflings from Twine grow greatly as the novel progresses and as Wilkins presumably grows more weary of the effort of recalling what took place on the stage, until, at the end of his work we are reading almost unadulterated Twine. In the equivalent of the first two acts of the play, the borrowings from Twine constitute about one-eighth of Wilkins's work; in the equivalent of the last three acts, the borrowings account for *one half* of the total. It is quite obvious that Wilkins, writing fluently but hastily, is little disturbed by his conscience for the accuracy of his work. Thaisa is resuscitated twice in the same paragraph—once as in the play and once as in Twine; Pericles, who "is now arrived at Tharsus" at the end of chapter two is still approaching it in the middle of chapter three.

Again, we must remember that Wilkins, though here a careless craftsman, was an able enough writer and rejoiced in a fertile fancy. He embellished his so-called 'report' of the play with his own inventions, either for simple adornment or to fill out passages and incidents forgotten. Half the difficulties found in trying to establish the relation between Wilkins and the Quarto disappear if it is borne in mind that it was far easier for Wilkins to rely on his own imagination than keep himself at the difficult task of reworking from memory someone else's material. We should be chary of leaping for the panacea of an earlier, lost play to account for the more staggering differences between novel and play; it may be noticed for example that the whole of the brothel-material from the capture of Marina up to her conversation with Lysimachus (which is peculiar to Wilkins, though loosely based on Twine) contains in its manner no vestiges of theatrical presentation; in those parts of the novel which run parallel with the play we find everywhere that drama has been but crudely converted into narrative; here there is no tell-tale evidence of the undigested conventions of stage-presentation.

We must also be ready to take into account, where play and novel diverge, the simple inaccuracies of memory, and this, of course, as has already been suggested, works both ways—

the reporters of the Quarto *or* Wilkins may be at fault in any given discrepancy. We find, as we should expect, that in a slow-moving piece of pageantry like the parade of the Knights (Act II) where there was time for the words spoken on the stage to be imprinted on the memory, the two versions run together almost word for word.

What follows is based upon the firm belief that Wilkins is 'reporting' the play given by the King's Men that is also reported in the Quarto of *Pericles*. But if, as I have just admitted, Wilkins is an imaginative and careless writer for whom the accurate reproduction of his original is by no means the cardinal aim, how can we possibly use his work as a 'control' for the Quarto? How can we be sure that a passage in Wilkins is 'correct' and proves that the Quarto is corrupt? There is only one way: to accept the Quarto as giving the skeleton of the play, and then to admit improvements from Wilkins using as an arbiter one's own (purely subjective) sense of fitness. For example, few would refuse to accept as improvements the verbal corrections of the Quarto that Wilkins gives and which are pointed out in all annotated editions—the most famous being *vncisserd* (unscissor'd) for *vnsisterd* (III, iii, 29). In these instances we accept the improvements by subjective standards, because we feel they are more right in the context, and by objective standards, because what is in the Quarto can be explained as a corruption of what is in Wilkins.

These principles also hold for the fragments of blank-verse embedded in Wilkins's prose and omitted from the Folio. The best-known example of these is Wilkins's passage:

Poore inche of Nature (quoth he) thou arte as rudely welcome to the worlde, as euer Princesse Babe was... (p. 44)

where the Quarto, omitting the striking "Poor inch of nature" runs simply:

... for
Thou art the rudelyest welcome to this world,
That euer was Princes Child: (III, i, 29–31)

We can in fact incorporate in the text of the Quarto, often with very little difficulty as in the following passage, verse peculiar to Wilkins (the words of the novel are in italics and divided as verse):

king. Traytor, thou lyest.
Peri. Traytor?
king. I, traytor.
That thus disguised, art stolne into my Court,
With the witchcraft of thy actions to bewitch,
The yeelding spirit of my tender Childe.
Peri. Euen in his throat, vnlesse it be the King,
That cals me Traytor, I returne the lye. (II, v, 55–7; Wilkins, p. 38)

Similarly we can admit from Wilkins such scraps of excellent verse as the following passage which clarifies the Quarto's presentation of Simonides's assumed role of heavy father (again I print as verse):

Is this a fit match for you?
A stragling *Theseus* borne we knowe not where...

But daughter...
Equalles to equalls, good to good is joined,

> This not being so, the bauine of your mind
> In rashnesse kindled, must againe be quenched,
> Or purchase our displeasure.   (Wilkins, pp. 39–40; cf. II, v, 74–87)

But there are instances of greater importance than these to point out the corruptness of the Quarto. Continually in the first two acts we find that although perhaps we may feel the Quarto has preserved in jumbled fashion more of the actual words of the original, Wilkins's paraphrase amplifies our understanding of the true import of the speeches. Such examples are Pericles's soliloquy (I, i, 121–42; Wilkins, p. 18) where he expatiates on the horror of Antiochus's incest and decides to flee from Antioch; the succeeding threatening soliloquy of Antiochus, where the crude melodrama of the Quarto becomes amplified into the Claudius-like perturbation of a guilty mind, with the sideways glance at Heaven and men's judgement and esteem; Pericles's true princely anxiety for the welfare of his subjects (I, ii; Wilkins, p. 19); the notion that the ruination of Tharsus is a judgement on its proud and luxurious ways (I, iv, 30–4; Wilkins, p. 21).

An incident from Act III shows how the second reporter, though not guilty of the gaucheness prevalent in the first two acts, may yet get hold of the wrong end of the stick.[17] Cerimon gazes at the still body of Thaisa, and suddenly takes the decision to try to restore her to life, reassuring the startled bystanders with the words:

> I heard of an *Egiptian* that had 9. howers lien dead,
> Who was by good applyaunce recouered.   (III, ii, 84–6)

One recalls the 'Ægyptian' in *Othello*: "She was a Charmer, and could almost read The thoughts of people" and one is at once inclined to prefer Wilkins's version which makes the Egyptian the restorer and not the restored:

> I haue read of some Egyptians, who after foure houres death, (if man may call it so) haue raised impouerished bodies, like to this, vnto their former health....   (Wilkins, p. 48)

One example will serve to show how Wilkins demonstrates the corruptness of the Quarto in whole scenes: the important scene between Lysimachus and Marina in the brothel. It will be useful to have the two versions before us. Lysimachus, the Governor, is questioning the youthful Marina who has just been brought before him as a particularly desirable prostitute.

Ly. Why? the house you dwell in proclaimes you to be a Creature of sale.
Ma. Doe you knowe this house to be a place of such resort, and will come intoo't? I heare say you're of honourable parts, and are the Gouernour of this place.
Li. Why, hath your principall made knowne vnto you who I am?
Ma. Who is my principall?
Li. Why, your hearbe-woman, she that sets seeds and rootes of shame and iniquitie.
O you haue heard something of my power, and so stand aloft for more serious wooing, but I protest to thee prettie one, my authoritie shall not see thee, or else looke friendly vpon thee, come bring me to some priuate place: Come, come.
Ma. If you were borne to honour, shew it now, if put vpon you, make the iudgement good, that thought you worthie of it.

Li. How's this? how's this? some more, be sage.

Mar. For me that am a maide, though most vngentle Fortune haue plac't mee in this Stie, where since I came, diseases haue beene solde deerer then Phisicke, that the gods would set me free from this vnhalowed place, though they did chaunge mee to the meanest byrd that flyes i'th purer ayre.

Li. I did not thinke thou couldst haue spoke so well, nere dremp't thou could'st, had I brought hither a corrupted minde, thy speeche had altered it, holde, heeres golde for thee, perseuer in that cleare way thou goest and the gods strengthen thee.

Ma. The good Gods preserue you.

Li. For me be you thoughten, that I came with no ill intent, for to me the very dores and windows sauor vilely, fare thee well, thou art a peece of vertue, & I doubt not but thy training hath bene noble, hold, heeres more golde for thee, a curse vpon him, die he like a theefe that robs thee of thy goodnes, if thou dost heare from me it shalbe for thy good. (IV, vi, 83–123)

But the Gouernour suspecting these teares, but to be some new cunning, which her matron the Bawde had instructed her in, to drawe him to a more large expence: He as freely tolde her so, and now beganne to be more rough with her, vrging her, that he was the Gouernour, whose authoritie coulde wincke at those blemishes, her selfe, and that sinnefull house could cast vppon her, or his displeasure punish at his owne pleasure, which displeasure of mine, thy beauty shall not priuiledge thee from, nor my affection, which hath drawen me vnto this place abate, if thou with further lingering withstand me. By which wordes, she vnderstanding him to be as confident in euill, as she was constant in good, she intreated him but to be heard, and thus she beganne.

If as you say (my Lorde) you are the Gouernour, let not your authoritie, which should teach you to rule others, be the meanes to make you misgouerne your selfe: If the eminence of your place came vnto you by discent, and the royalty of your blood, let not your life prooue your birth a bastard: If it were throwne vpon you by opinion, make good, that opinion was the cause to make you great. What reason is there in your Iustice, who hath power ouer all, to vndoe any? If you take from mee mine honour, you are like him, that makes a gappe into forbidden ground, after whome too many enter, and you are guiltie of all their euilles: my life is yet vnspotted, my chastitie vnstained in thought. Then if your violence deface this building, the workemanship of heauen, made vp for good, and not to be the exercise of sinnes intemperaunce, you do kill youre owne honour, abuse your owne iustice, and impouerish me. Why quoth *Lysimachus*, this house wherein thou liuest, is euen the receptacle of all mens sinnes, and nurse of wickednesse, and how canst thou then be otherwise then naught, that liuest in it? It is not good, answered *Marina*, when you that are the Gouernour, who should liue well, the better to be bolde to punish euill, doe knowe that there is such a roofe, and yet come vnder it. Is there a necessitie (my yet good Lord) if there be fire before me, that I must strait then thither flie and burne my selfe? Or if suppose this house, (which too too many feele such houses are) should be the Doctors patrimony, and Surgeons feeding; folowes it therefore, that I must needs infect my self to giue them maintenance? O my good Lord, kill me, but not deflower me, punish me how you please, so you spare my chastitie, and since it is all the dowry that both the Gods haue giuen, and men haue left to me, do not you take it from me; make me your seruant, I will willingly obey you; make mee your bondwoman, I will accompt it freedome; let me be the worst that is called vile, so I may still liue honest, I am content: or if you thinke it is too blessed a happinesse to haue me so, let me euen now, now in this minute die, and Ile accompt my death more happy than my birth. With which

42

wordes (being spoken vpon her knees) while her eyes were the glasses that carried the waters of her mis-hap, the good Gentlewoman [*sic*] being mooued, hee lift her vp with his hands, and euen then imbraced her in his hart, saying aside: Now surely this is Virtues image, or rather, Vertues selfe, sent downe from heauen, a while to raigne on earth, to teach vs what we should be. So in steede of willing her to drie her eyes, he wiped the wet himselfe off, and could haue found in his heart, with modest thoughts to haue kissed her, but that hee feared the offer would offend her. This onely hee sayde, Lady, for such your vertues are, a farre more worthy stile your beuty challenges, and no way lesse your beauty can promise me that you are, I hither came with thoughtes intemperate, foule and deformed, the which your paines so well hath laued, that they are now white, continue still to all so, and for my parte, who hither came but to haue payd the price, a peece of golde for your virginitie, now giue you twenty to releeue your honesty. It shall become you still to be euen as you are, a peece of goodnesse, the best wrought vppe, that euer Nature made, and if that any shall inforce you ill, if you but send to me, I am your friend. With which promise, leauing her presence, she most humbly thanked the Gods for the preseruation of her chastitie, and the reformation of his mind.

(Wilkins, Mommsen's reprint, pp. 65–7)

The elements of these two extracts are not really dissimilar, though the items in the colloquies are in a different order and though Wilkins treats the whole very much more fully. In both we have Marina's upbraiding of Lysimachus for setting foot in a place he has just spoken of with contempt; Lysimachus's unpleasant threats to employ the power of his authority; Marina's appeal to his honour and the responsibilities of his position; Marina's plea for death; Lysimachus's praise of Marina's virtue and his gift of gold to her. The major divergence is that in the Quarto Lysimachus, abandoning his apparent intention of seducing Marina, makes the strange remark: "had I brought hither a corrupted minde, thy speeche had altered it" and later: "I came with no ill intent"; in the novel we have no such protestations, but the penitent: "I hither came with thoughtes intemperate, foule and deformed, the which your paines so well hath laued, that they are now white."

This divergence between novel and Quarto is taken by Hardin Craig[18] (who believes that the Quarto is a good text) to show the measure of revision that the play of *Pericles* had undergone after it had been reported by Wilkins. He argues that the Quarto version shows the reviser attempting to present a more plausible and less objectionable Lysimachus, a Governor acceptable by modern standards as the future husband of Marina; Lysimachus is not genuinely a customer of the brothel—he is an observer like the Duke in *Measure for Measure*, hiding his real intentions from the heroine until he has tested her quality, whereupon he reveals the harmlessness of his purpose.

But I hold that the scene in the Quarto is not a revision but a corruption of the scene which Wilkins reports and of which he gives the true sense. A scene of dissimulation such as Hardin Craig suggests seems to me rather lacking in dramatic point; it can only be seen as showing a silly trick on Lysimachus's part, which hangs loose on the action of the play. A scene such as Wilkins gives us of a genuine conversion is far more relevant—we see the struggle of unarmed innocence that, having withstood the horrible and corrupting atmosphere of the brothel, is able to overcome the evil intentions of a temporal ruler and bring home a sense of sin to a thoughtless rake. It is perhaps worth recalling, if we are to talk of acceptable moral codes,

43

that in that same *Measure for Measure* where inhabits the Duke of dark corners is also one Angelo, who intends the filthiest crimes, who yet, when he is sincerely penitent, is thought no unfit husband by one who is all goodness and whose name is, by a strange mutation—Mariana. And it is most difficult to read into the scene in the Quarto—up to the point of Lysimachus's protestation—anything of the dissimulation theory. Lysimachus is surely portrayed as a rake. In the early part of the scene his arrival at the brothel is noted with the utmost casualness by Boult and the Bawd as though it were a customary thing. When he enters the three of them jest together with the grossest of innuendoes like old friends in lechery. There is clearly an excellent understanding between them:

> *Bawd.* Wee haue heere one Sir, if shee would, but there neuer came her like in *Meteline*.
> *Li.* If shee'd doe the deedes of darknes thou wouldst say.
> *Bawd.* Your Honor knowes what t'is to say wel enough.
> *Li.* Well, call forth, call forth. (IV, vi, 30–6)

Because Lysimachus's words to Marina are not brutal they are not therefore kind: the Governor is curious about this strange creature and speaks to her as Steerforth might have spoken to Little Em'ly before he seduced her. He is apparently convinced (ll. 93–5) that the girl is only angling for favours and his tone roughens: "Come bring me to some priuate place." Then the 'conversion' follows naturally.

What is perhaps most to the point is that *whichever* way we take the scene in the Quarto, it must be corrupt; if we were to accept Craig's theory there must be large omissions and perversions. Lysimachus gives no explanation of his terrifying conduct which has made poor Marina distraught. He has behaved abominably and offers no word of apology: as he hastily departs he gives her money and assures her that he "came with no ill intent" and that she is a "piece of virtue". There must have been something more than this in a "dissimulation" scene.

If we accept the much more probable interpretation of the scene, that it presents Marina's conversion of Lysimachus, then the omissions have to do with Marina's eloquence. The brevity of the two crucial speeches she addresses to Lysimachus which first sway and then overcome him is quite remarkable. After a mere sentence appealing to his honour, Lysimachus is marvelling at her *wisdom*, and after what is really only a passionate and inarticulate cry, he is marvelling at her *eloquence*—"I did not thinke thou couldst haue spoke so well, nere dremp't thou couldst." An affecting cry is not what the age called eloquence. What we need is amplification of these ejaculations into really persuasive arguments—and Wilkins at the relevant points supplies just that very eloquence that is needed; we are given finely phrased, finely argued appeals which have all the power required to amaze, shame and convince Lysimachus. Moreover, these appeals carry striking verse-rhythms. Surely they must represent parts of the scene omitted in the Quarto's report.

The ambiguous phrase "had I brought hither a corrupted mind" would lose its ambiguity if it stood in its ampler context; it may, of course, be possible that the words have become corrupted to the inversion of the meaning, as the equivalent passage in Wilkins may suggest, but it is perfectly possible to take them as having meant (and this being clear in the original context) that Lysimachus, confessing to foolish behaviour and thoughtlessness, yet assures

Marina that though his actions were dishonourable, his mind was not corrupted—he came with no ill intent: he is not to be thought of as a hardened villain, but only as a pleasure-seeker now seeing for the first time that thoughtlessness may be a crime.

CONCLUSION

It has been the purpose of the present paper to point out that the 1609 Quarto of *Pericles* is a debased text and to demonstrate the general nature of the corruptions. The argument has been based chiefly on self-evident confusions in the text, on confusions which become apparent by comparison with Wilkins's novel and on the evidence of the quality of the verse. It has also been argued that the reconstruction was undertaken by two 'reporters'; the first responsible for the first two acts, the second for the last three. These two work by quite different methods: the first welds into mediocre verse the words, phrases and general sense of the original so far as he can remember them. He is at his best in prose, where remodelling is not attempted. The second reporter, perhaps giving the original very much more faithfully than his predecessor, makes no attempt at rewriting, and after the first scene does not make more than desultory attempts to write down the verse in lines.

It remains to ask what would be the significance of such a theory on the question of authorship. Apart from the obvious fact that great caution would be needed in making any statement based on style since we are always at one remove from the original writing, there is one specific point that arises. Many critics have believed that *Pericles* is the work of two authors and that the second author's work begins with Act III. Peter Alexander, for example, remarks "few will doubt from the opening of the third act...with its sublime sea music, that they are listening to Shakespeare". But it is clear, if the present theory be accepted, that the *immediate* cause of the sudden and startling improvement in the style at III, i is the different capability and habits of the second reporter. The problem that has to be solved is whether the different aptitudes of the two reporters are the *sole* cause of the difference in literary value between the two halves of the play; whether, in fact, the original play of *Pericles* was all of one standard, all by one author, and that the first reporter, in his crude attempts to rebuild a verse structure and in his reliance on a palpably defective memory, has perverted language such as is found in the later acts. So extensive is the damage in the first two acts that it can never be known just what the original was like, and the question may remain a question for ever. But we can say that it would be a strange coincidence if the areas of the play covered by the two reporters exactly corresponded to the work of two distinct dramatists.[19]

NOTES

1. This article is an amplification of a brief paper read at the Shakespeare Conference, Stratford-upon-Avon, in 1948.

2. Malone, *Supplement to the Edition of Shakespeare's Plays Published in 1778*, II, 183; Collier, *Further Particulars Regarding Shakespeare and his Works* (London, 1839), pp. 29–54; Mommsen, *Pericles Prince of Tyre: A Novel by George Wilkins* (Oldenburg, 1857), p. iv.

3. Pollard, *Shakespeare Folios and Quartos* (1909), pp. 58–62, 79; Adams, *A Life of William Shakespeare* (1923), pp. 401, 515; Greg, *Editorial Problem in Shakespeare* (1942), pp. vii, 74, 187; Chambers, *William Shakespeare* (1930), I, 520–1; Kirschbaum, 'A Census of Bad Quartos', *Review of English Studies*, XIV (1938), 25.

4. See transcript in Greg, *Bibliography of the English Printed Drama*, I, 24.

5. It is by no means irrelevant that this Quarto was used as the basis for an acting text by a provincial company of players in 1610. See Sisson, 'Shakespeare Quartos as Prompt Copies', *Review of English Studies*, XVIII (1942), 130–43.

6. All act, scene and line references are to the Globe Edition of Shakespeare, although all quotations are taken from the 1609 Quarto. The facsimile of the Quarto published by the Shakespeare Association in 1940 conveniently gives the Globe line numbers in the margin.

7. Other scenes with omissions and consequent ambiguity are: IV, iv, which is discussed in detail later in the article; V, i, where the entry of Lysimachus and the business between Helicanus and the sailors are confused; I, iv, where Pericles enters, apparently briefed by a messenger sent to fetch him, before the same messenger has had time to leave the stage; II, iv, in which the 'rebellion' of the lords is quite unexplained.

8. E.g. Sir Henry Thomas, 'Shakespeare y España', *Homenaje a Menéndez Pidal* (1925), I, 226.

9. Greg, *Editorial Problem*, pp. 147–8; Hoppe, *The Bad Quarto of Romeo and Juliet* (1948), p. 111.

10. The first two acts omit no entries, the last three omit 7; the first two acts omit 9 exits, but 5 of these are at the ends of scenes; the last three acts omit 13 exits, only 3 of which are at the ends of scenes.

11. The first dumb-show treats the miming drily and gives technical instructions; the later ones describe the *emotions* to be expressed and talks of the actors departing instead of putting *exit* or *exeunt*.

12. See IV, iv, 48; IV, i, 64; III, i, 52; III, i, 61; III, iv, 5; V, Ch., 20. There is also slight evidence for a change in the hand in that certain spellings used consistently by all three compositors in the first two acts alter in the last three: *eies* (3 times in I and II) becomes *eyes* (5 times in III–V); *sed, ses, agen* are found only in III–V; the spelling *–ayn–* (e.g. *remayne*) occurs on 6 of its 7 appearances in III–V. The spelling shifts *mild* to *myld*, *blith* to *blyther*, *gift* to *gyft* and *honour'd* to *honor'd*, *tould* to *told*, *behoulding* to *behold* may also be significant.

13. rapture: the text reads 'rupture'.

14. Duthie, *The 'bad' Quarto of Hamlet* (1941), pp. 90–131.

15. Collier announced the discovery of Wilkins's novel in 1839; the copy he found, which lacked the dedication leaf that alone betrays the authorship of the novel, passed into the hands of Halliwell-Phillipps. The only other copy extant was found in 1857 in the Stadtbibliothek in Zürich. See *The Athenaeum*, 7 February 1857. Mommsen's reprint of the novel has been used for all quotations and references in the article.

16. Kenneth Muir's important article ('The Problem of *Pericles*', *English Studies*, XXX (1949), 65–83) came to hand after the major part of this article was completed. Much of the evidence he brings forward to show that Wilkins based his novel on an 'Ur-*Pericles*' seems to me to point equally clearly to the fact that he based it on the original of the Quarto.

17. This point was made by Collier.

18. *Studies in Philology*, XLV (1948), 600–5.

19. There are so many difficulties involved in claiming for Shakespeare the whole of *Pericles*—the lost, genuine *Pericles*—that I have avoided carrying my argument to its logical conclusion. But clearly, if indeed in *Pericles* we are concerned with but one dramatist, then Shakespeare, whose hand is so unmistakably present in the later acts, is the only candidate. So much of what happens in the first two acts is so akin to the world of Shakespeare's last plays that it seems to me that a strong case can be made out. In spite of the play's exclusion from the Folio, I feel we must be alive to the possibility that there once existed a *Pericles* wholly by Shakespeare.

APPENDIX

THE COMPOSITORS OF THE QUARTO OF *PERICLES*
(see p. 29)

Some of the principles that have guided bibliographers in distinguishing one from another the compositors of an early printed book may be examined in R. B. McKerrow, *Introduction to Bibliography*, p. 128 and *The Library*, 4th ser., II (1921–2), 106–8; A. K. McIlwraith, *The Library*, 4th ser., XI (1930–1), 88–91; E. E. Willoughby, *Printing of the First Folio*, pp. 54–9; Charlton Hinman, *The Library*, 4th ser., XXI (1940–1), 78–103; H. R. Hoppe, *The Bad Quarto of Romeo and Juliet*, pp. 45–56.

The work demands great caution; spellings alone are an insufficient guide in differentiating compositors, since ordinary human inconsistency, the alteration of spellings to 'justify' lines and the mingling of copy-spellings with compositor-spellings all confuse the issue. Safety would seem to lie in numbers: that is to say, *all* the phenomena of each printed page which show signs of varying in the whole work should be listed, from spellings to such mechanical things as the positioning of stage directions. It will then appear that certain pages contain the same collocation of variants, and that other pages contain a quite different one. Mathematics are unnecessary; examination will be enough to show the distinct patterns of variants among different groups of pages.

In *Pericles*, for example, the chief significant variants are seen in the abbreviations of the names in speech-headings, in methods of punctuation, in the use of capital names for nouns, etc., and in certain spelling features (shown in the Table below). The first pages of sheet A, which are quite consistent, show a compositor whose trade-marks may be briefly set out as follows: Heavy and varied punctuation; frequent initial capitals for nouns; preference for single -*e* in *he*, *be*, etc., but for -*ee* in *heere*; preference for final -*y* in (e.g.) *many*; preference for -'*d* or -*ed* in the unaccented suffixes for the past forms of weak verbs in stems ending in *l*, *m*, *n*, *r*, *v*; no distinction between *do* and *doe*.

Two clear changes take place within sheet B. The trade-marks of a second compositor, evident in the first four pages are: very scanty punctuation—mainly commas and periods with a rare colon and no use of brackets; very few initial capitals; spelling preferences (in the order given above) for *he*; *here*; -*ie*; -*d* -*ed* -*de*; *doe*. The trade-marks of the third compositor, similar to those of the second, are: scant punctuation, but more frequent use of the colon than in the second compositor; few initial capitals; preferred spellings of *hee*; *heere*; -*ie*; -'*de*; *doe*. Putting these selected spelling variants in tabular form may help to show, in little, how the 'pattern of variants' appears:

1st comp. (*x*):	he	heere	-y	-'d	-ed		do doe
2nd comp. (*y*):	he	here	-ie	-d	-ed	-de	doe
3rd comp. (*z*):	hee	heere	-ie	-'de			doe

It is clear from examination that the whole of sheets A, C, D, E is set by the first compositor (*x*). Sheets F–I3 v are equally clearly the result of alternate shifts between the second and third compositors (*y* and *z*), but one or two pages present insufficient evidence for them to be decisively assigned to either. These pages do not affect the argument presented in the article, but they have been assigned to their compositors on the basis of the number of black-letter full-stops a page contains. For in all the pages of compositors *y* and *z* black-letter full-stops are intermingled with ordinary ones, but '*y*' pages are distinguished by their far greater proportions of the intruding element (an average of 42 compared with 22 per cent). With this new aid, the only page in the Quarto that remains indecisive is F4v, which may either end a group belonging to 'z' or start one of 'y'. It must be the former: there must have been a change in the person setting up the text *after* F4v, because the word 'Bawd' occurs 8 times on the page—including the catch-word, but the next page, G1, begins with 'Baud' and so the word is spelt 6 times there.

Some rather important bibliographical questions are raised by the division of the Quarto among the three compositors as set forth in the table on p. 29. The sheets of the Quarto are typographically in two distinct groups: A, C, D, E and B, F, G, H, I. The groups are distinguished one from another by having different running-titles, different numbers of lines to a page (37 to 35) and different founts of type. Now we find that the divisions of the compositors' work corresponds to this division—one compositor is responsible for the first group and two others for the second. It seems to me highly probable that the two groups of sheets were set up in different printing-houses. The shares of *y* and *z* compositors in the second group of sheets work out as an exact halving of the work; it is hard to see any rhyme or reason in the capricious shifts of the three compositors, if we imagine them all working together on the text in one printing-house. In addition, the second and third compositors (*y* and *z*) seem to share the same general habits in their style of composing a page, as though they had been trained in the same house; the first compositor's style is utterly different. The problem is worth pursuing further, for it might throw light on how the copy came into the publisher's hands.

TABLE. *Distinguishing Features of the Compositors of Pericles*

I. Spellings

		x	*y*	*z*
he, be,	-e	183	119	58
she, we	-ee	26	38	102
	Totals	209	157	160
Final y/ie	-y	80	26	29
	-ie	39	54	69
	Totals	119	80	98
do, go	-o	15	6	4
	-oe	16	32	39
	Totals	31	38	43
here	here	4	13	5
	heere	27	1	20
	Totals	31	14	25
Words with *an*, e.g. dance, danger	-ange-	12	0	2
	-aunge-	0	2	3
	-ance-	3	2	6
	-aunce-	10	2	2
	-and	0	1	1
	-aund	1	3	0
	Totals	26	10	14

		x	*y*	*z*
Medial ai/ay in *faith*, *maid* and conjugates	-ai-	0	13	6
	-ay-	5	3	3
	Totals	5	16	9
Unaccented past forms of verbs with stems ending in l, m, n, r, v	-d	9	16	7
	-ed	19	15	6
	-de	1	9	1
	-'d	22	3	7
	-'de	0	0	13
	Totals	51	43	34
Miscellaneous -o- forms	tongue	3	1	0
	toung	0	0	2
	young	2	1	2
	yong	0	2	0
	hour	2	0	0
	hower	2	0	0

		x	*y*	*z*
Distinctive forms peculiar to one compositor		yeat	agen	syr
		togeather		

II. *Punctuation*

x	*y*	*z*
Heavy and varied: comma, semi-colon, colon, period, question mark, exclamation mark, brackets both parenthetical and vocative	Very light: comma, period, question mark, occasional colon	Light: comma, colon, period, question mark, three uses of semi-colon

III. *Average number of words to a page with initial capitals, excluding proper names*

x 17·5	*y* 7	*z* 7

IV. *Average number of black-letter periods to a page*

x 0·5	*y* 7·5	*z* 4·5

V. *Abbreviations of speakers' names*

	x	*y*	*z*			*x*	*y*	*z*
Per.	27	35	13		Mari.	—	10	13
Peri.	38	2	0		Mar.	—	17	2
Pe.	0	2	1		Ma.	—	1	20
Total	65	39	14		Total	—	28	35
Hell.	6	9	0		Lys.	—	15	1
Hel.	0	9	9		Li.	—	0	20
Helli/y.	0	0	2		Ly.	—	0	3
Total	6	18	11		Lysim.	—	0	1
					Total	—	15	25
					Bawd	—	0	31
					Baud	—	11	0
					Total	—	11	31

THE SHAKESPEARE COLLECTION IN THE LIBRARY OF TRINITY COLLEGE, CAMBRIDGE

BY

H. M. ADAMS

It is not easy to be precise about the beginnings of the Shakespeare collection in Trinity College, Cambridge, because of the absence of early and detailed records concerning the books in the Library. But one of the earliest and much the most notable component in that collection was the gift in 1779 of his books by Edward Capell, the Shakespearian editor. This contained, among other items, the four folios and fifty-one quarto plays, besides four quarto editions of the separate poems, and the octavo *Passionate Pilgrim*, 1599 and *Venus and Adonis*, 1620. Perhaps before the advent of the Capell books the College may have possessed two of its four Fourth Folios, and perhaps also the collected editions of Rowe, Pope and Theobald. Then in 1863 came second copies of the First, Second and Third Folios, part of the library of William Grylls, scholar of the College. In the second half of the nineteenth century the Library was enriched by W. Aldis Wright, one of the editors of the Cambridge Shakespeare and later Vice-Master of the College. He gave several eighteenth-century editions, besides other books which will be mentioned later. But it seems that donors were never lacking to provide the Library with editions of Shakespeare. From the early 1700's and excluding the Capell collection there are sixty-one editions in English up to 1900, besides one in French and two in German.

It may be of interest to make a rapid survey of the Capell collection as far as the Shakespeare editions go, and of its donor. He was born in 1713, came up to Catharine Hall, Cambridge, and after a few years as deputy inspector of plays devoted himself to his real interest, editing Shakespeare. As an example of his industry, he is said to have transcribed the whole of Shakespeare ten times. He published his edition of the text in ten volumes in 1767–8. He intended to follow this with a commentary of which the first volume appeared in 1774. This was not a success and he withdrew it; but the whole commentary was published posthumously in three volumes in 1783. During the last years of his life he lived in seclusion in Brick Court, Temple, London. He gave his collection of books to Trinity in 1779, two years before his death.

The 256 volumes of his Shakespeare collection contain the works of other authors besides Shakespeare—e.g. Chaucer, Spenser, Milton—but these are there, not, so to speak, in their own right, but simply as throwing light on Shakespeare.

To come now to the Shakespeare collection in more detail, we will first consider the Folios. Of these there are two complete sets and two additional copies of the Fourth Folio, 1685. The First Folios both have the second issue of the portrait and have misprints in signatures and pagination as mentioned in A. W. Pollard's *Shakespeare Folios and Quartos* (1909), p. 108, together with one or two others noted as occurring in the Grenville copy at the British Museum (G11631). In one of the Trinity copies the leaf of verses is in facsimile. In the Second Folio the Capell copy has the title containing the spelling "Coppies" in l. 6, the Grylls copy has

50

"Copies". (In R. M. Smith's *Variant Issues of Shakespeare's Second Folio* (1928), Allot title nos. 1 and 4.) Also the Capell copy has on A₅ Smith's Effigies A, with the reading "starre-ypointed" in l. 4 of the lower, Milton's, epitaph, the Grylls copy has on A₅ Smith's Effigies C, reading "starre-ypointing".

In the Third Folio the Capell copy has the "Seven playes never before printed in folio" bound up immediately following the preliminary leaves, and the original A₁ of the first issue of this edition, containing the Verses, is inserted after "To the great variety of readers". The misprints in pagination are as noted in Pollard.

There are four copies in Trinity of the Fourth Folio, one in the Capell collection and three others. William Grylls did not possess one. All the four have the imprint: "for H. Herringman, E. Brewster, and R. Bentley". Misprints in signatures and pagination are as noted by Pollard. Leaf L₁ is printed in smaller type, with a larger number of lines than is normal in the volume. One copy (H.18.11) has the price, "24/6", in an early hand at the top of the title.

Later editions of the plays are Rowe's, 1709 and 1714, Pope's, 1725, Pope and Sewell, 1728, and Theobald, 1733. In the Capell copy of this edition, facing the preface in the first volume, is the manuscript note in Capell's hand: "This copy of Mr Theobald's edition was once Mr Warburton's; who has claim'd in it the Notes he gave to the former which that former depriv'd him of and made his own, and some passages in the Preface, the Passages being put between hooks, and the notes sign'd with his name. E. C[apell]." Then follows another edition by Theobald, 1740. The Oxford edition "revised and corrected" by Sir Thomas Hanmer with Pope's preface and Rowe's life of Shakespeare is dated 1744. Then an edition in 1745 "revised and corrected by the former editions", in fact, as the Advertisement states, "exactly copied from the Oxford edition". Next is the edition of 1747 by "Mr Pope and Mr Warburton"—really Warburton's edition. Then we have Samuel Johnson's edition of 1765, the second one of that date, followed by Capell's own edition, put out without his name, ten volumes 1767–8, and by a reprint of Johnson's edition, also 1768. A Dublin edition, 1771, six volumes in twelve, has the prefaces of various editors and Capell's introduction.

From this point it seems hardly necessary to give a detailed list of the later editions in the Library, but it is worth mentioning that we have two sets of the printer's proofs of the Cambridge Shakespeare, edited by W. G. Clark and W. Aldis Wright, with some manuscript corrections of the editors.

Leaving the collected editions of the plays, we come to the separate plays, and of these only a selection of the editions here must suffice, taking the plays in alphabetical order: *Antony and Cleopatra*, fitted for the stage by abridging only, by Edward Capell and David Garrick, 1758; an edition in Greek translated by M. N. Damirale (Athens, 1882), and Cobden Sanderson's edition, printed at his own Doves Press, 1912. Of *Hamlet* the Library has the second issue of the Second Quarto, dated 1605 (22276ᵃ),★ the Third Quarto of 1611, lacking the title (22277), the Fourth Quarto, undated (22278), and the Fifth, 1637 (22279). *Henry IV, Part I* is represented by seven Quartos from 1598, the First (apart from the Folger fragment, Greg 145 (a)) to 1639 (22280–7, except 22283). *Henry IV, Part II*, has the first issue of the First Quarto, with the 4-leaf version of sheet E (22288). Of *Henry V* there are the First Quarto, 1600, the Second, 1602, and the Third, 1608, the latter one of the false-dated quartos, really printed in or about

★ Numbers in round brackets are the *STC* references.

1619. At this point, perhaps, it should be mentioned that the Library has all nine of these quartos with false dates, named and described by Sir W. W. Greg in two articles in the *Library* (n.s., vol. IX, 1908, pp. 113–31 and 381–409). In the Capell collection they are bound in two volumes, four and five plays together.

To return to the Quartos. Capell had *The First Part of the contention betwixt Yorke and Lancaster*, Second Quarto, 1600, and *The whole contention*, Third Quarto, 1619, now called *Henry VI, Parts II and III*. Of *King Lear* there is the First ('Pide Bull') Quarto, 1608, and the misdated Second Quarto, 1608 (really 1619), both "for N. Butter". Of this play we have a Hebrew translation published at Warsaw in 1899. Of *Love's Labour's Lost* we have the variant of the First Quarto, 1598, with l. 2 of D$_1$^{a}: *Ar...argument* and D$_2$^{b}, penultimate line: *fit* (see *Huntington Check List*, 1919, where a different reading is given). We have also the Second Quarto, 1631. The only noteworthy edition of *Macbeth* is a Hebrew translation printed at Drohobycz in 1883. Then follow three editions of *The Merchant of Venice*, the First Quarto, 1600 (22296), the Second, wrongly dated 1600, really 1619 (22297), and the Third, 1637 (22298). We have also a Quarto "for W. Leake, 1652". Of *The Merry Wives* there are the three Quartos, First, 1602, Second, 1619 and Third, 1630 (22299–301). The two editions of *A Midsummer Night's Dream* dated 1600 are here, the First and Second Quartos, the second one really 1619. The real 1600 edition, the First Quarto, "for T. Fisher", belonged to Theobald, who has written on the title: "Collated with the other old quarto, with the same title, printed by James Roberts in 1600. L. T.". The collations are entered in the margin. There is also a Danish translation by A. Oehlenschläger, of 1816. Of *Much Ado About Nothing* we have the only early Quarto, the First, 1600 (22304). *Othello* is represented by the two Quartos, First and Second, 1622 and 1630. Though part of the Capell Collection, the 1622 Quarto appears to be a made-up copy, the sheets I–M^{4}N^2 being narrower than the rest. A note by Dr Greg mentions that, though the last line on H$_4$^{b} is repeated at the head of I$_1$^{a} the supplied sheets are from the same edition as the rest. The repetition of that line is a peculiarity in the other known copies of the first edition. The Capell collection has also the edition published by Leake in 1655 which, though called the fourth edition, is really the third. Preserving alphabetical sequence I mention next *The late, and much admired play, called Pericles*, 1609 (First Quarto). The Capell copy has the stage direction on A$_2$^{a}: *Enter Gower* (22334). Another edition, the Fifth Quarto, 1630, is of the issue in which the imprint occupies four lines (22338). We have also the edition of 1635 (22339). Of *Richard II* there are four Quartos: the First, 1597, which collates A–I^{4}K^2 (22307), the Second, 1598, A–I^4 and has "sold" in the imprint (22308), the Fifth, 1615 (22312) collated throughout in Capell's hand with the 1608 edition, and the Sixth, 1634 (22313). For *Richard III* the Library has to be content with an edition later than the First. The Capell collection has the 1598 edition, the Second Quarto (22315), with the readings "maiestie", l. 22 on A$_2$^{b} and "thanke", l. 5 on F$_1$^{a}. This is followed by the Quartos of 1602 (22316), 1612, 1622, 1629 and 1634 (22318–21) the Third, Fifth, Sixth, Seventh and Eighth. The last lacks the title, which was supplied in manuscript by Capell. *Romeo and Juliet* is represented by the Quartos of 1597, the First (22322), 1609, the Third (22324), 1637, the Sixth (22326), and the Fourth, printed without a date but between the last two. Of the two issues it is the one with 'Shake-speare's' name on the title (22325^a). Of *The Taming of the Shrew* we have a copy of the only Quarto, 1631 (22327). For *The Tempest* there is the edition of 1670 published by H. Herringman, adapted by Dryden, and an edition "since altered by Sir William Davenant and Mr J. Dryden, 1710" which was in the Library of Sir Isaac Newton and which came with the gift to this College of his books by the Pilgrim Trust in 1943. Of the 800 books surviving together from a library of about 1800 this is one of the comparatively few volumes of pure literature in the collection. Next we have *Titus Andronicus*, 1611, the Third Quarto (22330), and lastly *Troylus and Cresseid*, 1609, the First Quarto, second issue, with cancel title and address to the reader.

Of the *Poems* there is the edition of 1640 (22344). Then follows a small octavo of quite extraordinary interest containing first the *Passionate Pilgrim*, 1599 (22342) and second the *Venus and Adonis*, 1620 (22362), the only recorded copy of this edition. The fly-leaf at the beginning has the rather boldly written signature "Tho: Martin", and below it "Anne Shute", followed by a note in a different and later hand: "Shakespeare was a Woolcomber. Ben Johnson a Foot Soldier in yᵉ Dutch Service says yᵉ Englishman's Evning Post. June 24, 1740". And below this, in the same hand

> Homer was a Beggar
> Euripedes an Herbgatherer
> Plautus a Baker's Servᵗ.
> Terence a Slave
> Virgil yᵉ Son of a Basketmaker.

The lower outer corner of C_7 of the *Venus and Adonis* is torn away, involving the loss of one or two words, and so there is a manuscript note on the blank D_4: "Not quite perfect, see 4 or 5 Leaves back, so it cost me but 3 Halfpence." The initials 'WB.' are at the top of this page. The 1598 edition of *Lucrece* appears to be unique. It is bound with the rare 1563 edition of Barnaby Googe's *Eglogs*. There is also one of two recorded copies of the 1607 *Lucrece*, the other one being in the Huntington Library. Of the *Sonnets* we have only an imperfect copy of the 1609 issue with Wright's name in the imprint (22353ª), in which the title is supplied in manuscript by Capell.

With the printed books in the Capell collection are a few volumes in manuscript, written by his own hand. The first is a "Catalogue of a Collection entitl'd Shakesperiana; comprehending All the several Editions of the Works of Shakespeare, old & new; divers rare old Editions of Writers, prose-men & verse-men; with a Variety of other Articles, chiefly such as tend to illustrate him;—made by his last Editor, E.C." Then follows a transcript of all the plays, in six volumes, being the text of Capell's own edition of 1768: and next three volumes of notes and various readings, etc. Then comes the text of *Paradise Lost*, with some additional pieces, the first of which is *Hermes, or, a guide to the elements, &c.* This edition of Milton was not published. And lastly a manuscript volume of the *Poems* which was published in 1709. So much for the Capell collection of Shakespeariana. Following the precedent of F. C. Francis in his account of the British Museum collection, it seemed worth while to go through Miss Bartlett's list of source books and see the proportion to be found even in so comparatively small a library. Without naming any book specifically except Caxton's *Troy book*, 1475, of Miss Bartlett's 89 books this Library has only 34, with another 15 represented by early, though not quite so early, editions. Of that total of 49 items, 25 are in the Capell collection. In addition it should be mentioned that the Library holds what is thought to be the unique copy of F. de Belleforest's *The hystorie of Hamblet*, 1608.

As an appendix it may be of interest to mention some Shakespeare items noted in other College libraries in Cambridge besides Trinity. Emmanuel has a 1630 Quarto *Othello*. King's has an imperfect First Folio and two Seconds (22274 and 22274ᶜ), a false-dated Quarto of *Henry V*, 1608 [1619] (22291), a *Romeo and Juliet* undated (22325ᵃ), and the 1640 *Poems*. Pembroke has a Second Folio, and the Fitzwilliam Museum two Seconds (22274 and 22274ᵃ).

In conclusion it would be lacking in piety to omit some more particular mention of William Aldis Wright, 1831–1914, editor of the Cambridge Shakespeare and a notable benefactor of this Library. He gave it no early editions of Shakespeare, but did add a large number of early editions of what is now generally called Background Literature, from Chaucer onwards. His interests were wide, Biblical (he became the Secretary of the Old Testament Revisers Company) as well as secular, and were reflected in the books he finally bequeathed to this College. Besides a large number of early editions of the English Bible these included a considerable number of pre-1640 English books.

Finally, it is of interest to record that in the list of librarians of this College will be found the names of W. W. Greg and R. B. McKerrow.

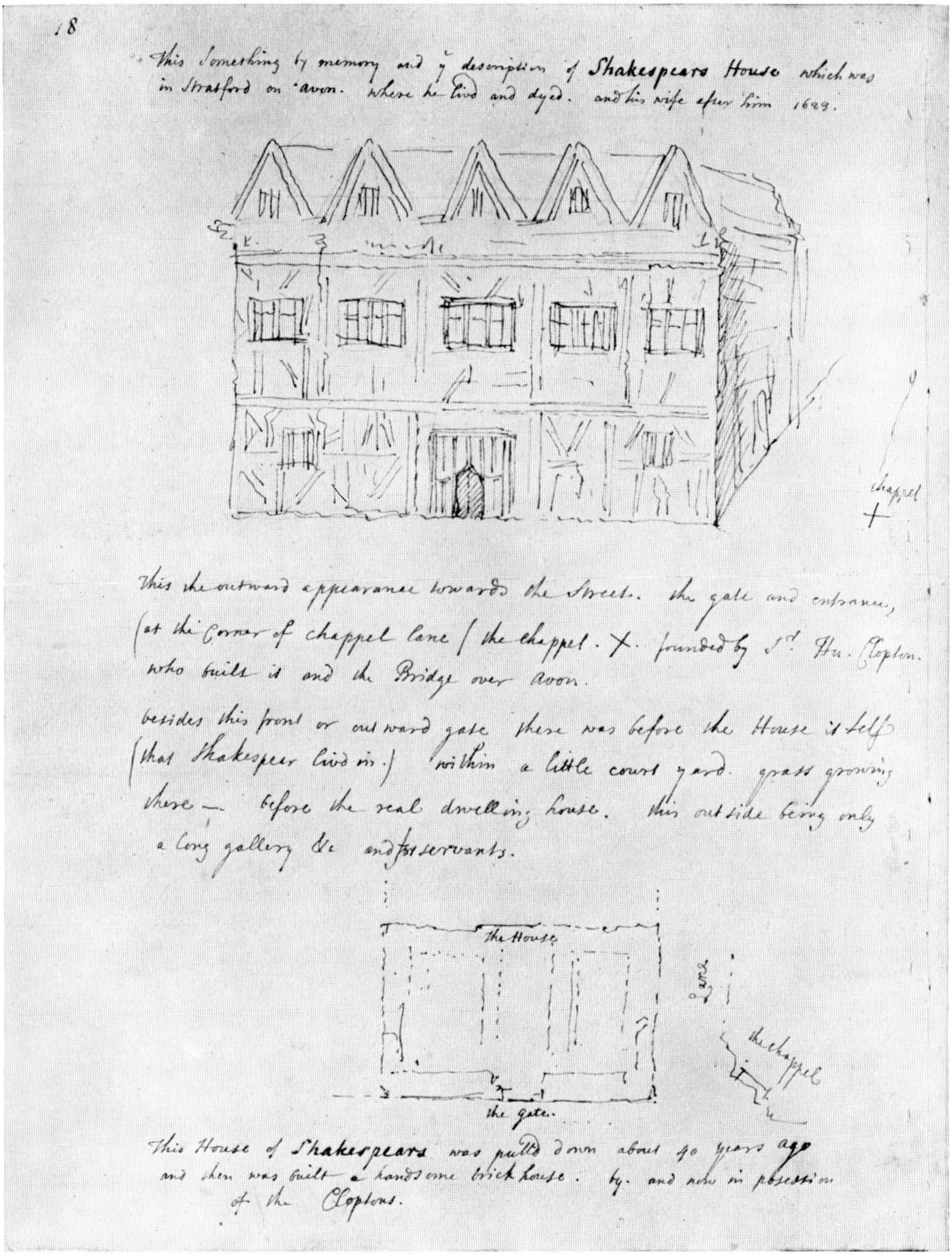

PLATE I

18

This Something by memory and y description of *Shakespears* House which was in Stratford on Avon. where he livd and dyed. and his wife after him 1623.

this the outward appearance towards the Street. the gate and entrance, (at the Corner of chappel lane) the chappel. X. founded by S.ʳ Hu. Clopton. who built it and the Bridge over Avon.

besides this front or outward gate there was before the House it self (that Shakespeer livd in.) within a little court yard. grass growing there — before the real dwelling house. this out side being only a long gallery &c and for servants.

this House of *Shakespears* was pulld down about 40 years ago and then was built a handsome brick house. by. and now in posession of the Cloptons.

VERTUE'S SKETCHES OF THE FRONTAGE AND PLAN OF NEW PLACE,
STRATFORD-UPON-AVON

PLATE II

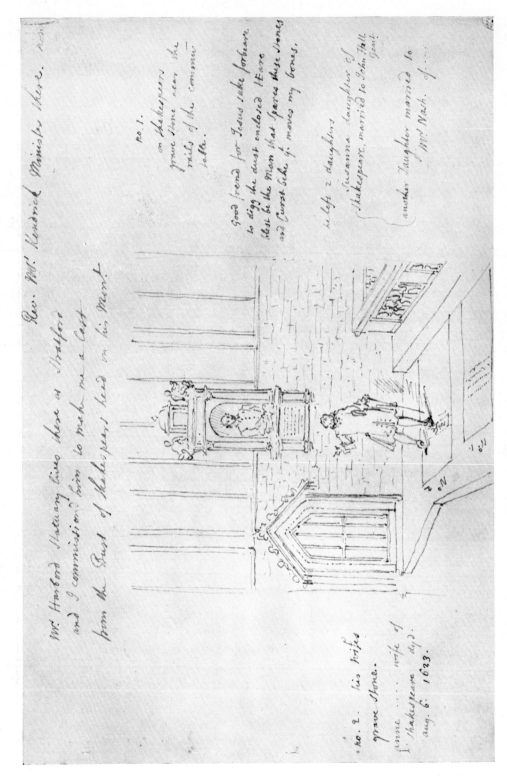

VERTUE'S SKETCH OF SHAKESPEARE'S MONUMENT IN STRATFORD CHURCH

NEW PLACE

THE ONLY REPRESENTATION OF SHAKESPEARE'S HOUSE
FROM AN UNPUBLISHED MANUSCRIPT

BY

FRANK SIMPSON

New Place holds a peculiarly important position among the landmarks of Shakespeare's life. At the beginning of his thirty-third year, at a time when his fame as a playwright was just becoming established, and several years before the period of his greatest triumphs, he seems to have put whatever money he had saved into the purchase of this, the second largest house in his native Stratford, described in 1496 by its original builder, Sir Hugh Clopton, as "my grete house in Stratford upon Avon". Later Shakespeare retired to New Place, and there he died.

The fortunes of New Place before its purchase by Shakespeare in 1597 and its vicissitudes after his death are well documented.[1] Unfortunately, however, the existing structure was pulled down about 1702, and a new house built in its stead, a house which in its turn was destroyed in 1759.

Apart from one or two brief and rather vague descriptions of the original "praty howse of brike and tymbar", nothing has hitherto been known of its appearance.[2] Hence the pen-and-ink sketch reproduced here has more than common interest (Plate I). The sketch itself shows the frontage on Church Street, but since this was only the gate-house and servants' quarters, behind which lay an inner garden-court leading to the 'Great House', we gain from the drawing the impression of a much nobler and more impressive mansion than we do from the extant descriptions. This was no ordinary Stratford dwelling but something much nearer to a manor house.

The author of this drawing was George Vertue, engraver, antiquary and collector of the materials from which Horace Walpole was to write his *Anecdotes of Painting in England; with some Account of the Principal artists*. In October 1737 Vertue accompanied the Earl of Oxford on a tour to Oxford, returning to London via Stratford-upon-Avon. A small quarto volume, now deposited at the British Museum by His Grace the Duke of Portland,[3] records the journey. Of their visit to Stratford Vertue writes:

[*folio* 17] went to see the church of Stratford / Several Monuments, one in the rails of the communion Table / For old John a Coomb a rich miser whom in Shakespeares time / he made an Epitaph —see Shakespears workes./ a monument for Sr Hugh Clopton and his Lady of that Town. / another Monument a Man and Woman hand in hand, not quite / half figures (erect) not lying this was made in memory of Judith / daughter of W^m. Coomb...she dyed 1649. but this Monument / was set up after the restoration—or about 40 years ago. only / upon one part of the Mon^t. is Tho: Stanton fecit Holb.

[Query?] who the Sculptor of the figures was / being done masterly. and some merit.

Rev. M^r. Kendrick Minister there. now /

M^r. Harbord Statuary lives there at Stratford / and I commissoind him to make me a Cast / from the Bust of Shakespears head on his Mon^t.

[*Here is drawn the sketch of Shakespeare's monument*]

[*folio* 18]   This Something by memory and yᵉ description of Shakespears House which was / in Stratford on Avon. where he livd and dyed. and his wife after him 1623. /

[Here is drawn the sketch of New Place]

This the outward appearance towards the Street. the gate and entrance, / (at the Corner of chappel lane) the chappel. X. founded by Sʳ. Hu. Clopton. / who built it and the Bridge over Avon. /

besides this front or outward gate there was before the House itself / (that Shakespear livd in.) within a little court yard. grass growing / there—before the real dwelling house. this outside being only / a long gallery &c and for servants.

[Here is drawn the plan]

This House of Shakespears was pulld down about 40 years ago and then was built a handsome brick house. by. and now in possession of the Cloptons.

[*folio* 19]   in Stratford Shakespeare had several houses. / besides some Land—the Maiden head & Swan an Inn / (now) did belong to him—and a house or two adjoyning. / These are actually in the possesion of Shakespeare Hart. / a glasier by profession, the remaining Heir˙ of Elisabeth—only / Sister to Wᵐ. Shakespear. she Married to…Hart / whose grandson George Hart. father of this present S. Hart / living, about 70 years of age..his right to this and all / Shakespeares estate appears by his Will, in case of / want of Issue Male or Female shoud descend to his / Sisters heirs. a Coppy of the original in poses—of this / Man. and may be Seen in Doctors Commons. from / whence they had it. /

also this which he now enjoys. came from /

Sʳ. John Barnards Lady of Northampton She was a grandaughter / of Shakespears daughter and left no Issue. /

octobʳ. 17.   Sʳ. William Kyte house. calld the College [… …]

Sʳ. H. Cloptons house. now is the ground where / Shakespears house stood. /

Orderd. the Monumental Inscriptions in Stratford church to be taken / and Copyed out exactly to be when done Sent to London / for the Rᵗ. Honᵇˡᵉ. the Earl of Oxford.   done and sent accordingly

Vertue's annotation to his sketch of New Place—"This Something by memory"—seems at first sight to suggest that he had visited Stratford before the demolition of the house in 1702, but it should be observed that, while such an earlier visit is not impossible, he himself was only seventeen years of age in that year. It may be, on the other hand, that he is referring to the 'memory' of another man. On folio 19 he made a point of recording that the poet's descendant, Shakespeare Hart, was "still living" and "about 70 years of age", while in his note-book[4] he states that "Shakespeare Hart *I saw*" [italics mine]: it is, accordingly, quite conceivable that the rapid sketch might have been made from a description given to him by one to whom the original house must still have been so familiar. Whether Vertue in his youth had actually seen Shakespeare's New Place or whether its appearance had been described to him by Hart, the fact remains that this is the only attempt, with any authoritative support, to represent Shakespeare's home, and for that reason it has great value.

Another sketch made by Vertue on this occasion (Plate II) has no less immediate interest. It is a charming sketch of the interior of Stratford Church, showing Shakespeare's monument as it appeared in 1737. Sometimes the assertion is made that this monument was "radically reconstructed" after 1748, and hitherto the only evidence available to disprove this statement was a painting by John Hall, made apparently before 1748, but of uncertain date.[5] Now, from Vertue's sketch, we know definitely that, eleven years before 1748, it presented the same appearance as it does to-day.

Attention should also be drawn to Vertue's reference to Shakespeare Hart's copy of the will (folio 19). Does not this provide the missing link in the history of the copy acquired by the Trustees and Guardians of Shakespeare's Birthplace in 1948?[6] Vertue saw it in Stratford, only ten years before the Reverend Joseph Green had made his copy for the Honourable James West; it was "a copy of the original...in Doctors Commons"; and who, better than a member of the family, could supply the copyist with the missing Christian name "Thomas" to fill a blank in the original will?

NOTES

1. The fullest record is that by J. O. Halliwell-Phillipps, *An Historical Account of New Place* (1864). A brief survey, with additional references, appears in Sir E. K. Chambers, *William Shakespeare*, II (1930), 95–9.

2. The engravings in Edmond Malone, *The Plays and Poems of William Shakespeare*, II (1821), 319, and Samuel Ireland, *Picturesque Views on the Upper, or Warwickshire Avon* (1795) have (rightly) been universally regarded as mere fabrications.

3. This is among the Portland papers at present deposited in the British Museum. These papers are quite distinct from the Vertue note-books and manuscripts in the possession of the British Museum, which have long been regarded as one of the most important eighteenth-century sources for the history of the Fine Arts in England and which are familiar from their publication by the Walpole Society (vols. XVIII, XX, XXII, XXIV, XXVI and XXIX, 1930–47).

4. British Museum Add. MS. 23072 (Walpole Society, XXIV; Vertue, IV, 1936, p. 138).

5. M. H. Spielmann, *The title-page of the First Folio of Shakespeare's Plays* (1924), Plate 16.

6. Levi Fox, 'An early copy of Shakespeare's Will' in *Shakespeare Survey*, 4 (1951), 69–77.

LETTERS TO AN ACTOR PLAYING HAMLET

BY

CHRISTOPHER FRY

In the summer of 1944 John Byron played Hamlet at the Memorial Theatre, Stratford-upon-Avon. I attended a performance while on sick-leave, and, in the actor's dressing-room afterwards, I evidently made some comment which needed to be expanded, and so began a succession of letters. The view of Hamlet they put forward is coloured by the circumstances in which they were written, but, coming to them again after an interval of six years, I see there are certain points which I would make again now. At any rate they add up to a *way* of playing the part, and so I have left them unaltered, except for a few omissions of sentences which were conversational rather than pertinent.

July 20th, 1944

My dear John,

This is being started at midnight, so expect no very clear thinking—I don't know when it will be finished. No preamble at this time of night: we'll plunge straight in. What I meant by the two climacterics of part 1—the two sentences which are like queen-bees to the swarm and clustering of the rest—are: first: "But break, my heart, for I must hold my tongue!"—It is the acceptance of his utter separation from all other life in the world: he is outlawed by his own nerves: there *is* no real way of expression for him, except for his heart to break and destroy him: the only possible expression of what he feels, is his death.... But there are two ways of death—physical death, which doesn't come until five acts further on: and personal death, the death of the *inner* person, which he at least begins to suffer now, though perhaps he doesn't innerly die until he has met with the spirit of his father. Once personal death has been suffered, the appearance of life is maintained by an over-consciousness of what it is to be alive—everything may seem to remain: ambition, laughter, personal relationships; but now they are made of the bone instead of the blood. It is no longer as though the body lives, but as though the skeleton dreams. Certainly there is still passion, vast, intimidating and driving passion, of a kind: but its kind is a kind of death: it is vast and intimidating because it is borne by a dead man—where can it flow to? With his mother and Ophelia his affection is the thrashing of a harpooned whale. With Horatio it is an adumbration of a relationship: he is never properly (because he *cannot* be) taken into Hamlet's confidence. Affection can only properly find its place in another dead man, one physically dead: his father. Horatio you can take (as you do) as Hamlet's occasional resting place on his flight to doom.—But how can you express all this? Perhaps by always remembering that life is finished, and as the play goes on, finished long ago: by your voice, in those lines which best permit of it, being a *scar*, a scar of this inner death-wound.

July 24th, 1944

I've been back in Nottingham for three days, but before we talk about that we'd better continue the quest for Hamlet.

Queen-bee Two: Haste me to know't, that I, with wings as swift
As meditation or the thoughts of love,
May sweep to my revenge.

This 'revenge' you can translate as 'resurrection'—it is the dying-inner-man's hope of a blessed resurrection and future-life—look how he couples it in his mind with what *had* been his life, the best of his life, the scholar-and-lover-life: as once he lived swiftly by meditation and the thoughts of love, so now he will live again by revenge.

But (as Shakespeare would say) Mark! what do you make of the complicated state of affairs in his next long speech? His murdered father is now the whole world he lives on; revenge is to be his life upon that world. "Remember thee!—while memory holds a seat"—and yet he must make a memorandum: he must jot down in his note-book "Uncle is a villain. Remember to avenge Father!" —Here is something that might well give us pause; and it is just here that I begin to see what I call the dreams of the skeleton. From here on, his actions and his conversations are a simulacrum of real life. This action of writing down the one thing he can never hope to forget is the action of a dream-world, a remembered action from an altogether different mode of Being: and much that follows can be understood by this: nightmare, but with this difference: that conscious and unconscious reign in his mind together. The joking, the swearing, the cunning of the scene with Horatio and Marcellus are both the remembrance of time passed and his effort to struggle through to his resurrection of revenge. He is living on two planes at one time: the planes of death-in-life and of resurrection-in-death. I think this letter had better come to you now and another one follow—I should like to spend some time with the god-kissing-carrion, the scene with Ophelia, and the closet, but there's one thing of importance I must add to this: your entrance into the graveyard: you arrive as though to a tea-party of dowagers, with a dove-grey cloak for full measure ("I am set naked on your kingdom", forsooth!). But: *can* this scene be played, as so often it is, as the actor's holiday, the relaxation and chance to show his matinee manner before he has to whirl first into Ophelia's grave and then into his own? You were Gray, charmingly contemplating his Elegy; but you should have already been eating the crocodile— yes, indeed, and being eaten *by* the crocodile of your resurrection. You are now three-times a murderer, three times as bloodied as your uncle: Polonius, Rosencrantz and Guildenstern have all gone. Doesn't that cast a different light on your first two sentences? The hand of not-so-little employment!

In this scene we see the dreaming skeleton looking upon the skeleton emptied of dreams; and the thought of "Cain's jaw-bone that did the first murder" isn't separate from the thought of other and nearer murder. This is no dowager's tea-party, or, if it is, it's at Lady Worm's.

I could start a new letter—I'd better start a new letter—about Hamlet and the problem of good and evil. It's the problem that has foamed uppermost in this century, and if we are anything at all, every one of us to-day is Hamlet in part. It is no longer possible—I can't see how it ever was possible— to think of him as a self-contradiction, or, in *himself*, as a problem. Isn't it a curious thing that the unbalanced man (one wholly and onesidedly devoted to action, for example) has always been considered by mankind to be more balanced than one who, poised between action and thought, is wide open to every true impact of the world?

August 26th, 1944

I haven't gone on writing to you about Hamlet partly because I only had a pencil to write with in hospital and pencil isn't one of my media, and partly because I didn't know how much or how little you wanted more words, words, words, from me. But now (and I still don't properly believe it) I am sitting at the same table at which I began my last letter to you, at about the same time of night, but a compleat civilian.... Here I have to stand for a moment on the brink of the next paragraph before I plunge into the ice-cold water of the problem of good and evil. I've refilled my fountain pen to get me off to a fair start.

It is the second important factor. First, his inner-death; then his attitude to good and evil. Perhaps it is curious, but I believe it to be true, that to a man innerly-dead the problem of good and evil comes particularly poignantly. To the man who has no very discernible hint of death in him, good and evil are dealt with straightly and according to his lights: for him they're no problem, any more than, to St George, the dragon was a problem. But let a man's Being withdraw from life, never so little, and he begins to be walled-up in this ubiquitous riddle. Once the ordinary actions of life are performed not as themselves but as actions-remembered, only two ambitions can remain to choose from (and Hamlet was ambitious and so desired these things most ambitiously): either the inner-death must become the complete, the physical death: or the riddle must be answered. Both may be—both are—desired at the same time; and since the riddle appears to be unanswerable, or answerable (in some sort) only *by* death, no choice eventually remains.—It was odd that immediately after I had started to put this to you in my last letter, but gave up for lack of time, I should have found myself in the midst of this very business. The hospital was mainly for severe cases of shell-shock, but also a good many men were there who had attempted suicide. They could see no particular reason for any life they might lead in the future, or no outcome for mankind generally, unless some clear outlines could be put to the inextricably wrestling muscles of good and evil. That's what I meant by our all being Hamlet, in part, to-day, to-day being out of joint, O cursed, etc.!

Now notice this: at Hamlet's very next entrance after vowing himself to the resurrection of revenge, we have the first hint of what has happened within him. There is already no clear Black's Black and White is White, as your fully *living* man, your man-of-action, your St George-Laertes, would feel. Already the uncle is the revengeful nephew, and the nephew is the murdering uncle, and Ophelia is the Queen and the Queen Ophelia, and all of them are something of dead dogs. His father was one man picked out of ten thousand, the sun, the god, who kissed a carrion-Queen, and bred a maggot-Hamlet—and there, by the way, if you can put up with the fancy, you have the double picture of him: the maggot-life and the maggot-sign-of-death ("We fat ourselves for maggots"). And so the revenge, to be wholly and clearly revenge, wholly and clearly a resurrection, should fall upon them all. They are all of the flesh of Claudius.

August 28th, 1944

I meant to have gone on with this last night, but I was too much i' the sun, it turned my stomach and I went to bed early.—There's so much to write about, and to get this letter finished at all I must jump over a good deal, but I think you'll find that the craving of Hamlet for *something* in this world to be Black or White, wholly black or wholly white, direct, unambiguous and reliable, governs much that follows. He welcomes the players because the melodramas they play have just that quality: they contain villains and heroes, as no-one in this world is villain or hero, and passion has the flight of an arrow and not (as with Hamlet) of a boomerang. His reaction to them is immediately in this key—hoping that there'll be nothing "cracked within the ring"—"We'll e'en to't like French falconers, fly at anything we see"—and he flies, like a thirsty man to water, at: "The rugged Pyrrhus, he whose sable arms, *Black as his purpose*"—and "this dread and *black* complexion," and the rest of the tale of direct action and undivided passion. If only he could be so lacking in death that his view of the world could be like that! That he could be sure of himself as worthy of life and his uncle as deserving of death—but we'll come back to that.

It is the same story in the scene with Ophelia. "Be white!" he says "Be completely, unnaturally white!" or if (I think it is Dover Wilson who suggests it) if 'nunnery' could also mean 'brothel' then "Be either white or black."—"I did love you once": but not in the white sense; in the black-white sense, which, to the inwardly-dead man, is to say "I loved you not". He is not—never for a moment is he—bullying her. He is *demanding* of her, without hope: he is wrestling from himself the admission that beauty cannot be loved as it must be loved; he is asking for beauty to be truth, and for truth to be revelation and rest.

Have you noticed that the soliloquy which has become the best-remembered, To be, or not to be, has nothing to do with Claudius at all? It has nothing *in particular* to do with Hamlet at all—proud man's contumely, pangs of despised love, law's delay, etc. are all general, not particular, ills. Hamlet, being (in everything but body) dead, is less 'a man' than Man: he is in arms not against one trouble or one villain, but a sea of troubles and a world of villains. How much, then, has to be crammed into the word 'revenge', how uncertain even what revenge consists of, and how increasingly difficult to narrow the eyes to an Uncle and the point of a poignard. He isn't living in procrastination but struggling towards comprehension of what deed is required of him. He is still unpregnant of his cause. His Uncle killed, what change comes over the world? What alteration in his mother, what black made white, what riddle unriddled? Indeed, since death is the only sound answer for mankind and since it is, in the end, *felicity* which he has to beg Horatio to absent himself from, can giving death be called revenge at all? To act thus is no more than inaction.—You may think I'm getting too far away from the acting of the part, but I believe there's more chance of it acting itself, to some extent, if all this is understood, if you see the play not as a study in procrastination but as one *action*, a difficult drawing-forth of the sword which has to consume *all* and Hamlet most of all because there is no other answer to the Ghost. By the time we come to the closet-scene he has begun to sense that 'revenge' means 'all'. Until now 'blood' has only meant 'uncle'. And when he fears that looking upon the Ghost again may mean "tears perchance for blood" it is because Revenge has become too big a word for Uncle and he feels (to quote another play) the pity, the pity of it. He still tries the other way: he still begs his mother to say that there is Black and White in the world, a white father and a black uncle. But he knows now that

> "heaven hath pleased it so,
> To punish me with this, and this with me,
> That I must be their scourge and minister,"

and he already sees the deaths of Rosencrantz and Guildenstern as part of the answer to the Ghost—"they must sweep my way, And marshal me to—" not to being a good son of his father but to 'knavery'—and here again we are trembling in the precincts of the terrible house of good and evil, face to face with the nonexistence of black or white. He is never, even at death, certain of himself. When at last action *has* the flight of an arrow he sees that it has gone o'er the house and hurt his brother. He touches, with Laertes, upon the outskirts of forgiveness. And that is, to a degree, perhaps the third answer to the riddle, which Shakespeare takes up in the last plays, but only when the things-to-be-forgiven have become mechanical and tired in his mind. Dostoievsky carries us further when he says, out of the middle of those things, "Compassion is the chief law of human existence."

SHAKESPEARE'S IMAGERY: THE DIABOLIC
IMAGES IN *OTHELLO*

BY

S. L. BETHELL

There is still no commonly accepted procedure in Shakespeare criticism. Yet method to a great extent determines results. Unfortunately no one to-day can have a specialist's familiarity with every department of Shakespeare studies: indeed, it is arguable that the talents of the critic and those required by the modern textual scholar are seldom to be found in the same person. The critic is usually willing to defer to specialist authority on textual and bibliographical questions, but other departments of scholarship, notably the study of Elizabethan thought and Elizabethan theatrical conditions, are indispensable. Without these safeguards the approach to Shakespeare's imagery is especially perilous.

I. METHOD

The study of poetic imagery is without doubt one of the most important innovations in Shakespeare criticism, but, unless a method is followed which brings imagery into due subordination to other aspects of dramatic expression, it can lead only to the construction of individual fantasies. There would seem to have been hitherto a good deal of confusion about the nature and function of Shakespeare's imagery and about the critical technique required to deal with it. It might be useful to examine some of the more important problems involved.

(*a*) There is a matter of definition. The late Caroline Spurgeon used 'imagery' in a strict sense: her elaborate tabulations refer only to such images as occur in rhetorical figures, metaphor and so forth. But direct reference is poetically as important as the oblique reference of a figure, and, moreover, since there is less likelihood of its being unconscious, it is more likely to be directly relevant to the main theme. In what follows I shall widen the scope of the term 'image' to cover any reference in word or phrase to a distinct object or class of objects, whether used figuratively or directly.

(*b*) There is also the problem of interpretation. Three methods are employed by different types of critic. (i) For the psycho-analyst, images stand for realities of the Unconscious very different from their apparent significance. Psycho-analytic criticism, however, can have little interest for those who do not accept the system of belief on which it depends. It is not just another tool, made generally available by the activity of a body of specialists; it has no validity outside the context of a particular group of psychological theories. (ii) Interpreters such as Wilson Knight are concerned with what the images mean to us, to the modern reader, apart from historical limitations, while (iii) a more recent group of scholars, mainly American, are engaged in discovering what they meant to the Elizabethans. Method (ii) seems to assume that Shakespeare's use of imagery was largely unconscious (i.e. indeliberate, a different connotation from the 'Unconscious' of Method (i)), that he habitually expressed profounder meanings than he was consciously aware of. Method (iii) stresses the learned and deliberate artist, employing his figures according to precept and with full awareness of their philosophical and other implications. The latter view is probably nearer to the truth, though we must also recognize that all poetry has an unconscious element which becomes clear only when a particular work is considered in relation to the wider framework of poetic tradition. It seems that Methods (ii) and (iii) might benefit from cross-fertilization. With Method (ii) there is a danger of 'reading in' to Shakespeare a modern—and perhaps a personal—set of attitudes and concerns; the danger of Method (iii) is that, in a purely scholarly application of Elizabethan poetic theory and philosophy, Shakespeare might be reduced to merely a typical Elizabethan. The two methods together are necessary if we are both to understand what Shakespeare was really doing and also to give him his place in a living tradition.

(*c*) The functions of Shakespeare's imagery require analysis. We can distinguish three main functions. (i) All imagery is used to assist in clarifying the meaning of the passage in which it occurs. Some imagery has no further use. This is most frequently true of such as is likely to have been employed unconsciously either because it is commonplace ("*fortune*, on his damned quarrel *smiling*" (*Macbeth*, I, ii, 14)) or because it is glanced at in passing and not dwelt on ("those honours *deep and broad* wherewith Your majesty *loads* our house" (*Macbeth*, I, vi, 17))— these two images do not form a 'mixed metaphor' in the bad sense, partly because they are so lightly touched on and also because they are treated intellectually, not sensuously). (ii) Sometimes imagery has the further function of establishing character (the most obvious instance is the exotic imagery in the speeches of Othello); (iii) sometimes it helps to elucidate a theme (the analogies from sub-human nature in *Lear* and *Macbeth*, which relate to the theme of order and disorder in the universe). I doubt whether the evocation of 'atmosphere' is an independent function; it is rather, I think, a by-product of thematic development—intellect and emotion were not separated in Elizabethan consciousness.

Perhaps we might consider more closely the relation of imagery to character and theme, since there are still occasional attempts to treat Shakespeare's dialogue naturalistically and the true significance of his imagery can never be appreciated on a basis of naturalism. Naturalism demands that no character shall use an image which would not be used by such a person in real life. Polixenes's reference to Judas Iscariot (*Winter's Tale*, I, ii, 419) and Macbeth's "poor player" (v, v, 24) would both be impossible to a naturalistic writer. If Shakespeare had been deliberately aiming at naturalism, he could scarcely have fallen into these errors by unconscious anachronism: he would be unlikely to associate Macbeth's Scotland with the drama, or, if this be not conceded, even Shakespeare would not naturally expect Gospel references from a pagan king. The case for naturalism collapses if it is punctured at any point, since a mixture of naturalism and conventionalism—which I have always believed to be Shakespeare's method —is itself conventional. The use of verse makes naturalism virtually impossible, even apart from the fact that people do not naturally talk in verse. The naturalistic playwright of to-day does not use his own prose style for all his characters indifferently; he attempts to write his dialogue in a variety of prose styles approximating to the styles which such persons would use in real life. He cannot often write in his own best prose, because usually his characters will be narrower in sensibility than he is himself. I believe that Shakespeare did sometimes write in a style inferior to his best in order to individualize his characters through the verse put into their mouths. He did so most notably with Othello and Iago. Othello's verse, noble as it is, has not the usual range and flexibility of Shakespeare, and Iago's pedestrian style is commonly recognized. But *Othello* was in this respect an experiment; thereafter Shakespeare rejected the method of characterization through verse style except in certain usually minor instances, such as the Shepherd in *The Winter's Tale*. It would be intolerable for a poet to have constantly to limit his poetic range to that of minds simpler and more stereotyped than his own: we can understand why Shakespeare for the most part preferred to use prose for less exalted characters and moods and, when writing verse, writes in his own style. Moreover, Shakespeare's method even in *Othello* is radically different from that of the naturalistic writer. Apart from its being in verse, the speech of Othello is not such as it would be in real life. He is a soldier, without the courtly refinements, rude in his speech,[1] as he says himself. Shakespeare suggests the much-travelled soldier in the exotic imagery of the Othello speeches, and the broad simplicity of syntax suggests a simple nature. But the eloquent poetry is of the medium, not the character. You cannot keep poetry out of poetic drama because the characters are not intended to be poetic themselves. Character may be suggested through the quality of the poetry, but in the nature of the case the one attribute that cannot be poetically expressed is that of poetic imagination. Those critics who still talk of the poetic imagination of Othello or Macbeth have surely not sufficiently meditated on the nature of Shakespeare's medium. We cannot judge the degree of a character's poetic imagination by the quality of his utterance; we must rely for such a judgement on direct indications. Othello is rude in his speech because he says so and it is what we would expect from what we know of his life and character; he has some imagination if he invents the handkerchief story, and a strong visual imagination helps to plague him in his jealousy; but there is nothing especially 'poetic' about him. To talk of Othello's poetic nature because he speaks of Anthropophagi, Arabian trees and turbaned Turks is to fall victim to a crude aesthetic. It is not the items mentioned, however romantic, that constitute poetry but the way in which they are treated. The famous Cydnus speech of Enobarbus depends considerably for its powerful effect upon the contrast between the luxurious barge and the everyday commercial associations of the "wharfs" and 'market-place" (*Antony and Cleopatra*, II, ii, 218, 220). Unless we are to ascribe to the character the composition of his own speech, we cannot claim him as 'poetic'. If we go so far as to allow Enobarbus an eye for luxurious appointments we have reached the limit of legitimate psychological induction.

Even the exotic imagery that Othello uses cannot, in the conventional framework of poetic drama, be claimed as revealing directly his mental operations. What it does is suggest his varied experience of foreign travel and the romantic aura which that cast about him. He is not a poet, nor necessarily highly imaginative, but he is seen to be a hero who would appeal to the romantic imagination of others. It is true, however, that many of the images employed are such as an Othello might well have used in real life. In contrast the magnificent imagery of *Antony and Cleopatra*—imagery of the heavens and the "ranged empire" (I, i, 34)—is not necessarily such as would naturally fall from the lips of a real-life Antony or Cleopatra. The poetry is not an outcome of their characters but their characters are created by the poetry. Indeed, the same imagery and the same poetic quality is given to other characters when speaking about them: to the unlikely Enobarbus, to a casual entrant such as Scarus, even to Octavius on occasions, though he has normally a well-marked 'deflated' style of his own. Thus we may conclude that Shakespeare's technique is not primarily naturalistic. He does certainly use imagery to help in characterization, but even then works more by poetic suggestion than by psychological realism. We can, however, distinguish in this connexion between images with a basis of naturalistic justification and those which have only poetic propriety. Shakespeare employs both types.

The remarks about *Antony and Cleopatra* lead to another consideration. Frequently imagery used in characterization refers not to the character of the speaker but to the person spoken about. When Octavius, in speaking about Antony or Cleopatra, uses the Antony-Cleopatra style we are not to ascribe their qualities to him. If we do we shall make nonsense of the play. An audience attuned to poetry will not be thinking of the speaker at such a time. When Valentine reports that Olivia will

> ...water once a day her chamber round
> With eye-offending brine: all this to season
> A brother's dead love, which she would keep fresh
> And lasting in her sad remembrance—   (*Twelfth Night*, I, i, 29)

we are to note how a ceremonial lustration with holy water—which is made with an admixture of salt—'fades into' the salting of beef for winter consumption. I do not think we are to admire the wit of Valentine or speculate on his religious leanings or association with the stockyard; but Olivia's mourning is seen for what it is, a sentimental and slightly ridiculous pose. Now the use of imagery to indicate the character of the person spoken about may itself involve a comment on the theme of the play, in this instance the theme of 'dream versus reality', the philosophic thread of *Twelfth Night*. So we may expect to encounter in the conventional drama of Shakespeare some groups of imagery which relate to theme rather than specifically to character, a use which I have already postulated and which I hope later to illustrate in detail. An immediate example is the theological reference of the Gentleman in *The Winter's Tale* to "a world ransomed, or one destroyed" (v, ii, 17); it has nothing to do with the speaker's character but everything to do with the underlying meaning of the play.[2] How are we to distinguish these uses of imagery? There are no rules; each instance must be treated separately in its context with all the resources of the critic's learning and sensibility. It is above all important that the first step should be in the right direction, that a proper distinction should be made between those images which have no significance outside their immediate grammatical and rhetorical function in the sentences in which they occur, and those which have a further significance either in relation to character or theme. To isolate a group of images and to deduce character or theme from them alone is to court every sort of freak interpretation. The images may be unconscious and their relationship to one another adventitious: the real significance of a chain of food images might be that Shakespeare had indigestion that morning. It is best to concentrate on those images which seem to express a quality of character or a theme for which there already exists good evidence of another kind (direct statement, implication of plot, etc.), or at least those which appear at important points in the development of the play and cannot be sufficiently accounted for in their immediate contexts. The truth is that no one method of approach to Shakespeare is adequate; the various approaches need to be balanced one against another.

2. APPLICATION

I propose to devote the rest of this essay chiefly to a consideration of the diabolic imagery in *Othello*, with some comparative study of *Macbeth* and *The Atheist's Tragedy*. Wilson Knight was, I think, the first to attempt what might be called a 'mystical interpretation' of *Othello*: his essay on "The Othello Music" in *The Wheel of Fire*[3] shows how the love of Othello and Desdemona is presented poetically in terms of heavenly bliss and cosmic order, while Iago figures as the devilish, disruptive force transmuting heaven into hell and order into chaos. Though I do not always agree with Knight's ingenious interpretations of Shakespeare's plays, I am surprised that this especially cogent essay has not received a greater measure of endorsement from other writers. The tendency is still to treat *Othello* purely as a domestic tragedy and to pay little attention to its profoundly theological structure.

With *Macbeth* it is different. Most recent critics agree in interpreting the later play, as I am bound to regard it, in the light of Christian theology. With whatever minor variations they take *Macbeth* to be a study of evil, the history of a soul's damnation. Consideration of the imagery, particularly as it relates to the doctrine of the Chain of Being, has done much to establish this interpretation. It has not yet been sufficiently realized, however, to what extent Shakespeare—deliberately, we must suppose—transformed the source-material of the play to give it theological precision. The renewed interest in Shakespeare's sources, which is a feature of contemporary scholarship, might well be directed to questions of this sort. Perhaps I may be allowed to give an example to which I have already drawn attention elsewhere. Holinshed, recounting the portents which accompanied the murder of Duff, states that "horsses in Louthian, being of singular beautie and swiftnesse, did eate their owne flesh, and would in no wise taste anie other meate". In *Macbeth* these become the King's own horses which, "turn'd wild in nature" and

> Contending 'gainst obedience, as they would make
> War with mankind,

"eat each other" (II, iv, 16). They are Duncan's horses so that there can be no doubt about where to apply the moralization of their behaviour. "Wild in nature" is a significant phrase: 'nature' is used many times in the play, frequently in connexion with ideas of order and disorder; wild nature to the Elizabethans meant disorder, nature escaped from the hand of man, her divinely appointed master. So the horses were "contending 'gainst obedience", against the graduated bond of duty and love which maintains the cosmic hierarchy; for them to "make War with mankind", a lower order in the Chain of Being against a higher, would imply rebellion, that most hideous word to an Elizabethan ear. As, however, the forces of evil, being centred in themselves and not in God, lack the cohesion which comes from mutual love and common duty, their power is limited and they ultimately turn to mutual destruction: Duncan's horses "eat each other". By comparing Shakespeare's words with those of his source we can thus see him defining and underlining the theological significance of the incident—and it becomes evident that the theology in Shakespeare's plays is not merely an unconscious reflexion of the age. The meeting of Malcolm and Macduff is usually said to be only a versification of Holinshed. Yet the scene (IV, iii) is full of religious imagery:

> new sorrows
> Strike heaven on the face;
>
> To offer up a weak poor innocent lamb
> To appease an angry god;
>
> Angels are bright still, though the brightest fell:
> Though all things foul would wear the brows of grace,
> Yet grace must still look so;
>
> Not in the legions
> Of horrid hell can come a devil more damn'd
> In evils to top Macbeth;
>
> I should
> Pour the sweet milk of concord into hell;
>
> Thy royal father
> Was a most sainted king: the queen that bore thee,
> Oftener upon her knees than on her feet,
> Died every day she lived;
>
> Devilish Macbeth
> By many of these trains hath sought to win me
> Into his power, and modest wisdom plucks me
> From over-credulous haste: but God above
> Deal between thee and me!

The description of Edward the Confessor and his touching for the Evil is full of religious imagery; St Edward is the positive contrast to "devilish Macbeth":

> He hath a heavenly gift of prophecy,
> And sundry blessings hang about his throne,
> That speak him full of grace.

When Ross arrives, Malcolm prays:

> Good God, betimes remove
> The means that makes us strangers!

So it continues:

> An older and a better soldier none
> That Christendom gives out;
>
> Not for their own demerits, but for mine,
> Fell slaughter on their souls. Heaven rest them now!
>
> Macbeth
> Is ripe for shaking, and the powers above
> Put on their instruments.

The scene is thus very full of religious images, several of them being direct references and so more likely to have been written deliberately. Not one of them, however, has any parallel in Holinshed. Shakespeare, it appears, had a habit of using religious imagery (including direct reference) which Holinshed—and how many others?—had not. It is not sufficiently accounted for by describing him as a typical Elizabethan.

It might be argued that *Macbeth* is a special case, being designed for a command performance before James I. There is a familiar list of the ingredients intended for his Majesty's pleasure: the good character of Banquo and references to his descendants, especially the show of kings; the 'equivocator' passage; touching for the King's Evil; the Scottish setting. The same intention might apply to the play as a whole. Not only is its demonology appropriate for the royal author of a treatise on that subject but the treatment of kingship (Duncan was "the Lord's anointed temple" (II, iii, 73)) and feudal hierarchy would appeal to the writer of the *Basilicon Doron*, while the strong theological flavour would surely win the approval of a king who notoriously enjoyed theological disputation and took the chair at the Hampton Court Conference with such manifest satisfaction. But these various ingredients are closely compounded; even the references to equivocation and the King's Evil take their place in the development of the theme. Shakespeare shows not only dramatic skill but a grasp of theology which could hardly be acquired for the occasion. Recent criticism of other plays, especially *Measure for Measure*, *King Lear* and the late romances, has revealed the same theological and philosophical concern, which I have myself also attempted to trace in the apparently alien atmosphere of *Antony and Cleopatra*.[4] If *Othello* should be found patient of a similar theological interpretation it would bring the play more into line with the other great tragedies.

Statistical methods are seldom satisfactory and never conclusive, but they can serve useful subordinate purposes.[5] I find thirty-seven diabolic images in *Macbeth*, i.e. images including such words as "hell", "hellish", "devil", "fiend", "fiend-like", "damn", "damned", or in some other way suggesting the notion of hell or damnation. In *Othello* I find sixty-four. *Macbeth* in the Globe Edition has 2108 lines and *Othello* 3316. A play the length of *Othello* with diabolic images occurring in the frequency of *Macbeth* would therefore have fifty-eight such images. Thus the frequency of their occurrence in *Othello* is greater even than in *Macbeth*, which recognizedly treats the theme of supernatural evil. There is something here, then, which calls for investigation. Every one has noticed the diabolic atmosphere of *Macbeth*, where "hell is murky" (v, i, 40) and its dun smoke (I, v, 52) hangs like a pall over the terrestrial scene. In *Othello* the image-hunter has been charmed by the exotic; the "antres vast and deserts idle" (I, iii, 140) have seized upon his imagination and distracted attention from the much more frequent and often no less vivid references to the "divinity of hell" (II, iii, 356). 'Exotic' is harder to define than 'diabolic', but, allowing for some subjectivity in interpretation, there are without doubt relatively few exotic images in *Othello*. I make the total fifteen[6] against the sixty-four images of hell and damnation.

The diabolic images in *Othello* cannot be adequately explained as purely local, exhausting their meaning in their immediate contexts. There are too many of them for that. Some are important direct statements, and several occur at turning-points in the drama, where they receive considerable emphasis. (This will appear later as we examine them.) Moreover, there is nothing in plot or characterization that is incongruous with their being given a wider significance. It appears, however, that they cannot primarily serve the purpose of characterization, either semi-naturalistically (like the exotic imagery of the Othello speeches) or by poetic convention. They can indeed be naturalistically justified, in that such expressions might be used on occasion by any one with a background of Christian thought—they are not out of character. But they are not characteristic of any particular person. They are widely distributed. Iago, surprisingly, has only eighteen to Othello's twenty-six; the remaining twenty are scattered among most of the other characters. Desdemona is the only important personage in the play to have none at all, and this, I think, has considerable significance for character: "O, the more angel she" (v, ii, 130). But they must have a more important function than the negative characterization of Desdemona.

Iago has only his fair proportion of diabolic imagery, yet we undoubtedly gain the impression that in this play the theme of hell, as it were, originates with him and is passed to Othello later as Iago succeeds in dominating his mind. Statistics show this impression to be well-founded. In Act I Iago has eight diabolic images and Othello none; in Act II he has six and Othello one. The change comes in Act III, where Iago drops to three and Othello rises to nine. In Act IV Iago has only one while Othello has ten, and in Act V Iago has none and Othello six. It all begins, then, with Iago.

Yet there is no obvious untheological reason why such imagery should be associated, either naturalistically or conventionally, with the type of character that Iago is meant to be. He has clearly much in common with the stage Machiavel; the fundamental principle he professes is that of pure self-interest:

> Others there are
> Who, trimm'd in forms and visages of duty,
> Keep yet their hearts attending on themselves,
> And, throwing but shows of service on their lords,
> Do well thrive by them and when they have lined their coats
> Do themselves homage: these fellows have some soul;
> And such a one do I profess myself.   (I, i, 49)

To "do themselves homage", as the phrase itself brings out, is the very inversion of feudal duty, a deliberate throwing over of the old morality based on traditional religion. To ascribe "soul" to such fellows gives the word a new and shocking significance. Iago's practical materialism is evident in his attitude to love, "merely a lust of the blood and a permission of the will" (I, iii, 339), and in his contemptuous remark to Cassio, bewailing his wounded reputation: "As I am an honest man, I thought you had received some bodily wound" (II, iii, 266). But all this has been noted often enough. Except that Iago never openly expresses disbelief in God, the nearest parallel to his view of life is that of D'Amville in *The Atheist's Tragedy*:[7]

> Let all men lose, so I increase my gaine,
> I haue no feeling of anothers paine;   (I, i, 144)

and

> All the purposes of Man
> Aime but at one of these two ends; pleasure
> Or profit.   (IV, iii, 125)

D'Amville's whole life is based upon the belief that "there's nothing in a Man, aboue His nature" (I, i, 16), and, although Iago is less dogmatically blatant, his "'tis in ourselves that we are thus or thus" (I, iii, 322) implies an equivalent rejection both of divine providence and grace and of diabolic inspiration. D'Amville and Iago are alike in self-regard and philosophic egotism. Both are also consummate hypocrites. D'Amville poses as a man of religion; Iago, more subtly, as an "honest" man with a rough tongue and a tendency to cynical utterance that fail to conceal his essential goodness. Iago, as we have said, has nothing comparable to D'Amville's exclamation to Castabella: "Nay then inuoke Your great suppos'd protectour" (IV, iii, 173), nothing that directly denies the existence of God. But there is no occasion for it, and *The Atheist's Tragedy* is much more crudely polemic than *Othello*. Shakespeare, though he has more direct doctrinal statement than is usually credited to him, was too good a dramatist to employ such professions gratuitously: he prefers to show belief in action and express philosophy in its poetic equivalent. The beliefs already ascribed to Iago are made with sufficient point for him to be recognized by an Elizabethan audience as an 'atheist'. It may also be some indication of Shakespeare's intention for Iago that Edmund in *Lear*, his literary scion, professes to worship Nature as his goddess (I, ii, 1). Perhaps it may be objected that Iago believes at least in the Devil and that this implies his acceptance of the Christian scheme. Indeed, he dwells lovingly on the "divinity of hell":

> When devils will the blackest sins put on,
> They do suggest at first with heavenly shows,
> As I do now.
> (II, iii, 357)

But does Iago give the impression of believing in the powers of darkness in the way Macbeth does? He admires their "divinity"; he seems to enjoy being taken for a devil at the end when his machinations have been revealed; but there is never any hint that he has commerce with infernal powers. "'Tis in ourselves that we are thus or thus." "Thou know'st we work by wit, and not by witchcraft", he admonishes Roderigo (II, iii, 378). Iago is a self-made devil.

How, then, are we to understand the great number of diabolic images in *Othello*? They are related closely to Iago, but in what way? I do not think that there is any Elizabethan convention by which the Machiavel or atheist is presented in such terms. I find only fourteen diabolic images in the whole of *The Atheist's Tragedy*: some are merely oaths and the rest have no great significance for character nor are they used to develop a theme. In *Othello* those employed by Iago himself are capable of naturalistic explanation up to a point. We might find credible the character of an evil man who, though an unbeliever, likes to dwell on that aspect of religion which fills others with dread and to model himself upon a Devil in whom he does not objectively believe. Alternatively, we could accept Iago as a 'practical atheist', one who lives by an atheistic code without making any deliberate intellectual rejection of religion. There are many such. If this were so, his enjoyment of the devilish might colour his language without implying either belief or disbelief. If naturalistic consistency of character is desired, I suppose that either of these readings might supply it. But Shakespeare leaves us small leisure for such speculation when we are watching *Othello*. What he does, however, is to assail our ears with diabolic imagery throughout, and by no means only in the speeches of Iago. A naturalistic solution is not quite impossible. Accepting either of the naturalistic explanations given above for Iago's use of this sort of imagery, we might argue that the other characters as they come into the circle of his influence take over his forms of expression. But would any Elizabethan, even Shakespeare, entertain such a notion—or even conceive such a character as either of the 'naturalistic' Iagos I have projected? Since we have established that Shakespeare's method was fundamentally conventional, there is no need to accept a fantastic naturalistic explanation if a plausible conventional explanation lies to hand.

I shall argue that the diabolic imagery is used to develop poetically an important underlying theme. Of the sixty-four diabolic images in *Othello* not one occurs in Cinthio's *novella*. We have found Shakespeare adding considerably to the number of religious images in the sources of *Macbeth* and sharpening those that were already there, so as to develop poetically a theological theme. Is it not likely that when he introduced a similar type of imagery into *Othello* it was with a similar purpose? There is a steady increase in the use of diabolic imagery from act to act, which looks like thematic development. The figures for each act are, respectively, ten, eleven, thirteen, fourteen, sixteen. I shall outline what I believe to be the general function of this imagery in *Othello* and then consider its operation in detail.

Othello can be interpreted on three levels, the personal, the social and the metaphysical. In *Lear* and *Macbeth* these three levels are so closely interrelated that it is impossible to make sense of the personal or story level without taking the others into consideration. In *Othello* the interrelationship is less complete: the story can be considered alone, with the result that the other elements often remain unnoticed. Unfortunately without them the story itself is liable to misinterpretation. On the personal level we have a straightforward domestic tragedy— Cinthio's *novella*, in fact, with modifications. On the social level we have a study of a contemporary problem, the clash between the 'new man' thrown up by certain aspects of Renaissance culture, the atheist-Machiavel with his principle of pure self-interest, and the chivalric type, representing the traditional values of social order and morality. That Iago is more intelligent than Othello reflects the usual ambivalence of Shakespeare's judgement. On the metaphysical level we see Othello and Iago as exemplifying and participating in the age-long warfare of Good and Evil.

These various planes of meaning coalesce into something like unity. It appears that to Shakespeare Cinthio's ensign suggested (*a*) the contemporary atheist-Machiavel, and (*b*) the Devil himself. It seems to follow that Shakespeare thought of the 'new man', with his contempt for traditional morality and religion, as a disintegrating force seeking to break down the social order that is a part of cosmic order—as, in fact, an instrument (no doubt unconscious) of the Devil in his constant effort to reduce cosmos to chaos. This would be a very natural attitude for a conservative Elizabethan, and to express this attitude is one main function—a general function —of the diabolic imagery in *Othello*: Iago is a "demi-devil" (v, ii, 301), worse than an ordinary devil, a bastard one,[8] and his philosophy is a "divinity of hell".

But Shakespeare's metaphysical interest is not wholly absorbed in the social issue. The problem of good and evil is also presented for itself and in much the same terms as we are familiar with from modern interpretations of *Macbeth*. L. C. Knights has drawn attention to the theme of "the deceitful appearance" in the later play.[9] Good and evil are so readily confused by fallen humanity: "Fair is foul, and foul is fair" (*Macbeth*, I, i, 11). "There's no art", says Duncan, "To find the mind's construction in the face" (I, iv, 11). This same theme of deceitful appearance runs its course right through the tragedies from *Hamlet* with its smiling villain to the final statement of *Macbeth*. In *Lear* Cornwall suspects Kent of being a sort of Iago:

> These kind of knaves I know, which in this plainness
> Harbour more craft and more corrupter ends
> Than twenty silly ducking observants
> That stretch their duties nicely.   (II, ii, 107)

I do not think that the ramifications of deceitful appearance in *Othello* have ever received comment. Of course there is Iago—"honest Iago" (II, iii, 177), who is in truth a "hellish villain" (V, ii, 368) but only so revealed at the end of the play. Cinthio's ensign is described as *di bellissima presenza*, a fact which actors would do well to note, for Shakespeare surely intended Iago to have this beautiful exterior, since it fits so well with his other arrangements for 'deceit'. His hero, Othello, is a black man, as calculated, in those times, to inspire horror as Iago to inspire confidence. It was well known that the Devil frequently appeared in the form of a black man to his worshippers. "There's no art To find the mind's construction in the face." Contrary to a 'Neoplatonic' doctrine much entertained at the time,[10] Othello and Iago are in appearance the exact opposite of their natures. Ironically enough, they both agree at one point that "men should be what they seem" (III, iii, 126, 128). Why, again, is Michael Cassio a Florentine? There is nothing in Cinthio to that effect. The Florentines were noted for their fine manners, a quality displayed by Cassio: "'tis my breeding That gives me this bold show of courtesy" (II, i, 99). Florence was also known as the birthplace of Machiavelli and a special degree of subtlety seems to have been ascribed to his fellow-citizens.[11] Cassio is an exception. His exclamation upon Iago, "I never knew A Florentine more kind and honest" (III, i, 42), has several layers of irony and reveals his own simplicity, which is evident also in the drunken scene. Expectation is again disappointed. Even Desdemona deceives expectation: though a Venetian, she is not a "cunning whore" (IV, ii, 89) as Othello was led frantically to believe. The cunning whores of Venice were well enough known to Elizabethan England: "the name of a Cortezan of Venice is famoused over all Christendome", says Coryate in his *Crudities*.[12] An Elizabethan audience might have expected fickleness in her, not chastity. Yet, though she "deceived her father", a point which is stressed (I, iii, 194; III, iii, 206), and tells a white lie about the handkerchief, she is the most innocent of all deceivers, dying with a noble lie upon her lips: "Nobody; I myself" (V, ii, 124). Emilia with her materialistic code ought to be a fitting wife for Iago, but her cynical professions conceal a golden heart—which is what Iago pretended about himself. Deceitful appearance thus characterizes all the main figures in *Othello*. Where is the evil one? Who is true and who is false? The play is a solemn game of hunt the devil, with, of course, the audience largely in the know. And it is in this game that the diabolic imagery is bandied about from character to character until the denouement: we know the devil then, but he has summoned another lost soul to his side.

It begins with Iago. In his opening speech he refers to Cassio as "a fellow almost damn'd in a fair wife" (I, i, 21). We know nothing of the wife and I do not find much significance in the phrase, except as an example of Iago's perversion of values. Perhaps Shakespeare originally intended to introduce Cassio's wife into the plot but omitted her on deciding to use Bianca. "Damn'd" is not important here—I shall try to avoid the image-hunter's fallacy of treating all similar images as equally significant in spite of their context. A more interesting remark occurs shortly afterwards: "I am not what I am" (I, i, 65). Iago expresses his policy of Machiavellian deceit in a parodied negation of the Scriptural words in which God announces his nature: "I am that I am" (Exodus iii. 14). His own diabolic nature is implied. I do not think that a point such as this is too obscure for an Elizabethan, bred on the Bible and trained in verbal wit, to have apprehended at a first hearing, especially if the actor knew what he was saying. Now comes the calling-up of Brabantio; Othello must be plagued with flies (I, i, 71). Edith Sitwell may be right in seeing a reference to the Prince of Flies,[13] though I should not wish to press the matter. (The association of flies with devils was ancient and well known: cf. "The multiplying villanies of nature Do swarm upon him" (*Macbeth*, I, ii, 11). The "summer flies" of *Othello*, IV, ii, 66 have no apparent relation to the diabolic imagery. If any connexion exists, it is surely unintentional and unimportant.) Iago warns Brabantio that "the devil will make a grandsire" of him (I, i, 91). In the same passage Othello is "an old black ram" (I, i, 88). Iago thus begins the 'devil-black man' reference which perhaps runs in Brabantio's mind later. The audience, not having listened to Othello yet, might be a little dubious about him. Almost at the same time, however, Iago takes the name of devil to himself: "you are one of those that will not serve God, if the devil bid you" (I, i, 108)—it is jocular, and meaningful only in the light of later developments. Its immediate value is that of iteration; the audience is being repeatedly assailed with the idea of the diabolic. A similar value, and no more, attaches to Iago's confidence to Roderigo: he hates Othello as he does hell-pains (I, i, 155). Brabantio, perhaps inspired by Iago's language earlier, accuses Othello: "Damn'd as thou art, thou hast enchanted her" (I, ii, 63)—the black man and black magic naturally falling together. But Othello has an opportunity of showing his true nature, first in preventing bloodshed and afterwards in his speech before the senate. The first endeavour to make a devil of the black man fails to convince the Duke and his senators and leaves the audience persuaded of his high character. No "practices of cunning hell" (I, iii, 102) have been employed. Desdemona "saw Othello's visage in his mind" (I, iii, 253), the sensible converse of popular 'Neoplatonic' theory; her love was unconstrained. So the Duke pronounces Othello "far more fair than black" (I, iii, 291), putting aside the deceitful appearance. Iago has suffered an initial defeat, but we hear him in good spirits rallying Roderigo: "If thou wilt needs damn thyself, do it a more delicate way than drowning" (I, iii, 360), hammering again on the theme of damnation. He calls on his "wits and all the tribe of hell" (I, iii, 364), and the Venetian scenes close with an ominous couplet:

> I have't. It is engender'd. Hell and night
> Must bring this monstrous birth to the world's light. (I, iii, 409)

On the shore at Cyprus Iago has a chance to vent his cynicism in the guise of entertainment. Women are "devils being offended", he says (II, i, 112), but the description would apply more appropriately to himself. There is a moment of high poetry when Othello and Desdemona meet after their safe passage through the storm:

> O my soul's joy !
> If after every tempest come such calms,
> May the winds blow till they have waken'd death !

> And let the labouring bark climb hills of seas
> Olympus-high and duck again as low
> As hell's from heaven! If it were now to die,
> 'Twere now to be most happy. (II, i, 186)

The tragic tempest[14] does indeed drive Othello's bark from heaven to hell; if he had died then in Desdemona's arms he would have been most happy. We move from exalted verse to the flat prose of Iago. What delight shall Desdemona have "to look on the devil?" (II, i, 229). The 'devil-black man' equation is revived for Roderigo's benefit. Cassio, too, is explained to be "a devilish knave" (II, i, 250). The limit of Cassio's devilry is reached the same night when he becomes successively possessed by "the devil drunkenness" and "the devil wrath" (II, iii, 297). Iago must have smarted under Cassio's eschatology: "there be souls must be saved, and there be souls must not be saved" (II, iii, 106), and "the lieutenant is to be saved before the ancient" (II, iii, 114). But he maintains his usual composure, no doubt taking comfort in the thought of the lieutenant's imminent downfall. Cassio, deprived of his rank, exclaims against drunkenness: "Every inordinate cup is unblessed and the ingredient is a devil" (II, iii, 311). "Come, come, good wine is a good familiar creature, if it be well used", says Iago reasonably, having just used it himself for a purpose devilish enough. Iago, it has often been observed, dominates the three night scenes; he is a Prince of Darkness and enjoys them thoroughly. Perhaps Shakespeare took a moment's thought before giving him the one appropriate exclamation as the bell rings out: "Diablo, ho!" (II, iii, 161). The second act ends as he concocts "divinity of hell":

> When devils will the blackest sins put on,
> They do suggest at first with heavenly shows,
> As I do now. (II, iii, 357)

Cassio was not a serious candidate for diabolic honours. His penitent self-accusations, the fact that he feels himself to have been possessed because he has been drunk and disorderly, serve merely to demonstrate the daily beauty of his life (v, i, 19). He has behaved badly, Iago apparently well. But the audience know the truth. Shakespeare has staged a pretty contrast between the apparent sinner and the hypocrite. Iago has not so far shared the stage very much with Othello, but we now pass to the main action, in which the handsome villain and his hideous but noble dupe stand together in the eye of the audience; fair face and black soul, black face and fair soul in double contrast. Desdemona is to become a devil to Othello, that Othello might become a devil in fact.

> Perdition catch my soul,
> But I do love thee! and when I love thee not,
> Chaos is come again. (III, iii, 90)

This is weighty irony at the turning-point of the play. When he loves her not, chaos does come again, his life is disintegrated, and perdition catches his soul. The Devil's aim, we remember, is to reduce order to its primal chaos once more. There is a microcosm-macrocosm parallel behind the image. Iago now goes to work to arouse Othello's jealousy:

> O, what damned minutes tells he o'er
> Who dotes, yet doubts, suspects, yet strongly loves! (III, iii, 169)

It would be wrong to make anything of the frequent association, in this play, of hell and damnation with sex. Heaven is equally expressed in terms of sexual love. The association is due merely to the particular dramatic medium. The war of good and evil is fought out in this intimate domestic field, just as in *Macbeth* the battleground is a kingdom and the most important relationships are political. Iago is duly warned: "If thou dost slander her...nothing canst thou to damnation add Greater than that" (III, iii, 368). When he is half convinced of Desdemona's infidelity, Othello exclaims at the thought of it: "Death and damnation!" (III, iii, 396). It is more than an oath. He loses his heaven with his faith in her.[15] Iago takes up the theme: "damn them then, If ever mortal eyes do see them bolster..." (III, iii, 398). At the end of the scene, Othello, fully persuaded, thinks of Desdemona as a devil while he confers upon Iago the coveted promotion:

> Damn her, lewd minx! O, damn her!
> Come, go with me apart: I will withdraw,
> To furnish me with some swift means of death
> For the fair devil. Now art thou my lieutenant. (III, iii, 475)

"Fair is foul, and foul is fair." Bemused by passion, Othello falls into the deep deceit of taking good for evil and evil for good.

At this point we can see how the study of imagery illuminates character problems, even when the imagery is not used for differentiation between characters. Iago is so strongly associated with the diabolic that we are justified in interpreting his character in terms of demonology. All his stated motives may be genuine, but the deepest, as Bradley saw,[16] is the desire to plume up his will (I, iii, 399). He is mastered by the sins which caused the angels to fall, Pride and Envy. He has already acquired, when the play opens, an habitual evil which is expressed in opposition to whatever is good and beautiful. Destruction is the only form of self-assertion left to the proud and envious. The diabolic imagery and the aura it casts about Iago cause the insinuation of jealousy into Othello to take something of the form of a temptation and fall. At bottom Othello's sin is the sin of Adam (as in *Paradise Lost*): he allows passion to usurp the place of reason. On the night of the brawl he felt passion assaying to lead the way (II, iii, 207). But Othello was expert in the command of soldiers; he never really lost self-control and so remained in control of the situation. In domestic affairs he was less expert; he had not formed habits of prudence and discretion in a way of life that was new to him. So passion had its way, in the form of jealousy, and like the Pontic sea (III, iii, 453) rushed on blindly to its end. He is to seek swift means of death for Desdemona, whom he sees as a "fair devil". The fair devil, however, is at his side. "I am your own for ever", says Iago (III, iii, 479), but it is Othello who has handed his soul into Iago's keeping. Confused by passion, Othello is on the devil's side without knowing it. Or perhaps he does know in part, for he has already called up "black vengeance from the hollow hell" (III, iii, 447).[17]

With a totally false view of her nature, Othello finds "a young and sweating devil", in Desdemona's palm (III, iv, 42). The importance of the handkerchief is underlined, for the audience as well as Desdemona:

> To lose't or give't away were such perdition
> As nothing else could match. (III, iv, 67)

"Perdition catch my soul": the handkerchief is central to the plot, and "perdition" to the argument. For a while the devil makes sporadic and rather casual appearances, important only because they keep the word dinning in the audience's ears. Iago compares a cannon to the devil (III, iv, 136); Cassio bids Bianca throw her vile guesses in the devil's teeth (III, iv, 184). The fourth act opens with a more serious passage:

> Naked in bed, Iago, and not mean harm!
> It is hypocrisy against the devil:
> They that mean virtuously, and yet do so,
> The devil their virtue tempts, and they tempt heaven. (IV, i, 5)

Ironic because, in spite of his morality, the devil has tempted Othello's virtue and he has fallen—into the sin of jealousy. When Othello drops down in a fit, his last words are "O devil!" (IV, i, 43). Iago continues to play upon him:

> O, 'tis the spite of hell, the fiend's arch-mock,
> To lip a wanton in a secure couch,
> And to suppose her chaste! (IV, i, 71)

(Bianca keeps up the theme for the audience: "Let the devil and his dam haunt you" (IV, i, 153).) At this stage Othello thinks continuously of Desdemona as a devil or a damned soul; this is the measure of his spiritual blindness, his enslavement by Iago: "Ay, let her rot, and perish, and be damned to-night" (IV, i, 191). His exclamations in the presence of Lodovico show how the thought has taken possession of his mind: "Fire and brimstone!" (IV, i, 245); then, as he strikes her, "Devil!" (IV, i, 251); and immediately after, "O devil, devil!" (IV, i, 255). This phase reaches its height in the terrible scene in which he treats Desdemona as a whore and her chamber as a brothel. Emilia, protesting her mistress's innocence, calls down "the serpent's curse" (IV, ii, 16) on the hypothetical beguiler of Othello, but alone with his wife he bids her swear her innocence and damn herself (IV, ii, 35),

> Lest, being like one of heaven, the devils themselves
> Should fear to seize thee: therefore be double damn'd:
> Swear thou art honest. (IV, ii, 36)

He is fully alive to the deceitful appearance; only he ascribes it to the wrong person: "Heaven truly knows that thou art false as hell" (IV, ii, 39). Even Patience, the "young and rose-lipp'd cherubin" must "look grim as hell" upon her fault (IV, ii, 63).[18] When he summons Emilia again it is as portress of hell (IV, ii, 90). The connexion with *Macbeth* is not irrelevant. The Devil is at work in Desdemona's chamber, not in the way Othello imagines but as surely as in the castle of Macbeth and with as bloody an outcome.

There is now a lull in the diabolic imagery except for another outburst of Emilia against the unknown villain who has poisoned Othello's mind. When Desdemona prays "If any such there be, heaven pardon him!" she retorts: "A halter pardon him! and hell gnaw his bones!" (IV, ii, 136). The irony of this, spoken in her husband's presence, is strong enough to link up with the denunciations of Iago later. Act IV, scene iii, the 'willow' scene, has no diabolic images, for Shakespeare is a master of decorum. It is more remarkable that Act V, scene i, Iago's last nocturnal scene of devilish activity, should produce only one reference of this kind, when the dying Roderigo recognizes the truth at last: "O damn'd Iago! O inhuman dog!" (v, i, 62). The murder of Desdemona is carried out, again appropriately enough, without any diabolical imagery: it is a moment for sympathy, not moral judgement. Thus between Othello's departure from Desdemona's chamber after the 'brothel' incident and Desdemona's last words to Emilia from her death-bed there are only two instances of diabolic imagery. In addition to the matter of local propriety this lull prepares very effectively for the continuous torrent of such imagery with which the play closes.

Hitherto the diabolic images have been frequently misapplied—to Othello in his innocence, to Cassio, to Desdemona. Now, immediately after Desdemona's death, the last misapplication is made and corrected. The same sort of images, with all the accumulated force of those that have gone before, will serve to give point and metaphysical depth to the denouement.

> Oth. She's, like a liar, gone to burning hell:
> 'Twas I that kill'd her.
> Emil.   O, the more angel she,
> And you the blacker devil!
> Oth. She turn'd to folly, and she was a whore.
> Emil. Thou dost belie her, and thou art a devil.   (v, ii, 129)

The formal stichomythia brings out the central importance of the passage. Desdemona quite certainly is angel, not devil, and she has gone to heaven. The imputation has passed from her to Othello, who this time can worthily sustain it. The black man is, after all, a devil: he has earned the title. He himself, however, still believes in the justice of his cause:

> O, I were damn'd beneath all depth in hell,
> But that I did proceed upon just grounds
> To this extremity.   (v, ii, 137)

His illusion is soon to be done away. Emilia challenges Iago and, when he maintains Desdemona's guilt, roundly accuses him of telling "an odious, damned lie" (v, ii, 180). Othello, not yet believing her, attempts to justify himself to Gratiano, whose only reply is to invoke Desdemona's father, now dead:

>   did he live now,
> This sight would make him do a desperate turn,
> Yea, curse his better angel from his side,
> And fall to reprobation.   (v, ii, 206)

It is to have that effect upon Othello.

Meanwhile the master devil must be identified:

> Let heaven and men and devils, let them all,
> All, all, cry shame against me, yet I'll speak,   (v, ii, 221)

says Emilia. When Iago's deceitful appearance has been penetrated at last, there is an end of the game. The devil stands revealed. This is sufficiently emphasized. "O cursed slave!" says Othello (v, ii, 276), and later:

> I look down towards his feet; but that's a fable.
> If that thou be'st a devil, I cannot kill thee.   (v, ii, 286)

Iago, wounded, accepts the imputation with what seems like vindictive satisfaction: "I bleed, sir; but not kill'd" (v, ii, 288). Montano calls him "damned slave" (v, ii, 243), and Lodovico has a variety of epithets of the same type: "damned slave" (v, ii, 292); "damned villain" (v, ii, 316); "hellish villain" (v, ii, 368). But Othello's "demi-devil" (v, ii, 301) is the most appropriate. Prospero explains the term as he applies it to Caliban: "For he's a bastard one" (*Tempest*, v, i, 273).[19] Iago has not quite the stature of a devil, for the devils *believe* and tremble.

As for Othello, he too has become willy-nilly of the Devil's party:

> when we shall meet at compt,
> This look of thine will hurl my soul from heaven,
> And fiends will snatch at it. (v, ii, 273)

This sounds definite enough, like a statement for the audience. The description of the torments of hell which follows seems to express not only Othello's present state of mind but his future fate:

> Whip me, ye devils,
> From the possession of this heavenly sight!
> Blow me about in winds! roast me in sulphur!
> Wash me in steep-down gulfs of liquid fire! (v, ii, 277)

In this speech he takes an eternal farewell of his heavenly Desdemona. Emilia's words have come home to him:

> This deed of thine is no more worthy heaven
> Than thou wast worthy her. (v, ii, 160)

His suicide, since he is a Christian, seals his fate. Shakespeare does not leave us in much doubt about the eternal destiny of his tragic heroes. Hamlet is attended to heaven by flights of angels. (It would be quite opposed to Elizabethan dramatic conventions for Horatio to be mistaken at this point about the hero's spiritual state.) This strengthens my conviction that the proper reading of the last act of *Hamlet* would see the Prince as returning to Denmark determined upon justice, but no longer desirous of revenge. That Claudius should be killed is a necessity, he sees, not only of personal but of social justice:

> is't not to be damn'd
> To let this canker of our nature come
> In further evil? (v, ii, 68)

He is confident that Providence ("there's a special providence in the fall of a sparrow" (v, ii, 230) and "a divinity that shapes our ends" (v, ii, 10)) will provide him an occasion to become Claudius's executioner. There are no more self-reproaches and no more feverish plots; Hamlet is quietly determined yet apparently quiescent. And, sure enough, the occasion is provided for him almost at once. This interpretation, which has been deeply influenced by the excellent analysis of G. R. Elliott in his *Scourge and Minister*,[20] would permit us to give full weight to Horatio's commendation—which I cannot imagine being uttered on the Elizabethan stage over a genuine avenger. Lear, after being bound upon his fiery wheel in this life, attaining humility and patience, is also fit for heaven. Macbeth's last stand, however, is no atonement for his sins: it is not manly but "bear-like" (v, vii, 2), beast-like. According to *The Governour* this is not fortitude but desperation; it has no moral value, for those who "hedlonge will fall in to daungers, from whens there is no hope to escape" are "rather to be rekned with bestes sauage, than amonge men whiche do participate with reason".[21] So Macbeth, though we may pity him, presumably goes to hell. The same with Othello. We may feel "the pity of it" (IV, i, 206), but the Elizabethans had a harder view of eschatology than is common to-day. After all, to the Middle Ages and to the century after the Reformation it seemed likely that the majority of people would go to hell. And the Elizabethans knew their ascetic theology: Othello shows no sign of penitence, only of remorse, which is another thing. How different is the behaviour of Leontes when he awakens from his jealous dream. Leontes prepares for a lifetime of penitent devotion, whereas Othello, self-willed to the last, commits the final sin of taking his own life. Shakespeare is no narrow moralist, and Cassio finds the motive for Othello's suicide in his greatness of heart (v, ii, 361). But Shakespeare was no sentimentalist either: even the great of heart might commit irrevocable sin. There is no contradiction between the feeling of sympathy and a recognition of objective justice in the Elizabethan mind. In *Othello*, as in all Shakespeare's plays, the deceitful appearance is torn away at the end: good and evil are seen for what they are; and, though one soul be lost,[22] good will triumph and order be restored. "Cassio rules in Cyprus" (v, ii, 332) and

> To you, lord governor,
> Remains the censure of this hellish villain.   (v, ii, 367)

I would not have it thought that, in proposing three levels of interpretation for Othello and in crediting Shakespeare with a considerable consciousness of what he was about, I intend to countenance any allegorizing of the incidents. The three levels coalesce into one; the deeper meanings, social and metaphysical, are directly applicable to the human story and necessary for a full understanding of its purport. The diabolic images we have considered do not carry us away from the characters into a world of metaphysical speculation in which they have no part. Rather they serve the true purpose of poetic drama, to show the underside, as it were, of ordinary life.[23] It is precisely in such sordid and—to the outsider—trivial domestic quarrels that the Devil is busiest. Shakespeare usually works as a romantic, raising his audience to the cosmic significance of his theme by setting it in remote ages and in the courts of kings. In *Othello* he goes differently to work, showing that the old war of Good and Evil has its centre everywhere, not least in the private household. *Othello* is Shakespeare's *Family Reunion*.

NOTES

1. See my *Shakespeare and the Popular Dramatic Tradition* (Staples Press, 1944; reprinted 1948), p. 65.

2. See my *The Winter's Tale: A Study* (Staples Press, 1947), p. 102.

3. I owe to Knight's essay the outline of the metaphysical interpretation of *Othello* and some particular points noted later.

4. See *Shakespeare and the Popular Dramatic Tradition*, pp. 116 *et seq*.

5. In counting images I have taken the complete sentence as my unit; i.e. if two or more images occur in a single sentence they count as one. This avoids dispute as to where one image ends and another begins. There is nothing sacrosanct about the punctuation of the Globe Edition, which has been followed—or perhaps of any other edition— but the principal aim has been to secure a firm basis for comparison.

6. I followed the method already described in note 5. It is only fair to notice that the "antres vast", the Anthropophagi and so forth are crowded into a single sentence and count as one image.

7. The edition of Tourneur used for quotation and reference is that of Allardyce Nicoll (1929).

8. See the Arden Edition of *Othello*, ed. H. C. Hart, p. 251, note.

9. *How Many Children Had Lady Macbeth?* (1933), p. 34. The essay is reprinted in *Explorations* (1946), where the reference appears on p. 18.

10. The belief, widely held in Elizabethan times, that moral character determines outward appearance is a popular misconception of Neoplatonic doctrine. It is expressed in Spenser's *Hymne in Honour of Beautie*, ll. 127ff.:

"So euery spirit, as it is most pure,
And hath in it the more of heauenly light,
So it the fairer bodie doth procure
To habit in, and it more fairely dight
With chearefull grace and amiable sight."

11. Sugden's *Topographical Dictionary to the Works of Shakespeare and his Fellow Dramatists* (1925) has a general statement about Florentine manners and two quotations concerning subtlety. The latter have the air of expressing an accepted opinion.

12. (Glasgow, 1905) I, 401. See also Deloney's *Gentle Craft*, ch. 2; in the *Works*, ed. Mann (Oxford, 1912), pp. 77 *et seq.*

13. *A Notebook on William Shakespeare* (1948), p. 118. I have not included this image in my total, but I have included "I am not what I am", which is not strictly an image at all. These are, I think, the only doubtful cases.

14. For the association of tempest with tragedy and an interpretation of its use in *Othello* somewhat different from that which I suggest, see Wilson Knight, *op. cit.* pp. 120 *et seq.*

15. Cf. Wilson Knight, *op. cit.* p. 127.

16. *Shakespearean Tragedy* (1905), p. 229.

17. I desert the Globe Edition here and give the reading of the Folio, which receives additional confirmation from the general run of diabolic imagery.

18. Our examination of diabolic imagery helps here to settle a textual crux. "Cherubin" must refer, as Johnson says, to a personified Patience and not, as Hart would have it, to Desdemona (*v.* Arden Edition, p. 202, n.). Othello consistently regards Desdemona at this time as a devil, whatever her appearance (in l. 37 she is merely "*like* one of heaven"). While rejecting Hart's reading of the Folio's "I heere", viz. "I here", there is no need to accept Theobald's emendation, "Ay, there". "Ay, here" gives perfectly good sense and is faithful to the Folio ("I" = "Ay", as frequently). The previous "there" ("Turn thy complexion there") might mean either that Patience is to alter her usually soft features at the theme of Desdemona's infidelity or, perhaps, in looking upon Desdemona. With either meaning the change from "there" in l. 63 to "here" in l. 65 would be dramatically effective if accompanied by a gesture focusing the audience's attention upon Desdemona.

19. See n. 8 above.

20. Duke University Press: Durham, North Carolina, 1951.

21. Bk. III, ch. 9; p. 229 in the Everyman Edition.

22. If we accept the Folio reading in l. 347, "Iudean" instead of "Indian", the case for Othello's damnation is strengthened. It seems the more likely reading, since it fits so well into the general pattern of the religious imagery and its apparent significance. Othello, like Judas Iscariot, has cast away the pearl of great price; he has rejected Desdemona and in so doing has rejected heaven. Like Judas, he fell through loss of faith.

23. T. S. Eliot writes in similar terms of poetic drama in his Introduction to my *Shakespeare and the Popular Dramatic Tradition*.

SUGGESTIONS FOR A NEW APPROACH TO SHAKESPEARE'S IMAGERY

BY

R. A. FOAKES

I

When in 1933 L. C. Knights[1] pleaded that "the only profitable approach to Shakespeare is a consideration of his plays as dramatic poems", he was putting forward an extreme point of view, reacting against what he considered the established way of regarding Shakespeare's plays, as studies in character. For at that time the study of Shakespeare's imagery, concentration on the poetry rather than on the action of the plays, was a comparatively new trend in Shakespearian criticism, although notable books had been published in the late 1920's and early 1930's by G. Wilson Knight, Elizabeth Holmes, H. W. Wells and others. More recently, and especially since the publication of C. F. E. Spurgeon's *Shakespeare's Imagery* in 1935, the volume of writings on the imagery of the plays has increased enormously. Discussion of verse and imagery appears in many books dealing mainly with other aspects of Shakespeare's plays, and a fair proportion of current Shakespearian criticism is concerned with imagery and language alone. By 1948 A. H. Sackton[2] could observe that

it is now becoming a commonplace of criticism that an Elizabethan play may be approached most profitably not as a study in human character, or as an expression of an individual philosophy, but as a dramatic poem.

The plea of 1933 has now become a commonplace.

In spite of a variety of methods and aims, this view that a play should be regarded primarily as a poem, has been the governing principle of nearly all writings on Shakespeare's imagery. Writers have disagreed over many matters, and there has been much mutual criticism, but it has been criticism of practice rather than of theory. Only a few, among them Caroline Spurgeon, W. Clemen, G. Wilson Knight and Una Ellis-Fermor, have made clear their method of analysing imagery and their reasons for following it. The majority seem either to have taken over another's method, usually Miss Spurgeon's, or to have criticized and adapted another's method of approach, without considering the attitudes upon which it was based. These common attitudes towards imagery, which are connected with the principle of regarding a play as a dramatic poem, may be conveniently considered under four headings.

I. CONCENTRATION ON POETIC IMAGERY

In the first place the study of imagery has generally been confined to poetic imagery, strictly interpreted as those metaphors and similes which provide a sensuous or pictorial image. Hence the poetic image is sometimes defined as a word-picture. Several critics have widened the meaning of the term 'imagery' to include iterative words,[3] but none has considered whether imagery in drama may not be something different from poetic imagery. For stage effects, properties and other direct 'images' all help to make a play, and many passages commonly classified as poetic images are metaphorical only in relation to the action, that is, in the sense that part of the image is provided by what is going on on the stage.[4] Perhaps Miss Spurgeon's work has influenced the majority in thus limiting their discussions. She restricted her discussion for a special purpose, to find out something about Shakespeare the man. She studied only "the little word-picture used by a poet to illustrate, illuminate, and embellish his thought", because she believed these images proceeded from "the storehouse of the unconscious memory", and would reveal "the furniture of his mind... the objects and incidents he observes and remembers, and perhaps most significant of all, those which he does not observe or remember".[5] She ignored references, as proceeding not from his unconscious but from his conscious mind, and as relating to the everyday world of trivialities.

Many critics, however, have concentrated on poetic imagery without having these special reasons for doing so. They have been concerned with a modern response to or interpretation of the plays, rather than with the imaginative picture in Shakespeare's mind.[6] They therefore have less justification than she had for ignoring the many other factors which help to create this response. In itself, however, Miss Spurgeon's method is open to certain objections, even when allowance is made for her special purposes.[7] She was inconsistent in applying her statistics, refused to allow that a simple reference may have any imaginative quality, and omitted to notice that much of Shakespeare's imagery is borrowed, proverbial or commonplace. She also made an arbitrary and unwarranted distinction between what is conscious and unconscious in Shakespeare's work. The borderline between the two can never be known, and recent research into the use of logic and rhetoric in Shakespeare's age suggests that figures of speech were artifices to be used deliberately for given effects. Sister Miriam Joseph, for instance, has pointed out that Shakespeare "employed all the rhetorical figures related to the several logical topics, sometimes adding comments which constitute a virtual definition of the figure".[8]

2. FURTHER LIMITATION OF INTEREST TO THE 'SUBJECT-MATTER' OF IMAGERY

The analysis of imagery has often been limited further to one term of the poetic image, to what Miss Spurgeon called the subject-matter. By this she meant the material illustrating the idea underlying the image; for her,

> Sleep that knits up the ravell'd sleave of care   (*Macbeth*, II, ii, 37)

was a "wonderful picture of knitting up the loose fluffy all-pervading substance of frayed-out floss silk";[9] she was interested only in the subject-matter, the "ravell'd sleave". She was not interested in the underlying idea, in what may be called the object-matter of the image, which in this instance is dramatically more important, the amplification of the idea of sleep as a supreme benefit.

Thus, when in the second part of her *Shakespeare's Imagery* she discussed iterative patterns in the plays, and spoke of the 'dominant' pattern of images, she was considering the subject-matter as providing a key to Shakespeare's imaginative vision of the play concerned. Numerous critics analyse imagery as she did and speak of the 'dominant' pattern of images when they mean the picture dominant in the mind of reader or audience, not in Shakespeare's mind. Miss Spurgeon realized that 'dominant' used thus in two senses could cause confusion, and it is perhaps for this reason that she condemned G. Wilson Knight's remarks on *Timon of Athens* as 'misleading'.[10] He said that 'gold-symbolism' is dominant in this play, where gold is referred to as many as twenty times in one scene and is used as a property; she pointed out that gold appears only once as the source from which a poetic image is drawn. Although both uses of the word 'dominant' may be legitimate, the important thing to recognize is that they represent two different ways of regarding imagery. Unfortunately, in the practice of criticism, confusion of these uses is general.

Most critics refer to groups or patterns of images as Miss Spurgeon did, meaning groups of which the subject-matter originates in the same source. Images are described and linked according to subject-matter, that is in terms of sensory experiences postulated as having influenced the author's imagination. The patterns thus formed are overall patterns extending throughout a play, and relating primarily to the author's mind. These overall patterns are often of only a dozen or so images scattered through two or three thousand lines, such as the clothing images Miss Spurgeon found dominant in *Macbeth*. They are important for the kind of study she undertook, but their contribution to the effect of the play on reader or audience is less obvious, their work being perhaps to help unobserved in the creation of the play's peculiar atmosphere, or what Wilson Knight called the 'spatial quality'.[11] It seems clear that the object-matter of images, their dramatic importance, and many other factors such as iterative words should receive attention in studies not having special aims such as Miss Spurgeon's had.

Here it is significant to note that writers concerned with the nature of imagery, its functions and effects, rather than with the particular study of Shakespeare, have regarded the object-matter as of prime importance. I. A. Richards claimed that poetic images do not necessarily appeal to the visual or other senses, but demand primarily intellectual awareness of implication.[12] D. G. James considered the "main use" of imagery to be "the expression of imaginative idea or object".[13] More recently Rosemond Tuve has shown that the Elizabethans thought of imagery as logically functional in poetry, its business being to persuade the reader and compel his understanding.[14] An image was effective, she claims, if its controlled suggestions illuminated the idea concerned, and caused the reader to forget irrelevant associations. The same conception is implied in H. W. Wells's names for the terms of an image: he calls the subject-matter the 'minor term', the object-matter the 'major term'.[15] These writers would presumably regard the image quoted above, "Sleep that knits up the ravell'd sleave of care", as an image about sleep, successful in so far as it causes the reader to ignore such associations as Miss Spurgeon's 'frayed-out floss silk'. In fact Sister Miriam Joseph cites this image and the lines following as an example of the use of systrophe, a figure which consists in heaping together definitions of one thing.[16] These writers, considering images in relation to the reader, not as an intimate expression of the author's mind, see a poetic image as a relationship between two terms, made so that the illustrative term, the subject-matter, illuminates, expands, and perhaps fuses into the underlying concept contained in the object-matter. Evidently the concept 'sleep' is dramatically important in the passage quoted; but most students of Shakespeare's imagery, following Miss Spurgeon, would still describe it as a domestic or knitting image, i.e. in relation to the author's mind or habits, not in relation to the play *Macbeth*.

It remains to consider how far Miss Spurgeon was justified in considering solely iterative patterns in the subject-matter of imagery as providing a key to Shakespeare's imaginative vision. Some objections have already been raised. Thus there seems to be no reason for her assumption that references are consciously made, having no bearing on his imaginative vision. For example, she included

A mote it is to trouble the mind's eye   (*Hamlet*, I, i, 112)

among the 'dominant' image group of sickness in this play,[17] yet omitted the far more powerful 'atmospheric' comment of Francisco in the same scene:

'tis bitter cold,
And I am sick at heart.   (I, i, 8–9)

If, however, as she claimed, Shakespeare saw *Hamlet*[18]

not as the problem of an individual at all, but as something greater and even more mysterious, as a *condition* for which the individual is apparently not responsible, any more than the sick man is to blame for the infection which strikes and devours him. . . .

if this was Shakespeare's imaginative vision of the play, then he must either have made references such as "I am sick at heart" unconsciously, or have made both references and images consciously.

Thus for the kind of study Miss Spurgeon undertook the scope of imagery should be widened beyond her definition; as indeed her staunch supporter, Una Ellis-Fermor, allows,[19]

in the special case of drama, there are sometimes reasons for extending it to include the frontiers of symbolism, description, or even, it may be, the setting itself.

For studies which have different aims, to interpret a play, to offer an appreciation, or to analyse its meaning, a conception of imagery different from and much wider than Miss Spurgeon's is clearly needed. Overall patterns in the subject-matter of imagery are often linked with, or based upon, what may be called primary patterns of word, idea, poetic image, or the direct visual or auditory images provided by the stage and its effects, patterns which may be local, existing only for a scene or an act. Reference and image work together; and the subject-matter of one image may occur as the object-matter of another, or as simple reference.

What is meant by primary patterns may be illustrated from *Macbeth*. The play opens with thunder and the appearance of the witches, and a succession of immediate and effective visual or auditory images is presented directly to an audience or imaginative reader by means of the bleeding sergeant, the bloody daggers and hands, the knocking at the gate, the banquet with the ghost of Banquo, the apparitions, and the sleep-walking. These effects establish the play's atmosphere, and form a kind of framework to the poetic imagery. The primary patterns of words and poetic imagery are those most closely linked to the direct visual and auditory 'images', that is, images and iterative stress on blood, sleep and sleeplessness, darkness and evil, and noise. These do not exist in a chain of a dozen or so images scattered throughout the play, but are concentrated at emphatic points. Of the many references to sleep, sleeplessness, and kindred ideas, eighteen occur in one scene (II, ii) and thirty-one in the whole of Act II. Macbeth has murdered Duncan in his sleep, and his punishment is:

> Glamis hath murder'd sleep, and therefore Cawdor
> Shall sleep no more; Macbeth shall sleep no more. (II, ii, 42–3)

It is also Lady Macbeth's punishment, as is seen in the sleep-walking scene (v, i). There is a concentrated emphasis on sleep which is dramatically very powerful in these two parts of the play. So also the stress on blood and noise is concentrated; blood appears on Macbeth's hands after the murder of Duncan, is stressed again in the banquet scene (III, iv), where Macbeth realizes the terrible fact

> It will have blood; they say blood will have blood, (III, iv, 122)

and again in the sleep-walking scene. There are ten stage directions for repeated knocking within fifty lines of Act II, together with alarms, bells and other noises, all associated with description and poetic images.

Blood, sleep and noise are stressed not only in primary patterns, but in patterns in the subject-matter of poetic imagery. Miss Spurgeon has observed the images of blood and noise, "the reverberation of sound echoing over vast regions",[20] but pays no attention to the associated properties, stage effects, or repeated words, or to the imaginative importance of sleep and sleeplessness in the play. Macbeth's murders bring not only fear and a guilty conscience to himself and Lady Macbeth, but inflict the sleeplessness of terror on the whole of his country. Besides the primary patterns, the dramatic stress in Acts II and v, there is an overall pattern whereby sleep and sleeplessness come to embody the one, health of mind and peace to the nation, the other, Macbeth's fear-haunted conscience and the terror he brings to Scotland. Men hope for his downfall so that

> we may again
> Give to our tables meat, sleep to our nights. (III, vi, 33–4)

Sleep forms both the object-matter of images, as in "Sleep that knits up the ravell'd sleave of care", and the subject-matter, as in "Macbeth does murder sleep, the innocent sleep"; both certainly contribute to our understanding and appreciation of the play, and both may have formed part of Shakespeare's imaginative conception.

For the study of drama a new definition of imagery, one derived from drama, is needed. The general tendency to approach Shakespeare's plays as dramatic poems has led critics to stress poetic imagery, and its subject-matter especially, above all things. G. Wilson Knight, for instance, while approaching the plays in a more general way than many who concentrate on imagery, wants to "see each play as an expanded metaphor".[21] S. L. Bethell is inclined to regard *King Lear* as a "poetic treatise in mystical theology".[22] This kind of approach links up with the criterion Cleanth Brooks derived from studying metaphysical poetry, "The comparison (i.e. the poetic image) is the poem in a structural sense",[23] a criterion which others have applied to drama, so that R. B. Heilman speaks of "the large metaphor which is the play itself".[24]

While it is possible for a poem to be a metaphor, to exist only in an image or images, this cannot properly be said of a Shakespearian play. The poetic image in a play is set in a context not of words alone, but of words, dramatic situation, interplay of character, stage-effect, and is also placed in a time sequence. Yet these critics want either to find the whole meaning and importance of a play in its poetic imagery, or even to see it as an extended metaphor, a kind of poetic allegory, with the characters as symbols. Many other means besides poetic imagery contribute to the effect and meaning of a play, but these they ignore.

3. CLASSIFICATION OF IMAGES

The classification or description of images according to the source of the subject-matter is very convenient, but it is dangerous for two reasons. First, it refers only to one term; the object-matter has no place in such classification. So Miss Spurgeon classified

> To take arms against a sea of troubles
> And by opposing end them   (*Hamlet*, III, i, 59–60)

as an image of war. In its context it might equally appropriately be described as an image of suicide. Secondly, many images derive from composite sensory sources, and may be classified under several heads. It seems, however, to be customary to classify images under one head. The choice of head must depend on the critic's personal feeling or on his particular aims. Thus the above image, instead of being put under war, could have been classified as a sea image. Another example is provided by an image already considered; Miss Spurgeon classified "knits up the ravell'd sleave of care" as a domestic image, but she might equally well have placed it among her 'dominant' clothing images. Neither she, nor Cleanth Brooks,[25] who tried to fit many more images into this group, have considered it in this way.

It is true that other methods of classifying imagery have been used. For his study of the characteristic imagery of various Elizabethan poets H. W. Wells differentiated images into eight kinds, defined according to the relationship between the subject-matter and object-matter;[26] and Rosemond Tuve suggested that images should be classified as the Elizabethans classified them, according to the logical categories or places of invention derived from Aristotle.[27] These methods of classification, however, like Miss Spurgeon's, reflect the particular purposes or interests of the critic concerned, and since there are many ways of describing images, critics should be careful not to assume, as some seem to do, that their method is the complete and only way of describing an image.

Another danger in classifying imagery is the tendency to rely on statistics, to decide the most important group of images according to its numerical size. Miss Spurgeon did so, and it is significant that she was forced to reject the implications of her statistical method,[28] thereby acknowledging that the largest group is not necessarily the most important or the 'dominant' one. R. D. Altick adopted her statistical method to decide which were the most important groups of iterative words in *Richard II*, choosing those for which Bartlett's *Concordance* showed "a definite numerical preponderance".[29] He, too, rejected the implications of this method by admitting that the word 'blood' occurs less frequently in *Macbeth* than in the history plays, yet has a richer and more vital meaning in that play. Statistics form no reliable guide in such a subjective matter as the discussion of imagery, and are valuable merely for the immediate force they can give to other evidence.

4. INTERPRETATION OF IMAGES

The picture, impression or idea evoked by the subject-matter of images is likely to be quite different for different people, as has in fact been demonstrated by experiment.[30] What is prosaic and unimaginative to one person may be vitally significant to another. It is not surprising then that images have often been strangely interpreted. For instance, Cleanth Brooks, eager to enlarge Miss Spurgeon's pattern of clothing imagery in *Macbeth*, would include in it "the blanket of the dark" (I, v, 50), where 'blanket' suggests rather the obscurity of the night and the bed on which Duncan is to be murdered. Roy Walker suggests that the greeting given by the Witches to Macbeth, the repeated "All Hail", has a special religious significance, though Shakespeare is here merely quoting Holinshed, not the Bible.[31] Again it may be said that, while such interpretations are possible, there is no justification for assuming that they are the only possible interpretations.

The kind of error R. B. Heilman makes when he quite misinterprets the following passage from *King Lear* is less common:

> Love's not love
> When it is mingled with regards that stand
> Aloof from the entire point. (I, i, 241–3)

In order to fit these lines into the pattern of 'sight' images which he wishes to find everywhere, Heilman takes them as meaning "that is, his (Burgundy's) seeing is directed by the wrong values",[32] 'regards' being for him something to do with Burgundy's eyes. A greater emphasis on the meaning of the image in its context, on the primary purpose of the subject-matter as illustrating an idea, thing or being expressed in the object-matter, might prevent unlikely or impossible interpretations from being made.

In this connexion, writers interested in poetic plays as drama rather than as poems have emphasized the need for ready intelligibility in an author's language. H. Granville-Barker has said[33]

The actor's speeches must be so written that not only the sound but the sense—even if a word or two should go wrong on the way—will travel easily and effectively.

G. H. W. Rylands observed how Shakespeare reduced blank verse to the level of prose in his mature plays;[34] and T. S. Eliot has said that dramatic verse differs from the verse of poetry, for the dramatist speaks through the medium of actors, and his language must be the language of a world of people, connected, if it is to be effective, with the rhythms of normal speech.[35] For any study of the plays where there are not special reasons such as those Miss Spurgeon put forward for excluding much material, the simpler, dramatic sense of images and language emphasized by these critics should surely be considered together with the poetic associations which are commonly analysed.

II

This discussion has shown that although 'poetic imagery' is usually defined as metaphor and simile, nevertheless a variety of meanings may be attached to the term; many, like Miss Spurgeon, use the term in a dual sense, speaking generally of an image as metaphor, but restricting their discussion for the most part to one term of the metaphor, the subject-matter. Others, such as R. D. Altick and Moody Prior, would include iterative words; a few such as G. Wilson Knight refer also to the symbolic use of words or properties. The tendencies to treat drama as poetry, to stress the subject-matter of imagery alone, and to classify imagery by subject-matter as though this were the only way of doing so, have been noted. The variety of aims in the study of imagery has also been indicated. Some critics have tried to discover facts about the author, or have used Miss Spurgeon's methods to compile biographies of Shakespeare based partly on inferences drawn from the subject-matter of his imagery.[36] Some, like Miss Spurgeon, have set out to reconstruct Shakespeare's imaginative vision, or more often, to offer their own interpretation and appreciation of a play based on an analysis of its image structure.[37] Some have discovered a play's meaning in patterns of metaphor, and have usually contrived to resolve a complex play into an abstraction or conflict between abstractions; such is R. B. Heilman's verdict on *King Lear*:[38]

The play's ultimate refinement of statement...is that man is wholly evil when reason and animality work together....

A few studies of imagery have also been made for limited and special purposes, and no criticism is intended of these. Such are M. M. Morozov's examination of the relation of imagery to character in Shakespeare's tragedies, and E. A. Armstrong's study of image-clusters, groups of related ideas or images recurring in several or all of Shakespeare's plays.[39]

The vagueness of the term imagery, and the variety of purposes which studies of imagery are expected to serve, add to the reasons already offered for formulating an adequate conception of dramatic as distinct from poetic imagery. The need for such a conception is further illustrated by considering the differing functions poetic imagery is said to have in poetry and in drama. C. Day Lewis found it possible to describe the function of imagery in poetry in one sentence, as that of creating a poetic world which

has meaning for us in so far as any given poem by virtue of its image-pattern, has correspondences with the pattern of the real world.[40]

i.e. draws things into affinity in a patterned whole, thereby suggesting pattern and order in the external world. On the other hand, Una Ellis-Fermor has said that there is no limit to the number of functions of poetic imagery in drama:[41]

...it would be foolish to suppose that those of us who have discovered some five or six have come to the end of the story.

Nearly all the functions she enumerates, revealing relations between the world of the play and the outside world, knitting together the plot by iteration, revealing and keeping in mind the underlying mood, etc.[42] are functions not peculiar to imagery, but shared by many other factors, stage effect, use of property, iterative language and so on. One other function she mentions is that of doing the work of argument or reflection, as in the political discussions in *Troilus and Cressida* or the soliloquies of Hamlet, and this is not a dramatic function of imagery at all; it is a function performed by imagery in all reflective poetry. What she has really observed here is that several if not all of the kinds of imagery differentiated by H. W. Wells occur in Shakespeare's plays, and this again is another difference between drama and poetry. Whereas most poems, particularly short poems, are written in a homogeneous style, so that for instance Donne or Spenser use chiefly one kind of image, Shakespeare and most good dramatists of his time are masters of all.

For imagery is used in a play not only with the general functions enumerated by Miss Ellis-Fermor, but has many particular functions. The playwright may differentiate his characters by means of poetic imagery, in fact must do so to some extent, since they exist only through their language. Imagery may be used in relation to plot, and perhaps because of this overall patterns occur throughout the play as a whole; or it may be used in relation to situation, which would account for the occurrence of smaller or primary patterns within a single scene or group of scenes. Imagery can be used also for special functions, to describe an event or scene which has an importance in the play, as in Enobarbus's famous description of Cleopatra (*Antony and Cleopatra*, II, ii, 195–245), to relieve tension, to close a scene, to provide information, to create a setting, or to show powerful emotion on the part of a character, when the lines may become almost unintelligible. Evidently different kinds of images will be used for these different purposes; and not only to distinguish character, but to mark those occasions when a character steps out of role to some extent, to act as chorus like Enobarbus, or to provide necessary relief from tension, as does Horatio in the opening scene of *Hamlet*—with for him an unusually vivid pictorial image:

> But look, the morn, in russet mantle clad
> Walks o'er the dew of yon high eastward hill.   (I, i, 166–7)

The general functions of poetic imagery in drama are shared by many other factors, the most notable perhaps being direct visual or auditory imagery provided by property or stage effect, for instance the repeated display and talk of gold in *Timon of Athens*, or the repeated knocking in *Macbeth*. Poetic imagery should be considered together with other factors in the play which share its functions; and together these constitute dramatic imagery. Nor are these other factors limited to direct visual and auditory imagery, and iterative words, or words associated with imagery. Historical and geographical placing, description, and the use of proper names and generalized characters have a bearing on dramatic imagery. Such things have been ignored except in the case of *Othello*, where the many references to remote places and to Othello's ancient lineage have such an obvious function in the play. In any drama, references to the external world have some imaginative power in establishing the events of a personal tragedy or story in events or places in the world outside, thus building up a background; in this, of course, reference and poetic image interact as in all things. Setting the action of a play against the background of an apparently real world or nation and linking it with events in that world, paradoxically universalizes the action through this localization of a special kind and gives it greater magnitude, by providing contrast between the deeds of which one man is capable, e.g. Macbeth, and the humdrum nature of life in general.

The tragic hero can be isolated only in the context of a world or nation, not in a geographical vacuum. So in *Macbeth* references to Macdonwald, Sweno King of Norway, to Scottish place-names, Forres and Dunsinane and Birnam, 'place' the play in a definite locality. At least one generalized character is used to enlarge the stature and crimes of Macbeth, giving the play also a setting in time, in the scene between Ross and an old man, any old man, who says

> Three score and ten I can remember well:
> Within the volume of which time I have seen
> Hours dreadful and things strange; but this sore night
> Hath trifled former knowings. (II, iv, 1–4)

Complementary to this is what may be a special function of poetic imagery in a play, at least in tragedy; that is to display a particular situation as symbol or type of a universal condition. Una Ellis-Fermor has said that imagery "reveals the relations between the world of the play and a wider surrounding world or universe", and "often reveals the presence of a surrounding or accompanying universe of thought or experience",[43] and other critics have observed this too. These general functions are shared by other effects, but the particular function of universalizing the immediate situation, not the play as a whole, has been overlooked. The images which perform this function are often common or proverbial generalizations, true in relation to their immediate context, but possibly contradicted by other generalizations in the same play, as in *King Lear*:

> The gods are just, and of our pleasant vices
> Make instruments to plague us. (v, iii, 170–1)

> As flies to wanton boys, are we to the gods,
> They kill us for their sport. (IV, i, 38–9)

The second of these is a comment by Gloucester on his own miserable condition after the blinding; the first a comment by Edgar upon the justice of Gloucester's losing his sight,

> The dark and vicious place where thee he got
> Cost him his eyes, (v, iii, 172–3)

as well as upon the fall of Edmund. Both are appropriate to the situation concerned, but it would be interesting to know which of these two passages has validity for those critics who find the play's meaning in its imagery.

A discussion of dramatic imagery then would include reference to the subject-matter and object-matter of poetic imagery, to visual and auditory effects, iterative words, historical and geographical placing, and to both the general and particular uses of these things. Dramatic imagery would be examined primarily in relation to context, to dramatic context, and to the time-sequence of a play; the general or overall patterns of word and image would be examined in relation to other effects, as well as for their own value. Considered in this way, dramatic imagery would offer a more adequate field of study than the analysis merely of poetic imagery.

As a final word it should be said that there is no suggestion intended here that Shakespeare used conscious artifice in building his play upon word- or image-patterns; rather that these patterns naturally occur in all good poetry or drama—whether consciously or unconsciously we can never know—and 'pattern' or 'chain' are the most convenient words to apply to them.[44]

NOTES

1. L. C. Knights, 'How Many Children had Lady Macbeth?' (1933) in *Explorations* (1946), pp. 1–39; the quotation is from p. 6.

2. A. H. Sackton, *Rhetoric as a Dramatic Language in Ben Jonson* (1948), p. 4.

3. See, for example, R. D. Altick, 'Symphonic Imagery in *Richard II*' in *PMLA*, LXII (1947), 338–65, and J. C. Maxwell, 'Animal Imagery in *Coriolanus*' in *Modern Language Review*, XLII (1947), 417–21. These were perhaps influenced by F. C. Kolbe's *Shakespeare's Way* (1930) in which iterative words are studied in the belief that the unity of Shakespeare's plays is due in large part to "deliberate repetition throughout a play of at least one set of words or ideas in harmony with the plot" (p. 2).

4. As, for example, Cleopatra's lines,

> Peace, peace !
> Dost thou not see my baby at my breast
> That sucks the nurse asleep.   (*Antony and Cleopatra*, v, ii, 311–13)

These are figurative only in relation to her action in putting the asp to her breast; in fact, in the absence of stage directions, her action has been inferred in order to make the lines explicable. Another example is Hamlet's remark as he leaves Claudius to go to his mother.

> This physic but prolongs thy sickly days   (*Hamlet*, III, iii, 96)

where "this physic" refers to Claudius's action of praying.

5. C. F. E. Spurgeon, *Shakespeare's Imagery, and what it tells us* (1935), pp. 9, 4, 43 ff. The phrase "the storehouse of the unconscious memory" is taken from her letter headed 'Shakespeare's Imagery' in *Times Literary Supplement*, 14 December 1935, where she makes clear her distinction between images (referring to the unconscious mind) and references (conscious and deliberate).

6. U. M. Ellis-Fermor noted this distinction, when criticizing H. W. Wells, J. M. Murry, F. Kolbe, and several other Shakespearian critics for being 'subjective', and praising W. Clemen to some extent, and C. F. E. Spurgeon wholly, for being scientifically objective; cf. *Some Recent Research in Shakespeare's Imagery* (1937).

7. Cf. the criticism of her work by L. H. Hornstein, 'The Analysis of Imagery' in *PMLA*, LVII (1942), 638–53; and by W. T. Hastings, 'Shakespeare's Imagery' in *Shakespeare Association Bulletin*, XI (1936), 131–41.

8. Sister Miriam Joseph, *Shakespeare's Use of the Arts of Language* (1947), p. 172.

9. C. F. E. Spurgeon, *op. cit.* p. 125.

10. *Ibid.* pp. 344–5.

11. G. Wilson Knight, *The Wheel of Fire* (1930), pp. 3 ff.

12. I. A. Richards, *The Philosophy of Rhetoric* (1936), pp. 127 ff.

13. D. G. James, *Scepticism and Poetry* (1937), p. 73.

14. Rosemond Tuve, 'Imagery and Logic: Ramus and Metaphysical Poetics' in *Journal of the History of Ideas*, III (1942), 365–400. This article is a summary of part of her *Elizabethan and Metaphysical Imagery* (Chicago, 1947). See especially pp. 370 ff. in the former and pp. 120 ff. in the latter.

15. H. W. Wells, *Poetic Imagery* (1924). Cf. also I. A. Richards's names for the terms of an image: 'tenor' = object-matter; and 'vehicle' = subject-matter. Other writers who take a similar view of imagery are S. J. Brown, *The World of Imagery* (1927), and Maud Bodkin, *Archetypal Patterns in Poetry* (1934).

16. Sister Miriam Joseph, *op. cit.* p. 109.

17. C. F. E. Spurgeon, *op. cit.* pp. 317, 369.

18. *Ibid.* p. 319.

19. Una Ellis-Fermor, *The Frontiers of Drama* (1945), p. 78.

20. C. F. E. Spurgeon, *op. cit.* p. 327.

21. G. Wilson Knight, *The Wheel of Fire*, p. 16.

22. S. L. Bethell, *Shakespeare and the Popular Dramatic Tradition* (1944), p. 80.

23. Cleanth Brooks, *Modern Poetry and the Tradition* (Chapel Hill, 1939), p. 15.

24. R. B. Heilman, *This Great Stage: Image and Structure in King Lear* (Louisiana, 1948), p. 12.

25. See his essay on *Macbeth*, 'The Naked Babe and the Cloak of Manliness' in *The Well Wrought Urn* (1947), pp. 21–46. To a Jacobean audience this image may have suggested an emblematic figure, 'Care', though there seems to be no evidence of this.

26. H. W. Wells, *Poetic Imagery*; these eight kinds are listed on p. 225.

27. Rosemond Tuve, *Elizabethan and Metaphysical Imagery*, pp. 261 ff.

28. Cf. her analysis of the images in *Hamlet*, *Shakespeare's Imagery*, pp. 367–71; she finds the largest groups relate to Nature (32), Animals (27), Sport and Games (22), Body, Sense and Sleep (21), yet she claims that the dominant image in the play is that of sickness (p. 316).

29. R. D. Altick, 'Symphonic Imagery in *Richard II*', *PMLA*, LXII (1947), 341 n.

30. See C. W. Valentine, 'The Function of Images in the Appreciation of Poetry', *British Journal of Psychology*, XIV (1923), 164–91; and D. A. Stauffer, *The Nature of Poetry* (1946), pp. 138 ff.

31. Roy Walker, *The Time is Free* (1949), pp. 15 and note, 54–5; cf. Josephine and Allardyce Nicoll (ed.), *Holinshed's Chronicle as used in Shakespeare's Plays* (1927), p. 210.

32. R. B. Heilman, *This Great Stage*, p. 62.

33. H. Granville-Barker, *On Dramatic Method* (1931), p. 32.

34. G. H. W. Rylands, *Words and Poetry* (1928).

35. T. S. Eliot, *The Music of Poetry* (Glasgow, 1942). See especially p. 20.

36. E.g. K. Muir and S. O'Loughlin, *The Voyage to Illyria* (1937); Frank O'Connor, *The Road to Stratford* (1948). Cf. also William Bliss, *The Real Shakespeare* (1947).

37. E.g. Moody E. Prior, *The Language of Tragedy* (1947); Donald A. Stauffer, *Shakespeare's World of Images; The Development of his Moral Ideas* (1949); Roy Walker, *The Time is Free* (1949).

38. R. B. Heilman, *op. cit.* p. 105. L. C. Knights, G. Wilson Knight, S. L. Bethell and the 'New Critics' of America all tend to approach Shakespeare's plays in this way.

39. M. M. Morozov, 'The Individualization of Shakespeare's Characters through Imagery' in *Shakespeare Survey*, 2 (1949), pp. 83–106; E. A. Armstrong, *Shakespeare's Imagination* (1946).

40. C. Day Lewis, *The Poetic Image* (1947), p. 28.

41. U. M. Ellis-Fermor, 'The Poet's Imagery', in *The Listener*, 28 July 1949, p. 158.

42. U. M. Ellis-Fermor, *The Frontiers of Drama* (1945), see pp. 77–95.

43. *Ibid.* pp. 80 and 83.

44. Since this article was written, W. Clemen's *The Development of Shakespeare's Imagery* (1951) has appeared, a much revised version of his earlier *Shakespeares Bilder* (Bonn, 1936). It is interesting that he stresses the interdependence of poetic imagery and other factors in a drama, and recognizes that "images in a play require another mode of investigation than, say, images in a lyric poem" (p. 5).

SHAKESPEARE'S INFLUENCE ON PUSHKIN'S DRAMATIC WORK

BY

TATIANA A. WOLFF

I admit quite frankly that I would be upset by the failure of my tragedy, for I firmly believe that the popular tenets of Shakespearian drama are better suited to the Russian theatre than the courtly habits of the tragedy of Racine, and any such failure might slow down the reformation of our stage. (Draft preface to *Boris Godunov*, 1829–30?[1])

Pushkin was born in 1799. He wrote at a time when Russian secular literature emerged from a period of apprenticeship to one of mastery, a time which saw the composition of most of Russia's finest poetry, and finally one in which English literary influence predominated. He had himself an enormous field of creative activity which he was constantly enlarging, for his mind was always alive and receptive to new ideas. He found inspiration in English literature for his poetry, his drama and his prose.

In accordance with the custom of his class Pushkin was versed in French from childhood. As a boy he read widely among the French classics that filled his father's library. His first literary homage was given to Voltaire; his juvenilia were Epicurean and lightly sceptical, in imitation of Parny and Grécour. When he read the works of authors of other countries he read them in French translations, which were perceptibly moulded to suit French taste. In an early poem, 'The Little Town', he listed his favourite authors and they were all classicists, French and Russian. But the poets of death and melancholy, of nature and night, were soon to penetrate into the classical stronghold of his tastes. Fired by his school-teacher's enthusiasm he wrote imitations of 'Ossian'.

In 1820, because he had expressed politically 'dangerous' opinions in his poetry, Pushkin was exiled to the south of Russia. It was there that he fell under the spell of Byron; and the Caucasian mountains afforded an effective background for the Byronic heroes, who for several years stalked through his poems. But the influence Byron exercised on him at that time was conditioned by Pushkin's previous poetic development. In style he always remained a classicist: he wrote with clarity and restraint, aimed at lightness, grace and conciseness, avoided the careless and the hazy. In outlook he moved steadily towards realism.

Pushkin's interest in Russian history moved the Byronic Mazeppa from the centre of *Poltava*. He remained the hero of the romantic narrative, but in the epic of national destiny his place was taken by Peter the Great. Pushkin gives a great deal of attention to Mazeppa, but he writes of him objectively, he is not himself emotionally involved in his glory or in his downfall. In Byron's poem, Mazeppa is the central character, and Byron, in sympathy with him, follows his fortunes after his defeat at the battle of Poltava. But, as the difference in titles suggests, it is the battle and its victor, Peter, which were the centre of Pushkin's interest.

In *Evgeny Onegin* the Romantic hero of the early chapters was in the course of the book overshadowed by the heroine, Tatiana, both of them being seen in the normal perspectives of Russian life, as it was lived in the country and in the capitals.

Byron's influence waned. Small details like broken pieces of a mosaic remained scattered in Pushkin's poetry: the hero's Byronic cloak, here and there a word full of the romantic overtones of the East to give 'local colour'. Relics without integration, seeds that have not taken root, they act as reminders of the hold Byron once had on the author.

The use of dramatic scenes to mark the significant moments of the action in the *Gypsies*, the breaking of the romantic framework of *Poltava* in order to include national epic material, an interest in the part played by the crowd in history, particularly when in conflict with its rulers, were all pointers in the direction of *Boris Godunov*. Pushkin turned to drama to express his conception of tragedy; to the intensity and directness which it alone could provide in dealing with the conflict of man with man, of the individual with the crowd, and of that within a man's own soul. And in turning to drama he turned to Shakespeare.[2]

Pushkin, already at work on *Boris Godunov*, outlined his dramatic principles in a letter to Raevsky.[3] He considered it ludicrous to seek verisimilitude by observing the Unities of Time and Place, when the very medium of dramatic art required the improbable situation of two thousand spectators in one half of a hall watching an action taking place on a three-walled stage in the other half. It was equally childish to avoid 'asides' as being unnatural, only to replace them, as Alfieri had done, by longer soliloquies. Shakespeare was far above such nonsense.

…je n'ai pas lu Calderon ni Vega mais quel homme que ce Sch[akespeare]! je n'en reviens pas. Comme Byron le tragique est mesquin devant lui!

Pushkin now saw clearly the limitations of Byron's dramatic powers. Byron, he wrote, created only one character, his own; and in his plays he had handed out the different traits of that character to his dramatis personae, giving to one his pride, to another his hatred, to a third his melancholy. In this way from one powerful and energetic personality he created several insignificant ones. He did not make allowance for the fact that every person loves and hates, sorrows and rejoices in an individual fashion, and can experience many of these emotions concurrently. Similarly types do not always act in character, a conspirator does not ask for a drink in a conspiratorial whisper. Shakespeare's characters always speak naturally, for Shakespeare knew that, when it was necessary, he could make them reveal their true natures by their words.

"Read Shakespeare, that is my refrain" is the keynote of this letter, which ends with the words: "Je sens que mon âme s'est tout-à-fait développé, je puis créer."

Boris Godunov was completed in 1825.[4] Pushkin was delighted with it: Shakespearian in content, style and structure, it also satisfied the antiquarian tastes of the age of Scott, for it was permeated with the spirit of the Russian past.

Boris Godunov deals with the problem of usurpation and civil war, a problem as relevant to Pushkin's contemporaries as to Shakespeare's. Pushkin lived in a Europe of revolution and dynastic change. At the very time of writing, the radical elements of the Russian aristocracy were preparing their final plans for the December rising, the aim of which was to force the new Tsar to grant a constitution. The historical period chosen by Pushkin for his tragedy also resembles that of Shakespeare's history plays. Boris's accession to the throne, following the murder of the rightful heir in the preceding reign, was the prelude to a series of usurpations, known as the 'Time of Troubles', which bridged the gap between the dynasties of Rurik and Romanov; events which can be compared to the murders, usurpations and wars of the Houses of York and Lancaster.

Pushkin accepted the view put forward by Karamzin in his *History of the Russian State* that Boris was the murderer of the Tsarevich Dmitri, but Pushkin does not allow his own personality to intrude, disguised as noble or serf, to point a moral. Like the monastic chronicler Pimen he presents his characters neither in pity nor in anger, but divides his sympathy between the murderer Boris and the Pretender 'Dmitri'. In that he resembles the Shakespeare of *Richard II* and *Henry IV* rather than of *Richard III*.

The tragedy does not trace Boris's rise to power, but shows him in the first scene on the brink of realizing his high ambitions. Having cleared the way to the throne Boris proclaims that he has decided to renounce the world, and he then retires to a monastery. The people of Moscow, led by the Patriarch and clergy, flock to him to beg him to accept the crown. Boris feigns hesitation and timidity, saying that he is afraid to take upon himself the heavy burden of sovereignty. Meanwhile the crowd stands outside ready to weep or shout to order. At a sign from the boyars they fall in waves onto their knees, trusting that they are made to do so for good reason. Finally Boris yields to the prayers of the Church and the cries of the people, and in a speech filled with humility prays that he may prove worthy of the task he accepts.

This episode provides a good example of Pushkin's use of Shakespearian material. The situation on the surface is almost exactly parallel to Richard III's devotions, which start at precisely the same moment as the Lord Mayor and Buckingham begin to exhort the people of London to cry "Long live King Richard!". There is the same false humility, the same sudden decision to forsake the world, followed by a gradual compliance with the wish of the populace. Fundamentally, however, the attitude of the two kings to religious observances is completely different. They both use them as a mask for their true intentions, but whereas Richard throws the prayer-book over his shoulder when it has served its purpose, Boris, having a religious and even superstitious nature, continues to seek in the Church comfort for his troubled spirit.

Once Boris is enthroned the play moves quickly forward in time, to the moment when external circumstances will reawaken his guilty conscience; for Boris, like Richard, has ascended the throne over the body of a murdered child. That fact seals his fate: that poison in his soul brings him to his downfall. Six years have passed. A Pretender appears and incarnates the secret fears that have long been tormenting Boris. His spirit is exhausted, and he cannot summon the energy and courage needed to meet the situation.

Boris's soliloquy "I have attained the highest power" is that of a man on the razor's edge. Power has brought little satisfaction. He does not yet know of the seed which the chronicler Pimen has sown in Grigory's mind, but he feels his life-blood draining away. He finds himself accused of every misfortune, named the murderer of every dying man; and is unable to combat with his accusers. Preyed upon by hallucinations, he seeks the advice of magicians and astrologers. He does not however, like Macbeth, advance on the path of guilt until he is hardened by blood; on the contrary, Pushkin shows him weakened and despairing, supporting with difficulty the burden of kingship. This was an aspect of kingship Shakespeare often stressed—the human frailty beneath the robes of state, with its consciousness of responsibility, its ever-present fear of treachery. Boris had feigned at first this desire to retreat from the world and from supreme rule, but it is with deep conviction that he now exclaims

How heavy art thou, crown of Monomakh!

This speeech of Boris and his next appearance are intended to awaken sympathy for him in preparation for the news he is soon to hear of the rise of the Pretender: a sympathy, and a pity, similar to what we feel while listening to the soaring flights of Macbeth's terrified imagination. Only it is increased by the fact that Boris is opposed not, like Macbeth, by the rightful heir to the throne, but by an upstart monk led by dreams along the cruel road of usurpation.

Boris is now seen talking with his daughter, whose betrothed has recently died: he is gentle and compassionate. He then turns to his son Feodor, who prattles in the artless way so typical of Shakespearian children whose elders, wittingly or unwittingly, are leading them to death. The ensuing scene is intensely dramatic and moves very quickly. Boris, on hearing that Shuisky has been in communication with Cracow, summons him to his presence. The wily Shuisky, prepared for the onslaught, is already in attendance; and in the thrust and counterthrust that follow both men try to discover how much the other knows, until Shuisky deals his final blow and discloses that the Pretender claims to be Dmitri, son of Ivan the Terrible. When he pronounces the name 'Dmitri', Shuisky realizes that the Tsar does not know the news he brings, for Boris is horror-struck by that name. Boris orders the Tsarevich to leave the room, and then shouting at Shuisky asks if he has ever heard of the dead rising from their graves to mock at anointed kings.

To Boris at that moment the fact that he has been anointed seems of greater significance than that he is a usurper; for he places the same trust as Richard II in the balm that has been poured on his head. He makes Shuisky repeat for his satisfaction that he did indeed see Dmitri in his coffin. Shuisky affirms this, and with every word of his description of the murdered child he stabs the raw conscience of Boris. When Shuisky is gone Boris tries to regain his self-control, to persuade himself that he is afraid lest a shadow, an empty name, should take the crown off his head and rob his children of their inheritance. Such thoughts led Macbeth to further crime, they lead Boris to despair.

Boris continues to seek confirmation of the death of Dmitri although every new testimony is torture to his spirit. One day on coming out of the palace Boris is accosted by a Yurodivy, a Fool of Christ, who asks the Tsar to kill the boys that are tormenting him as he killed the Tsarevich. Boris, stopping the boyars from chasing the prattling Fool away, asks Nikolka to pray for him, but the Fool replies that he cannot pray for King-Herod. In Russia Fools of Christ were considered saintly and none were allowed to harm them. The licence that Boris allows Nikolka in this scene is typical of the respect they were afforded; but Pushkin's use of a Fool of Christ in a play was unprecedented, and was obviously inspired by Shakespeare's use of court fools, notably in *King Lear*. The Yurodivy expresses the feelings of the people, among whom he alone is permitted to speak thus to the Tsar.

In the next scene Boris is on his death-bed; and asking to be left alone with his son, counsels him in words very similar to those spoken by the dying Henry IV to Prince Hal. As a usurper he speaks to an heir who will succeed him in his own right, and so, forgetting the sins of his father who will answer for all before God, should rest happy in that he will never know the anguish of an unclean conscience. He advises Feodor to choose prudent councillors, liked by the people and respected by the nobles, and continues

> Speak not too much, for the Tsar's voice
> Should never idly on the air be lost;
> Rather, like holy chimes, it only should announce
> The general sorrows and the greatest feasts.

Henry had stressed the importance of the king being rarely seen, so that his appearance should be "wondered at" as a "robe pontifical" marking some great solemnity. By making Boris advise silence instead of rare appearance, Pushkin underlines another similarity in the characters of Boris and Henry IV, as he is portrayed by Shakespeare. Having given his last counsel Boris, as was customary for Russian monarchs, takes the monastic vows preparatory to death.

It is in the comic scenes of *Boris Godunov* that the other Shakespearian parallels are to be found. They do not form a sub-plot but are directly connected with the main action. Here in a frontier inn are found Russian counterparts to Falstaff's companions, mendicants, drinking down all they collect in alms for their monastery, whose speech varies from proverbial jingles to pious Old Slavonic as the occasion demands. The situation they are involved in is delightful, and, although it has no direct parallel in Shakespeare, is written in the Shakespearian comic manner. In this scene Pushkin, having caught the spirit of Shakespeare's humour, has adapted it to a Russian setting with complete success.

Grigory, fired by the idea that he might be the son of Ivan the Terrible, flees from his monastery, and comes to the inn with two mendicants he has met on the way. But he does not make a very good drinking companion, and is more concerned with finding out from the hostess the nearest road to the Lithuanian frontier. At that moment some guards enter, who have on them a written order for Grigory's arrest. They suspect him to be one of the mendicants, but they are not sure, for they cannot read the order. Grigory volunteers to read it for them, and as he reads he glances at the fatter monk and closely describes him. When the guards go to seize him, the old monk grabs the paper from Grigory, and in his indignation remembers how to read. As he slowly picks his way through the description of Grigory all eyes turn towards him, only in time to see him snatch out his knife and leap out of the inn window.

The other comic relief is provided by the foreign mercenaries recruited by the Pretender in Poland. They include a Frenchman and a German, who mix their native tongues with their inadequate Russian, and engage in vituperation very similar to that of their prototypes, the Captains Fluellen, Gower, Macmorris and Jamy.

Finally, an important part is played in the tragedy by the crowd, the common people: at times easily swayed from anger to pity, as is the Roman mob in *Julius Caesar*, or silent and obstinate, as in *Richard III*; ignorant, as in *Coriolanus*, or humorous, as its representatives in *Henry IV* and *Henry V*. It symbolizes the shifting foundations on which autocracy rests. In the first draft, the play ended with the crowd, typically compliant, shouting "Long live Tsar Dmitri!" But Pushkin changed this ending and gave it a deeper significance. In the play as it now stands, at the proclamation "Long live Tsar Dmitri!", "The People are silent". This silence is an ominous portent of the fate which awaits the Pretender, a fate similar to that which has struck down the House of Godunov. It is the result of the crowd's horror at the fresh crimes perpetrated in the name of lawful succession.

Unlike most of Shakespeare's plays, *Boris Godunov* closes on a hopeless note. There is no harmony or order at the end; the tragedy has not been an expiation which leads to peace. Instead of the trumpets of the victors, the last sounds are the cries of Boris's family as the Tsarevich is slain: a new usurper has replaced the old, and once more he has reached his throne over the body of a murdered child. The play does not end with the conqueror ordering the solemn burial rites of the victims and promising reparation and reward, but with a silent crowd standing before the palace where once more blood has been spilt.

In style and structure, *Boris Godunov* also owes much to Shakespeare: in the use of blank verse, in the mingling of verse and prose, with prose used chiefly in the comic scenes and blank verse in the tragic, often with rhymed endings for closing emphasis; in the long period of time the play covers; and in the constant change of scene from court to monastery, from patriarch's palace to frontier tavern, and from public square to battlefield, with corresponding transitions of mood from tragedy to comedy, and from calmness and serenity to storm and anguish.

After the completion of *Boris Godunov* Pushkin wrote a number of articles in which he set out some of the principles which had guided his work. He returned to the attack which he had launched in the early 1820's on the outworn forms of French classicism and the deadening influence of Boileau's criticism. Urging a change of allegiance, he had then welcomed English influence as being more beneficial to Russian letters than that of the "timid and mincing" poetry of France.[5] He again contrasted Shakespeare's dramatic talent with Byron's, repeating what he had long ago said of the latter's shortcomings; and in this depreciation of Byron as a playwright identified himself with Hazlitt and other English critics. Being convinced that people were tired of the lifeless forms of neo-classical literature, and were eager for innovation, especially in the drama, he had taken the first step and written his play on the lines of "our father Shakespeare". He had dispensed with the Unities of Time and Place, and almost with that of Action; and had replaced the Alexandrine by blank verse in pentameters, and even occasionally by prose. But he realized that his innovations might not meet with success, for the public brought up on French drama would view all departures from the canons of Boileau with suspicion.

The reading of Shakespeare, Karamzin and medieval Russian chronicles gave him the idea of presenting in dramatic form one of the most stirring epochs of Russian history. Believing that tragedy is increased by a sense of contrast, as for example in the 'cellarage' scene in *Hamlet*, he had placed comic scenes immediately after tragic. Believing that every literature came to a point when the language it was written in became stereotyped and tedious, and in great need of a new vitality, he had turned to the hitherto despised language of the common people. Dramatic language had to be appropriate to both speaker and subject; the French, by never allowing their tragedies to leave the salons, had spoiled their effects by timidity and bombast. Pushkin saw that the problem before Russian dramatists lay in bringing tragedy back from the aristocratic milieu in which it moved to the public squares where it had once flourished. But he asked

...where, from whom can one learn the dialect which is understood by the people, what are the passions of these people, of what nature are the sinews of their hearts, where will it find an echo, in short, where are the spectators, where is the public?[6]

In 1826, after the failure of the Decembrist rising and when its leaders were awaiting the Tsar's sentence, Pushkin, deeply concerned for the safety of his friends, wrote to Baron Delvig urging that they should both, in their attitude to the case, exercise restraint from bias, a failing of French dramatists, and ended, "let us rather view this tragedy as Shakespeare would have done."[7] Here was contained the germ of his definition, in the article quoted above, of the qualities necessary to a dramatist: "a philosophy, impartiality, the political acumen of an historian, insight, a lively imagination, no prejudices or preconceived ideas, FREEDOM."[8] The dramatist's aim in tragedy was to reveal the destiny of humanity, and it was in the achievement of this aim that Shakespeare was great. The need for impartiality Pushkin stressed again:

The dramatic poet, impartial as Fate...must not lean surreptitiously to one side, thus sacrificing the other. Neither he himself, nor his political opinions, nor his secret or open prejudices, must find expression in his tragedy—but only the people of the past, [their] minds, their prejudices. It is not his business to excuse, condemn, or prompt; it is his business to resurrect the past in all its truth...these [are the] primary and fundamental conditions.[9]

The final negotiations for the publication of *Boris Godunov* were in progress between Pushkin and his censor, Nicholas I, through an intermediary, Count Benckendorf. The Tsar, when first approached by Pushkin in 1827, though pleased with the play, had written on the manuscript

I consider that Mr Pushkin's aim would have been achieved if he had, with the *necessary expurgations*, changed his play into a historical narrative or novel in the manner of Walter Scott.[10]

In 1829 Pushkin once again approached the Tsar on the question of publication, this time through Zhukovsky. Before handing the play to the censor Zhukovsky had changed the wording in a few places, which he thought might meet with disapproval. This did not help: the censor remained adamant. Benckendorf reminded Pushkin that the Tsar had expressly stated that he would prefer the work changed into a historical novel in the manner of Scott, naturally with some alterations. He added, however, that if Pushkin effected the few changes he had indicated, he would once again approach the Tsar.

Pushkin was loathe to abandon his favourite composition which he had thought out so carefully, and worked on for so long. Replying to this request to effect a few changes in the dialogue where the Tsar had found it too applicable to contemporary events, he said that he could not be held responsible for the words spoken by historical personages, for it was his duty as a dramatist to make them speak in character. He agreed, however, to exclude the crowd scene before the monastery, and to make a few other minor alterations in the language, especially in that used by the mendicant monks and foreign mercenaries. On 28 April 1830 permission was granted for publication.

On the eve of publication, Pushkin wrote that his play was written in a manner quite different from that which had won him such unmerited popularity in the past, but his conviction that it was one best suited to the Russian stage prompted him to present *Boris Godunov* to the public, although he feared it would meet with little success.

Pushkin wrote *Boris Godunov* for the stage—it was not intended as closet drama. He had hoped that it would serve as a model for a new school of Russian drama; but, from the first, insurmountable obstacles were raised to prevent his plans from becoming effective. If the censor had been hesitant about publication, he had no doubts about presentation. "It is obvious that it is both impossible and undesirable to stage it, for we do not allow the Patriarch and monks to be represented on the stage."[11] And the presence of the Patriarch among the dramatis personae was not the only feature of the play distasteful to the Tsar. With the Decembrist rising still fresh in memory, any revival of disturbing events in Russian history was looked on with disfavour. The figure of the Pretender 'Dmitri' was banned from the stage. A request in 1833 by two famous actors for permission to present the Fountain scene between 'Dmitri' and Marina was refused on this ground.

No further attempt to gain permission to stage *Boris Godunov* was made till 1866, when permission was given on the condition that no ecclesiastical figure or any church ritual was represented. The project was dropped, and only on 17 September 1870 was *Boris Godunov* finally produced, even then in a censored version with shortened crowd scenes. By that time Mussorgsky was completing his opera *Boris Godunov*, which was to eclipse Pushkin's play, on which it was based, in public favour.

Boris Godunov was published in St Petersburg in the beginning of January 1831. Four hundred copies were sold on the first day, and Pushkin, who was in Moscow at the time, was delighted with the rumours that were reaching him of the success of his play in St Petersburg. He wrote round to all his friends expressing his astonishment, his delight, his bafflement. In one of these letters he suggested that this success might be due to the popularity of Walter Scott, presumably because of the general interest in history his novels had aroused.

But the play did not meet with unqualified praise. There were many people, as Pushkin had feared, who were disappointed; for it proved very different both from the drama they were accustomed to and from the kind of work they had come to expect from Pushkin's pen. Pushkin was grieved that the one work that he was most anxious should astonish and delight was misunderstood by the public, that had for so many years lavished praise on his other productions.

Before its publication Pushkin had read *Boris Godunov* to circles of his friends, who had at once been struck by its Shakespearian affinities. Pogodin recorded that Pushkin had said that he was 'giddy' from reading Shakespeare for it was like gazing into the depths.[12] Bulgakov wrote of his "Shakespearian strides", spanning the whole of life;[13] Polevoy, that Pushkin had in his work reflected the whole progress of Russian literature—starting from an education on foreign models, he had passed from one influence to another until he came to express in his poetry the spirit of his own country, and after a struggle with the Giant of English letters had emerged as his follower but not his imitator.[14]

The Shakespearian quality of *Boris Godunov* was now discussed by the critics. One attributed the growth of interest in Shakespeare to two causes: the influence of Schlegel, and the fascination for the past aroused by Scott's novels.[15] Another deplored the imitation of a man who wrote at a time entirely devoid of elegance and taste.[16] This was echoed in advice to Pushkin to cease imitating Byron and Shakespeare, who, had they been alive now, would be writing differently.[17] Perhaps the most discerning criticism was Kireevsky's. He suggested that the true core and 'hero' of the play was an idea—"the consequence of murdering an heir to the throne"; that the spirit of the murdered Dmitri played the chief part in the tragedy from beginning to end;

and that the allegation made by Prince Shuisky in the first scene, that Boris was his murderer, ran like a red thread through every subsequent conversation. The whole movement of the play was determined by that fact, which drew together all the characters and all the scenes; everything took place under that bloodstained shadow. Thus, judging the play from a Shakespearian angle, Kireevsky saw in it the unity of idea rather than of structure.[18]

Boris Godunov was not the only play Pushkin wrote under the impetus of his admiration for Shakespeare; but it was his only attempt to write a tragedy in the purely Shakespearian manner. In the *Little Tragedies* Shakespeare's influence is felt in the spirit of the whole, in single phrases or incidents, or in the development of character. In them Pushkin at times reaches Shakespearian heights, and transmutes his material with Shakespearian fire. They were all written in 1830; and both before and after their composition Pushkin continued to write both of Shakespeare's dramatic method and of his creation of particular characters.

In *Boris Godunov* Pushkin was concerned with the interaction of the people's fate with that of single personalities; in the *Little Tragedies*, or *Dramatic Scenes* as they were called after those of Barry Cornwall to which they owed their form, Pushkin is concerned only with the fate of individuals. Whereas in *Boris Godunov* he had aimed at breadth in his development of character, in these plays he aimed at depth; where previously he had concentrated largely on unique historical figures, he now concentrated on universal types, consumed by some overriding passion.

The Covetous Knight, the first of these plays, has for its theme the passion for wealth. Pushkin ascribed to it a fictitious source which long caused mystification to its critics, describing it as a translation of a tragi-comedy by Shenstone. To understand Pushkin's intention in this play one should read it in the light of his criticism of *The Merchant of Venice*, in which he contrasts the dramatic methods of Shakespeare and Molière. Molière when creating a miser was conscious only of his miserliness, and presented him as a man whose one abiding and all-embracing passion was gold. Shakespeare, on the other hand, in Shylock showed a man compact of many passions, of vindictiveness, pride and avarice.[19]

Pushkin, following Shakespeare's example, saw his covetous knight as a complex character, whose love of gold is complementary to his love of power, the power which that gold bestows. He desires not so much the tangible products of wealth, but the knowledge that the power to obtain such possession lies in his cellars. He worships gold because it raises him above his fellow-men and allows him to contemplate the vast estates and palaces that could be his. So Shylock seeks wealth because it is the one thing which gives him self-confidence against the hate and the disdain of the Venetians. Further, in *The Covetous Knight* the type of miserly Jew is separated from the character of the avaricious knight; and the cringing shiftiness of the one is opposed to the cruel yet magnificent vision of the other. Written in blank verse more mature and flexible than that of *Boris Godunov*, the play in its short span rises to great intensity of feeling.

The same can be said of *Mozart and Salieri*, where again Pushkin shows the working on man of an overruling passion, in this case envy. Salieri, the hard-working and talented composer, is counterpoised to the playful and carefree genius, Mozart. Salieri, almost overcome by the glory of Mozart's music, poisons him, because he feels that he is destined thus to save the musicians who have to seek and work for that inspiration which comes to Mozart without effort. It is the study of conflict between envy and admiration, of the impact of natural genius on trained mastery.

The dominating passion in the *Stone Guest* is the desire to achieve perfect love, burning through Don Juan, its hero. This play has a curious Shakespearian parallel, for Don Juan woos a lady, whose husband he has killed, in words strikingly similar to those addressed by Richard of Gloucester to Lady Anne. He confesses to Donna Anna that he has killed her husband. He meets with a rather half-hearted rebuff—which contrasts with Anne's curses to Richard—but the parallel is resumed in the sequel, for on offering to kill himself Don Juan captivates the heart of his lady.

The last work which Pushkin wrote under Shakespeare's influence, and the last in which he used dramatic form, was his part translation, part adaptation of *Measure for Measure*, which he wrote in 1832. He had started with the intention of simply translating *Measure for Measure*, but that proved cramping to his creative powers, and so he decided to change the whole into a narrative poem with a few dramatic scenes. For this he freely translated the five scenes which lie at the core of the play and relate directly to the conflict that divides the soul of Angelo, and to the ordeal that tests Isabella's chastity.[20]

In the article already mentioned in which Pushkin compared Shakespeare's and Molière's methods of creating characters, he contrasted, for illustration, Angelo and Tartuffe. Tartuffe is simply and wholly a hypocrite. All he does he does hypocritically. Hypocrisy is written all over him. Angelo on the contrary is divided within himself: he sees justice and acts accordingly, but in such action he reads his own death sentence, for he condemns a sin which he himself commits. He has become a hypocrite, for his passions have led him into an abyss which is repulsive to his reason.

Concentrating on the psychological problem of Angelo's dualism, Pushkin discarded all extraneous elements. He linked together the dramatic centres he translated with narrative verse, in which he epitomized all the rest of the action that was relevant to his theme. When actually translating he kept fairly close to the original, although throughout he shows a tendency to condense. He followed the main plot closely, with only a few slight alterations, such as changing the scene to Italy, making the Duke older, and Mariana the deserted wife of Angelo. The poem is interesting as an example of Pushkin's use of Shakespearian material for his creative needs, but it lacks the strength and originality of the *Little Tragedies*; and shows that Pushkin was nearer realizing the spirit and power of Shakespearian composition when he was creating independently than when translating, however freely, and constrained by an original.

All these works were received comparatively coldly by the critics and public, and it was only after Pushkin's death that the same critics, who had lamented his decline, came to wonder at this seeming blindness which had beset them in the 1830's, and had rendered them incapable of recognizing the amazing achievement of the *Little Tragedies*.

The theatre which Pushkin wished to reform was both well ahead of, and far behind, that in which Shakespeare worked and for which he wrote. The technical possibilities were infinitely wider and more elaborate; the stage could be adapted to every kind of pageant, spectacle and dance, with fountains, horses and flamboyant scenery. But this varied apparatus was cumbrous, and it broke down when a play like *Boris Godunov*, in which there were endless changes of scene, required staging. The result was that the play was immediately declared unsuitable for the stage, on the grounds that the scene-shifters would be exhausted by having to move so many sets, and a myth arose, that proved as tenacious as it was unjustified, that *Boris Godunov* was unactable—all this being quite apart from the censorship difficulties already mentioned.

What was worse was the tremendous poverty of dramatic material, the stagnation in infancy, which reigned in the Russian theatre in the beginning of the nineteenth century. The *élite* of both capitals would assemble in the theatre almost nightly, to be presented exclusively with poor translations of French neo-classical drama, even poorer Russian imitations of such plays, or with pageants or melodramas. The public was superficially amused and pleased, and used the theatres as convenient meeting-places: but there was no vitality, no creation, no criticism.

Pushkin realized very clearly how this situation had arisen, and described the process by which the dramatist had changed from being a spokesman, or even teacher of the people, in the court-yard, to being a cringing servant of the sensibilities and tastes of the *élite*, in the salon. Pushkin did all he could to acquaint himself with the methods and practice of dramatic art. He visited the theatre often, knew all the dramatists and actors of his day, and possessed in his library a large collection of dramatic literature, containing the works of all the major European dramatists, as well as much dramatic criticism. But he never knew the pulsating reciprocity of actor, dramatist and audience, such as existed in the Elizabethan theatre; he was never abroad, and therefore never encountered a theatrical atmosphere more alive and virile than the Russian; never saw the knowledge of dramatic method he had acquired from books put to use on the stage.

Shakespeare was a man of the theatre at a time when it was at the height of achievement and vitality. He was well versed in all the technical details that go to make a successful play, and was fully acquainted with the demands of his critical public. His aim was to expand, transcend and deepen, but not to reform. Pushkin was the leader of a band of reformers, wishing to replace the existing form of drama with one they considered more suitable and compact of great possibilities; and it was a very uphill fight against tradition, prejudice and conservatism.

In his adaptation of Shakespearian drama to the Russian stage Pushkin at one point found himself under the influence of two contradictory tendencies. He lived in the age of Scott and consequently wanted to combine with the Shakespearian drama of universal humanity the romantic drama of historical reality. But he realized that excessive historical realism was limiting to great tragedy, binding it by a fear of anachronism and a too great concentration on insignificant detail. Speaking of the *Little Tragedies* Dostoevsky said that Pushkin was more universal than Shakespeare because he could create characters true to whichever country or period he chose, whereas Shakespeare's Romans and Italians always remained Englishmen.[21] Dostoevsky is here judging Shakespeare's art by the standards of nineteenth-century realism; not understanding that, just as in his own novels time and place are irrelevant to the central core of the action and thought, so in Shakespeare's plays a more complete universality is achieved by his comparative indifference to historical detail.

Pushkin expressed this conflict in his criticism. He claimed that the great dramatists did not observe details of costume and setting; that to write a 'national' tragedy it was not enough to choose a subject from Russian history and pepper one's dialogue with archaisms. He saw that Shakespeare's anglicized Romans by their common humanity transcended limits of time and place.

On the other hand, in his draft preface to *Boris Godunov* he said that he had tried to replace the traditional habits of drama by a faithful representation of an historical period—in short, had written a truly romantic tragedy. He had urged that the richest source of inspiration for Russian writers lay in the Russian faith, the former Russian way of life, and in the chronicles, songs and proverbs in which these are revealed. Pushkin's aims in studying such material were fundamentally different from Shakespeare's when he used Hall and Holinshed. Pushkin searched for historical detail and the flavour of the past, where Shakespeare had looked for events which could serve as plots to be charged with contemporary application.

Boris Godunov is a combination of the tragedy of character and the drama of social custom. Pushkin was soon to turn to another medium which would afford him wider possibilities of developing his interest in social history. He was, in *The Captain's Daughter*, to write what the Tsar had long before requested of him, an historical novel in the manner of Walter Scott.

Pushkin's hopes for the 'Shakespearization' of Russian drama were not realized; and although many plays appeared about Ivan the Terrible, Godunov, and the Pretender 'Dmitri', there was nothing on the level of *Boris Godunov* until Count Alexis Tolstoy wrote his trilogy, *The Death of Ivan the Terrible*, *Tsar Feodor Ivanovich* and *Tsar Boris*, between 1865 and 1870. But by his inspiring criticism Pushkin raised Shakespearian studies in Russia to a new plane, and with the final disappearance of the canons of neo-classicism from the Russian stage, Shakespeare could at last be seen and read in unexpurgated form and free of his eighteenth-century mask.

Pushkin's death in 1837 was an irreparable loss to Russian letters. No other Russian writer had so wide a scope, or was so ready to experiment with new forms in which to express the new ideas that he was constantly evolving in his mind. Most of his contemporaries were carried away by one or other of the great literary influences of the time; Pushkin assimilated them all and yet throughout remained original, and true to his own genius. Byron, Shakespeare and Scott each contributed to his literary development. He learned from them himself, he encouraged others to learn from them; but he showed his contemporaries by his example that to learn is not to imitate but to assimilate, to mould, to select and to adapt. He never lost his critical faculty in a welter of enthusiasm. His exclamation that Byron and Scott were "food for the soul" and "Read Shakespeare, that is my refrain!" were expressions not of empty adulation but of a great intellectual vitality, which enabled him to imbue himself with the spirit of one writer after another, take all he could from each, and then return to his own writing enriched by new experience, and with a widened literary horizon.

NOTES

LIST OF ABBREVIATIONS USED

[All Russian titles have been translated]

Pushkin—Pushkin, A. S., *Complete Edition of the Works*, edited by M. A. Tsyavlovsky, 6 vols., Academia, Moscow/ Leningrad, 1936.

Pushkin, *Letters*—Pushkin, A. S., *Letters*, edited by B. L. and L. B. Modzalevsky, 3 vols., Academy of Sciences U.S.S.R., Moscow/Leningrad, 1926–35.

Pushkin and his Contemporaries—Pushkin and his Contemporaries, documents and research. Issues I–XXXIX, Academia, 1903–30.

Zelinsky—Zelinsky, V. A., *Russian Critical Literature on the Works of A. S. Pushkin*, 3 parts, Moscow, 1887–8.

1. Pushkin, vol. v, p. 228. All excerpts from Pushkin's letters and articles cited in the text are translated by the author, who has a translation and edition of Pushkin's literary criticism in active preparation.

2. For the earlier history of Shakespeare in Russia see Lirondelle, A., *Shakespeare en Russie (1748–1840)*, Paris, 1912, and Simmons, E. J., *English Literature and Culture in Russia (1553–1840)*, Cambridge, U.S.A., 1935.

Pushkin possessed the following editions of Shakespeare: *Œuvres complètes de Shakespeare*, traduites de l'anglais par Letourneur. Nouvelle édition par F. Guizot, Paris, 1821, and Shakespeare's *Dramatic Works*, printed from the text of S. Johnson, George Steevens and Isaac Reed, Leipsic, 1824.

It is not certain when Pushkin actually came to read English freely. Some claim that he was already able to do so when living in St Petersburg before his exile—he borrowed Hazlitt's *Table Talk* to practise on. His father maintained that he had learnt it as a boy at home before going to the Lycée. There is, however, no evidence to confirm either of these claims. In September 1825, when working on *Boris Godunov*, Pushkin wrote to his friend Prince Vyazemsky: "I need a knowledge of English—it is one of the disadvantages of my exile that I have no opportunity of learning while the time is ripe" (Pushkin, *Letters*, vol. I, p. 160). It therefore seems likely that though he might have started dabbling in English when he was staying with the Raevskys in the Crimea, using *The Corsair* as a text-book, he did not master the language till about 1828. For a fuller discussion of this question see *Pushkin and his Contemporaries*, Issues 17/18, M. A. Tsyavlovsky, 'Pushkin and the English Language'.

3. Rough draft in French (end of July, 1825, Mikhailovskoe). Pushkin, *Letters*, vol. I, pp. 147–8. This letter shows the influence of A. W. Schlegel's *Lectures on Dramatic Art and Literature*, which Pushkin was reading at the time.

4. There are only two English translations of *Boris Godunov*: in *The Works of Alexander Pushkin....Selected and edited by A. Yarmolinsky*, New York, 1936. Reissued in London by the Nonesuch Press, 1939, and *Boris Godunov: a Drama in verse...Rendered into English verse by A. Hayes*, London, 1918. Also two of the scenes are translated by C. H. Herford, in the course of his paraphrase of the play, in a paper on Pushkin published in *The Bulletin of the John Rylands Library*, vol. 9, no. 2, July 1925, and reprinted in *The Post-War Mind of Germany and other European Studies* by C. H. Herford, Oxford, 1927. Not one of these versions affords any idea of the poetic quality of the original.

5. See Pushkin to Gnedich, 27 June (1822, Kishinev), Pushkin, *Letters*, vol. I, pp. 31–2.

6. Pushkin, vol. v, pp. 333–4.

7. (About 15 February 1826, Mikhailovskoe) Pushkin, *Letters*, vol. II, p. 5.

8. Pushkin, vol. v, p. 330.

9. *Ibid.* p. 334.

10. Pushkin, *Collected Works*, published by the Academy of Sciences U.S.S.R., 1935–7, vol. VII, pp. 412–15.

11. *Ibid.*

12. *Pushkin and his Contemporaries*, Issues 19/20, p. 77.

13. A. Y. Bulgakov to his brother; see N. N. Ardens, *Pushkin's Dramatic Work* (Moscow, 1939), p. 131.

14. *Moscow Telegraph*, 1829, pt. 27, no. 10; see Zelinsky, pt. III, pp. 138–48.

15. 'More about *Boris Godunov*, a work by A. S. Pushkin', article by I. S. Kamashev in the *Son of the Fatherland* (1831), vol. 23, pt. 145, nos. 40/1; see Zelinsky, pt. III, pp. 93–106.

16. *About 'Boris Godunov', a work by A. S. Pushkin* (Moscow, 1831); see Zelinsky, pt. III, pp. 106–15.

17. 'Remarks on A. S. Pushkin's work, *Boris Godunov*.' Article by V. Plaksin in the *Son of the Fatherland* (1831), vol. 20, pts. 142/3, nos. 24/8; see Zelinsky, pt. III, pp. 171–213.

18. 'Survey of Russian Literature for 1831.' *The European*, 1832, pt. I, no. 7; see Zelinsky, pt. III, pp. 146–51.

19. 'Table-talk' (1834–6), Pushkin, vol. v, pp. 463–4.

20. The parts translated are approximately: Act I, sc. 4; Act II, sc. 2, ll. 27 to the end; Act II, sc. 4, ll. 31–171; Act III, sc. 1, ll. 53–149; and single lines in Act v, sc. 1.

21. *A Wreath for Pushkin's Monument* (St Petersburg, 1880), pp. 243–58.

It is interesting that Pushkin specifically praised Shakespeare in his 'Note on *Romeo and Juliet*' (1829), for the way in which he permeated his play with an Italian atmosphere. Pushkin may have had this romantic view of *Romeo and Juliet* in mind when, in the following year, he wrote his description of a Spanish summer night in the *Stone Guest*.

SHAKESPEARE ON THE FLEMISH STAGE OF BELGIUM, 1876–1951

BY

D. DE GRUYTER AND WAYNE HAYWARD

The way in which Shakespeare's plays have been incorporated into the literary traditions of countries other than his own is of no greater interest than his incorporation into the theatre—his reappearance year after year on their stages. When did this incorporation start? Which plays are most popular? Has production method followed the same changes it has in England? Are the roles given similar interpretations by the actors? These are some of the questions this paper will attempt to answer for the Flemish-speaking stage of Belgium.

Shakespeare as a part of the Belgian theatrical tradition is difficult to survey, for (as is perhaps too little realized) even the Belgian National Theatre is, in reality, two distinct theatres representing two linguistic and cultural groups.

Information of all kinds coming from Belgium is in French, and it may be a surprise to some to learn that four and a half of its eight million inhabitants speak, not French, but Flemish, and that the Belgian National Theatre, founded in 1945 by the Ministry of Education, has one French-speaking theatre to three that perform in Flemish. In other words, Le Théâtre National de Belgique sponsors one theatre in Brussels, while Het Nationaal Tooneel van Belgie, out of an equal grant of four million Belgian francs, sponsors De Koninklijke Nederlandse Schouwburg van Antwerpen, De Koninklijke Vlaamsche Schouwburg van Brussel and Het Reizend Volkstheater, a touring group with headquarters in Antwerp. These theatres do not represent the entire theatrical activity of the country, but merely those which are subsidized by the State.

Of the Flemish-speaking theatres, the one in Antwerp with a regular public of about 4000 is the largest and its development may be taken as being representative of the development of the Flemish theatre as a whole.

Since 1876 when Shakespeare was first performed in this theatre, his plays have been a regular part of its repertory. So revered a place does he now hold that one of his plays is chosen for the gala opening every season. Each of the other theatres produces one or two of his plays a year. Thus, in any single season one could see at least three Shakespearian plays performed by professional companies in Flemish.

The audience for these performances is mainly centered in the five provinces of East and West Flanders, Antwerp, Limburg and Brabant, where Flemish is the principal language. Of these, Antwerp is the most predominantly Flemish, and Brabant, because it contains French-speaking Brussels, the least. In the five provinces there is at the present time a theatre public of around 15,000 for plays performed in the Flemish language. Theatregoers beyond reach of the two groups operating permanently housed repertory companies are served by the Volkstheater touring company and by dozens of amateur groups.

Historically, the development of these theatres is similar to that of the theatre in England, with mystery and miracle plays performed by amateurs appearing as early as 1275. Typical

Flemish drama was developed during the next century with the Abele Spelen ("beautiful, artistic pieces") such as *Esmoreit, Gloriant* and *Lancelot van Denemarken*. The performances of Abele Spelen were followed by amusing little farces called Kluchten ('jokes') or Sotternien—rude playlets with the battle of the sexes forming the theme, much in the style of Punch and Judy.

In the fifteenth century religious drama was of sufficient interest to inspire Petrus Dorlandus, a member of a Chartreuse cloister at Zeelem, near Diest in Limburg, to write the morality play *Den Spieghel der Salichiet van Elckerlyck* (printed in Delft in 1495) which some scholars believe found its way to England as *Everyman*.[1]

From the Middle Ages until 1853, the Flemish stage was served wholly by amateurs and the literature of their theatre was dominated by Germany, Spain and France. No professional theatre and no outstanding playwright developed. In the sixteenth century, it is true, the Rederyker Kamers, societies for the preservation and performance of drama, music and literature, came into existence, but these were riddled by political and religious quarrels and in many cases did more to deter the artistic development of these arts than to foster them.

In 1830 Belgium became an independent nation and in 1853, two Flemish actors, Victor Driessens and Frans Van Doeselaer, founded the first professional company of actors under the protection and subsidy of the Town Council of Antwerp. From this troupe grew the Royal Netherlands Theatre of Antwerp which was taken over by the National Theatre of Belgium in 1945.

This repertory theatre in its early days drew heavily on translations of French melodramas, on fantasies from England, Germany and Italy, and on the violent plays of some young Flemish dramatists which had no permanent literary or dramatic value.

Against this background Shakespeare appeared on the Belgian stage when the Italian tragedian, Ernesto Rossi, presented *Othello* and *Hamlet* (in Italian) in March 1876, and again in January and February, 1877. The first production of Shakespeare in Flemish was seven years later, in 1884, when Jan Dilis appeared as Romeo in a translation of *Romeo and Juliet*.

In the spring of 1886 the Duke of Saxe-Meiningen brought his company to Belgium, playing *The Winter's Tale, Julius Caesar, The Merchant of Venice* and *Twelfth Night* in German. The Belgian critic, Pol de Mont, praised the force of the individual actors in the troupe, the *mise en scène*, the psychological depth and truth of the performances, all of which, he felt, gave the productions their peculiar realism.

So inspiring were the performances and so popular was Shakespeare that in the same year the Royal Netherlands Theatre of Antwerp presented *Hamlet*, starring Jan Dilis, and revived his earlier (1884) production of *Romeo and Juliet*. Both were successes, but the critics particularly acclaimed Dilis's interpretation of Hamlet (in preparation for which he had visited England to study Irving's performance), saying he "carried Hamlet, with all the subtleties, from the depth of pain to the height of joy". Audiences were tense and silent, and at least one critic was surprised that their interest extended beyond Hamlet and Ophelia to the other characters. This suggests that Dilis's production was an interpretation of the whole play, in the Meiningen tradition, and not merely a star-vehicle as was common on the English and Belgian stages of the period. It was acclaimed as a triumph for the Royal Netherlands Theatre, and the hope was expressed that further Shakespearian productions would follow.

In fulfilment of this desire, there has been at least one Shakespearian play in every repertory season except for the period 1914-19. To some extent, this is less an indication of Shakespeare's popularity with the audience than a tribute to the meaning his plays will always have for the actor and producer. It should be noted that the Flemish theatres are operated on a repertory basis; in a single season of twenty-four weeks, the company may perform as many as thirty different plays. Thus in the earlier days a work by Shakespeare might have been prepared for a single performance. Between 1886 and 1914, for example, *Hamlet* was produced four times for only one or two performances. Almost the same was true of *A Midsummer Night's Dream* and *Romeo and Juliet*. *Othello* was produced once for only one performance. *The Merchant of Venice*, on the other hand, always the most popular on the Flemish stage, was produced eight times for a total of twenty-five performances.[2] Inevitably, but none the less unfortunately, these productions fell short of the standard set by Dilis's *Hamlet*, and tended to revert to conventional groupings of star actors and to sacrifice the full dramatic value of the text.

Altogether, between 1884 and 1914, there were twenty-three productions of nine of Shakespeare's plays with a total of fifty-seven performances. Then came the period of the First World War, when, unlike the situation during the recent war, Shakespeare was not performed in the Flemish theatre. With the resumption of normal production in 1919 came a general reform in method. Each play was produced systematically and scheduled to run one week.

In 1921 J. O. De Gruyter became director of the Royal Netherlands Theatre of Antwerp. Under his management Shakespearian productions reached a high standard. De Gruyter was a producer and actor as well as general manager of the theatre. His production of *The Taming of the Shrew* in 1927 was seen by W. T. Grein, the English critic, who, after praising the setting—Italian Renaissance in style, flanked by mighty pillars of gold with a terrace-like elevation looking out upon a panorama of town and country and allowing for action on different levels—found that each actor was a character and not merely a reciter, and that the play had a sense of buoyancy, of satire, and a feeling of the joy of living often lacking in English productions of the time.[3]

In his first year as director, De Gruyter employed the actor and producer Charles Gilhuys, and to him has fallen the task of producing the majority of Shakespearian plays. Although his productions during the early 1920's when he collaborated with De Gruyter received critical acclaim, he did not really attain unity of dramatic impact until his own production of *The Merry Wives of Windsor* in 1929. Falstaff, in this production, was played as a Flemish type, and the sets, although they were not new, were well adapted and brilliantly lighted so that each scene became more like a Flemish painting than a stage set. Besides Gilhuys, Joris Diels, Gaston Vandermeulen and M. Balfoort were successful directors. Their productions have been praised by the critics for their homogeneity; their use of side lighting—termed 'Rembrandt lighting'; their speed, achieved through the skilful use of unit sets and rapid changes; and, above all, their integrity in following the text and allowing Shakespeare to speak for himself.

Jos Gevers, the leading actor in Flemish Belgium, has had thirty years on the Flemish stage. During his career he has appeared in ten Shakespearian plays and was outstandingly successful in the roles of Shylock, Richard III, Iago, Aguecheek, Angelo and Leontes. In common with other Flemish actors he has many qualities which assist him in performing Shakespeare: a good sense of humour, emotion, understanding—and the Flemish language itself, which, while slower in rhythm than English, has many similarities with English.

The standard translation of Shakespeare used in the Flemish theatre is that of L. J. Burgersdyk, although, since 1946, this has been in the process of some revision and modernization of spelling by Fr. de Backer. Of Burgersdyk's work W. T. Grein declared that it was "the finest equivalent of the original in the whole of Europe", since it "has a particular idiomatic flavour...germane to Shakespeare's words".[4]

The Flemish theatres have produced no brilliant innovations in Shakespearian production to impress the world, but its producers have placed the plays ahead of their own interests, and its actors, seeking in the text for the key to their roles, have had their interpretations co-ordinated into productions which strive always to project the essential meaning of Shakespeare. There is undoubtedly something in Shakespeare which can be fully appreciated only by one who is, as he was, a worker in the theatre, and every honest professional is as likely as the scholar to find a true interpretation of his lines.

The purpose of this article has been to show that, though slow in gaining a foothold, Shakespeare is now part of the classical repertory of the Flemish-speaking Belgian theatre, and that his plays will continue to be performed and enjoyed as long as the theatre exists. If the time ever comes when an International Shakespearian Festival is held, the authors feel certain that Flemish-speaking Belgium would be represented with a production both honest and sincere, and one that would not fall far short of those of other nations.

CHART LISTING SHAKESPEARIAN PRODUCTIONS IN DE KONINKLIJKE NEDERLANDSE SCHOUWBURG VAN ANTWERPEN

Play (in order of popularity)	1884–1914		1919–1950	
	Productions	Performances	Productions	Performances
Merchant of Venice	10	25	7	50
The Taming of the Shrew	—	—	3	35
Hamlet	4	6	5	25
Twelfth Night	1	5	3	25
As You Like It	1	6	3	25
Merry Wives of Windsor	—	—	2	22
Much Ado About Nothing	—	—	3	18
Othello	1	1	2	15
A Midsummer Night's Dream	1	1	1	12
The Winter's Tale	—	—	2	12
Richard III	1	5	1	6
Julius Caesar	1	5	1	6
Macbeth	—	—	1	11
Romeo and Juliet	3	3	1	6
Measure for Measure	—	—	1	9
Cymbeline	—	—	1	9
King Lear	—	—	2	6
All's Well That Ends Well	—	—	1	6
18 Plays	23	57	40	298

NOTES

1. Henry De Vocht, *Everyman—Comparative Study of Texts and Sources* (Leuven, 1947); Henri Logeman, *'Elckerlyc'—A Fifteenth Century Dutch Morality and 'Everyman'—A Nearly Contemporary Translation* (Gent, 1892).
2. Chart appended.
3. W. T. Grein, Theatre Review in *Illustrated London News*, 22 October 1927.
4. *Ibid.*

Other works consulted: Lode Monteyne, *Drama en Tooneel* (Brussels, 1949), *Over Shakespeare* (Antwerp, 1948); Th. De Ronde, *Het Tooneel en Vlaanderen* (Antwerp, 1930); Maurits Sabbe, Lode Monteyne, Hendrick Coopman, *Het Vlaamsch Tooneel* (Brussels, 1927); Joseph Gregor, *Weltgeschichte des Theatres* (Zurich, 1933).

INTERNATIONAL NOTES

A selection has here been made from the reports received from our correspondents, those which present material of a particularly interesting kind being printed wholly or largely in their entirety. It should be emphasized that the choice of countries to be thus represented has depended on the nature of the information presented in the reports, not upon either the importance of the countries concerned or the character of the reports themselves.

Austria

In the summer of 1950 Shakespeare's *Twelfth Night* was included in the performances of the Salzburg Musical and Theatrical Festival. The actors were of the Vienna Burgtheater, which, in the autumn, brought this comedy into its regular repertoire.

The *Klassiker-Verlagsgesellschaft*, Baden-Vienna, has issued a reprint of the well-known German translation of Shakespeare's dramas by Schlegel and Tieck in nine handsomely bound and well printed volumes. The text is that of the translators' last edition of 1839–40 and the editing is well done by Edwin Zellwecker of Vienna, who has also added introductory essays to the single groups of plays. A short biographical sketch in the first volume has been written by myself. The new edition, which is the first reprint of this well-known translation that has appeared since the War in any German-speaking country, is sure to make Shakespeare's works better known again, the more so as it is circulated among the members of the Book-Club attached to the publishing house at a cheap price and sold in Germany by a Book Guild in Munich. KARL BRUNNER

Belgium

On 9 January, in Brussels, the company of Claude Etienne ('Rideau de Bruxelles') played, for the first time in Belgium, a French translation of *King Lear* (French text by Romain Sanvic). The production was very good. André Berger in the title-role was extremely successful. He was impressive, moving and full of majesty. Emile Lanc's decoration was simple and effective, with very swift changes of scenery. The tempo of the whole production was remarkable.

A few days before the first performance of *King Lear*, the weekly paper *Les Beaux Arts* issued a special number devoted to Shakespeare. In addition to an article on *Lear*, another appeared on *Othello*—which the Comédie Française presented at the Théâtre Royal du Parc for a few performances. Aimé Clariond played Othello; Jean Debucourt, Iago, and Renée Faure, Desdemona. It was extremely interesting to watch the acting of these great players, more accustomed to Corneille and Racine, in the Shakespearian parts. The settings were by Cassandre. The French adaptation by Georges Neveux (who had already translated *A Midsummer Night's Dream*) is extremely lively and Neveux's rhythmical prose is eminently actable.

The company of the Théâtre National de Belgique, to whom we have been indebted in the past for successful performances of *Othello*, are preparing a revival of *Richard III*, in the French translation of André Obey. The play is to be directed by a well-known English producer, Michael Langham. ROBERT DE SMET

Czechoslovakia

Shakespeare is more alive in our country than ever, even although some recent productions have failed to do justice to his scenes and although, regrettably, the present favourites among his dramas are the farcical *Merry Wives of Windsor* and *The Taming of the Shrew*. In Prague, audiences have recently seen a rather unfortunate *Hamlet*, a *Romeo and Juliet* behind barbed wire, a misunderstood *Macbeth*, two productions of *A Midsummer Night's Dream* (one, at the Komorní divadlo, 'The Chamber Theatre', very delightful, with a boy-actor as Puck), two productions of *The Taming of the Shrew* and three of *The Merry Wives of Windsor*. The producer of *The Taming*, who had already handled this play before the War, is still searching for the correct interpretation to be given to it: in his third production he has laid greatest stress on presenting the characters realistically.

The National Theatre plans a series of the tragedies—beginning with *Othello*, in which, it is announced, Iago's 'fascist' tendencies and the 'racial' element in the plot are to be emphasized.   B. HODEK

Germany

A total of 107 Shakespeare productions covering 23 plays and comprising 1545 performances shows the undiminished popularity of Shakespeare on the German stage. As in previous years *Hamlet*, *Twelfth Night*, *A Midsummer Night's Dream* and *The Taming of the Shrew* reached the highest figure of performances, an exceptional case being *Othello*, which was produced eleven times and was played on more than 125 nights. For the first time after the war, *King John* was produced on the occasion of a Shakespeare week at the Dresden State Theatre. Noteworthy events were performances of *King Lear* with Werner Krauss as Lear and of *Julius Caesar* at the Ruhr festival held at Recklinghausen in 1950. There was a notable increase of open-air performances given at small medieval towns like Feuchtwangen in Franconia, where *Twelfth Night* was played 30 times. Heinz Hilpert, the former director of the 'Deutsches Theater', Berlin, went on tour with *Much Ado about Nothing*, copiously accompanied by incidental music from Schubert. The tendency to stylize was counterbalanced by other tendencies towards modernization in costume as well as in production, so that no special feature could be singled out as prevailingly characteristic of the whole.

After a three-year interval (due to post-war conditions) the German Shakespeare Society resumed publication with the *Jahrbuch* 84–6 (1948–50) which, after the death of Max Deutschbein, is now edited by Hermann Heuer, Wolfgang Clemen and Rudolf Stamm. The annual meetings of the German Shakespeare Society are still held at Bochum, where Saladin Schmitt, President of the Society and director of the Bochum theatre for many years, succeeded in establishing a solid and individual tradition of Shakespeare production. After Schmitt's unexpected death in March 1951, the famous German author and poet Rudolf Alexander Schröder was elected president. The Shakespeare festival 1951 at Bochum was begun by a performance of *Much Ado about Nothing* and ended by *The Winter's Tale*.   WOLFGANG CLEMEN

Greece

Two important Shakespeare productions are to be chronicled during recent months, both of comedies. In May 1950 the National Theatre, under the direction of D. Rondiris, presented *The Tempest* in a translation by D. Economidis, and in October, under the direction of Al. Solomos, gave *As You Like It* in a translation by M. Skouloudis.

A new collection of Shakespeare's works in Greek has now been launched, with versions by V. Rotas of *Twelfth Night*, *A Midsummer Night's Dream*, *The Tempest* and *Much Ado about Nothing* and by K. Karthaios of *Macbeth* and *Romeo and Juliet*.   GEORGE THEOTOKAS

Israel

The main event in the Hebrew theatre in Israel this past year was the production of *Othello* by the Habimah Players. Julius Gellner, a former director of the State theatres in Prague and Munich and well known in Britain, was invited by Habimah, after his production of *Othello* at the Old Vic, to do the same play with them. (This was Gellner's second production with Habimah; he had produced *A Midsummer Night's Dream* before.)

The opening night was 3 March 1950—an event of note in literary and artistic circles. The Habimah worked most seriously on the play, giving it its very best: Aharon Meskin, an actor of extraordinary personal power, in the role of Othello; Simon Finkel, one of Habimah's most gifted and intelligent players, as Iago; and its leading lady, Hannah Rovina, as Emilia; and last but not least, one of its younger set, Shoshanna Ravid, as Desdemona. There have been 84 performances throughout the year before full houses in ten different theatres (in city, colony and communal settlements). The Israel audience, both young and old, was most enthusiastic about Gellner's masterful production and the players' serious acting.

Our theatres being repertory, it is a usual thing to see on the bill-boards announcements of performances prepared in former years. Thus Habimah recently gave *A Midsummer Night's Dream* and *Hamlet* on more than one occasion, while the Ohel Theatre revived its productions of *King Lear* and *The Merry Wives of Windsor*.

Shortly after the première of *Othello*, the Hebrew version of the play was published by Sifriath Poalim (Workers' Book-Guild). Nathan Alterman, who had prepared the translation for the Habimah, dedicated his translation in book form to "the great Hebrew actor, Aharon Meskin", who played the leading role. The Hebrew version reads smoothly; it is poetic and charming at times and often shows a skilful hand, but it is in no way comparable with the translation made seventy years ago in England by Isaac Edward Zalkinson, which is Biblical in style and spirit, and, therefore, always lofty and worthy of the original.

The Am Oved Publishing House is about ready now to carry out its carefully prepared plans of the past few months—giving the Hebrew reader one large volume of Shakespeare's tragedies in Hebrew translations done by different Hebrew poets. The book will have an introductory essay on Shakespeare, the man and his work, and each play will have its own introductory notes and annotations. S. Halkin and Reuben Avinoam are to collaborate in editing the volume.

REUBEN AVINOAM

Italy

The most remarkable book on Shakespeare to appear in Italy in the latter part of 1950 is Valentina Capocci's *Genio e mestiere, Shakespeare e la commedia dell'arte* (Bari, Laterza). Following the lines of Croce's distinction between *poesia* and *non poesia*, this critic finds that all the prose passages in Shakespeare's plays are mediocre, betray improvization according to set formulae, in a word, are the work of the actors; and this is the reason— she argues—why Shakespeare, while he saw his poems through the press, took no interest in the printing of his plays "which must have appeared to him for the first time what they actually were, a product of collaboration, nay, an actual travesty" ("doveva apparire a lui per primo ciò che è in realtà, una collaborazione, e, nel fatto, una vera e propria contraffazione"). Preposterous as it may appear in its conclusion, this book is valuable in so far as it shows for the first time the close resemblance between certain Shakespearian scenes and traditional scenes of the *commedia dell'arte*. Valentina Capocci's book has been severely criticized, among others, by one of the most cultured and distinguished Italian actresses, Elsa De' Giorgi (*Shakespeare e l'attore*, Florence, Electa Editrice, 1950).

The most remarkable performances of Shakespeare's plays during the twelve months have been: *Twelfth Night* in the gardens of the Villa Floridiana at Naples (July 1950), with Salvo Randone in the role of Malvolio and Anna Proclemer as Viola; *The Taming of the Shrew* at the Teatro Ateneo, Rome, with Carla Bizzarri as Katharina reminding one of the vehement and elegant attitudes of Fuseli's women; *Romeo and Juliet* at the Teatro Valle, Rome, with Edda Albertini in the role of Juliet and Vittorio Gassmann as Romeo; *Othello* at the Greek Theatre of Taormina, with Annibale Ninchi as Othello; and *Much Ado about Nothing* at the Amphitheatre of Verona, with Memo Banassi as Benedick and Pagnani as Beatrice.

A new translation of Shakespeare's plays having an Italian background has been published at Turin, Utet, 1950: *Shakespeare degli italiani*, Contents: *I due genti-luomini di Verona*, translated by Gino Caimi, *Romeo e Giulietta* by Luciana Milani, *Il Mercante di Venezia* by Maria Antonietta Andreoni, *La bisbetica domata* by Silvio Policardi, *Molto rumore per nulla* by Carlo Aldo Menetto, *Giulio Cesare* by Nicoletta Neri, *Otello* by Lorenzo Gigli, *Antonio e Cleopatra* by Ercole Angelo Gambino, *Coriolano* by Lella Aimerito, *La tempesta* by Gigi Cane, Introduction by Annibale Pastore and an essay on 'Interpreti di Shakespeare in Italia' by Bruno Brunelli.

MARIO PRAZ

Norway

Two Shakespeare plays were presented in 1950: *Twelfth Night* in an open-air theatre outside Oslo and *The Merchant of Venice* at the National Theatre. The open-air frame was admirably suited to *Twelfth Night* and made it a very sweet and agreeable thing; one critic called it "an innocent Shakespeare for family fare". Remarkable in the *Merchant* was a very original Shylock, played by Havrevold, a Shylock somewhat younger than the traditional one, no patriarch, but imperious, wise and dignified even in submission, and growing to impressive dimensions in the great scenes. It may be noted, however, that one critic pretended that on the very first night Shakespeare had, from his seat on Olympus, written a note which he had dropped down on the head of the theatre manager. It read:

"Dear Knut,

I have written 37 plays. In the course of fifty years the National Theatre has staged no more than 16 of them. Please find something new instead of trotting out this well-worn play with Shylock in it, which everybody knows by heart.

Yours

W. S."

LORENTZ ECKHOFF

South Africa

At least four of Shakespeare's plays have been translated into Afrikaans in the last three years, but probably the most important dramatic event in South Africa during 1950 was the Afrikaans production of *Macbeth* by the National Theatre. The translation was made by L. I. Coertze, Dean of the Faculty of Law at the Pretoria University. Though the play had an enthusiastic press wherever it was performed, it was coolly received in academic quarters, and has fewer merits than the same author's translation of *Hamlet* in 1947. Miss C. van

Heyningen in *Vista*, 1950 (a publication of the Cultural Societies of the University of Witwatersrand, Johannesburg) argued that to offer Afrikaans-speakers (who also know English) a translation of Shakespeare, is to do them and the dramatist a disservice; it is not possible, she feels, to make the speech of people who lived before the middle of the nineteenth century sound natural in a homely modern language like Afrikaans. She believes, also, that the Afrikaans translations offered reveal an insensitiveness to the beauty, power and rhythm of Shakespeare's verse. In Coertze's version "so many stumbling-blocks of metre and syntax have been laid across the path that meaning breaks its shins against them and comes out rather bruised and hard to recognize". Selected examples of the nobler passages undoubtedly illustrate her point; but whether she has gained the more contentious one—that no translation into Afrikaans is necessary—can be answered only by future generations.

A. C. PARTRIDGE

Sweden

1948 brought a record in the history of Shakespeare on the Swedish stage. This year we had six new productions in our principal theatres. One theatre, Stockholmsteatern, even had two plays in the same season: *Hamlet* and *The Taming of the Shrew*—those works through which Shakespeare has always been popular to the Swedish theatregoer. Interesting has been the staging of *Macbeth* at the Gothenburg Stadsteater with many thrilling effects carried out under Ingemar Bergman's inspiring leadership.

In 1949 not quite so many performances can be registered, but that year we had what was considered the best staging of a Shakespearian comedy in our country: the *Much Ado about Nothing* at Malmö Stadsteater (director: Torsslow). As the year ended another comedy success lay in waiting, *The Taming of the Shrew* produced at Gothenburg. We must add to this many open-air performances in summer and many attempts and experiments by amateur troupes among the university youths.

Looking back upon the time when Shakespeare the 'classic' was more or less dutifully acted once a year, there is a notable change in the attitude. The characteristic feature of our days is the real and warm interest with which he is met by young stage-managers and young actors.

The acting of Shakespeare in 1950 has been concentrated on *The Taming of the Shrew* (except for a new *Hamlet* at Linköping by the youthful Ingemar Pallin). No less than three separate productions can be recorded:

in Gothenburg, at the Skansen open-air theatre, and at the Dramatiska Teatern. It seems that for the immediate future we have had our fill of this popular comedy.

NILS MOLIN

Switzerland

Robert Fricker's *Kontrast und Polarität in den Charakterbildern Shakespeares* has just been published as the twenty-second volume of our 'Swiss Studies in English' by A. Francke in Bern. It is sure to be widely discussed, and we need not say more about it here than that it is a most serious attempt at reconciling the views of Schücking and Stoll with those of the more traditional students of Shakespeare's characters. A new edition of Alfred Günther's *Der junge Shakespeare*, which was briefly reviewed in *Shakespeare Survey* 3, p. 138, was issued in Zurich by the Ex-Libris Verlag as a handsome volume enriched by a number of excellent illustrations. In the September–October (1950) number of the Lausanne periodical *Études de Lettres*, Adrien Bonjour has printed an article on 'Le problème du héros et la structure du Roi Jean de Shakespeare', in which he tries to prove that Faulconbridge is the hero of *King John* in the second part of the play only, the King himself being the hero in the first part, the whole play being built on the contrasted decline of the King and ascension of the Bastard. In the same number Pierre Cherix has shown, in an article entitled 'L'évolution de la pensée de Shakespeare: la thèse de Max Deutschbein', that the German scholar has been drawn to the study of Shakespeare's spiritual and intellectual development by his own experiences and that, if he has shed some genuine light on this or that aspect of Shakespeare's inner life, he has too often lent him his own conceptions.

There were many Shakespearian performances in the course of the year. At Basel, as H. Lüdeke tells us, "three plays were given by the Municipal Theatre. During the latter part of the 1949–50 season, Walter Richter's highly interesting and extremely powerful interpretation of *Richard III* resulted in a figure that in its emphasis on the King's physical ugliness and moral sliminess was more like Dostoievsky than Shakespeare and lacked the remnant of nobility and charm that is necessary to make the winning of Anne a convincing possibility. In May, Ernst Ginsberg produced a charmingly agile performance of *As You Like It*, in which the slightly too realistic Audrey was more than compensated for by Anne Marie Blanc's intellectual vitality and force as Rosalind. In December Käthe Gold's poignant rendering of Hermione, supported by Ginsberg's Leontes, gave, in its marvellous wealth of psychological detail, a weight to the serious parts of the play that the pastoral fourth act could not bear up against and that seriously impinged on the character of the whole as merely *The Winter's Tale*." At the Zurich Schauspielhaus the Old Vic Company gave four performances of *Hamlet* (30, 31 May and 1, 2 June), and the repertory company of the same theatre performances in German of *Romeo and Juliet* and *The Merchant of Venice*. *Romeo and Juliet*, with Will Quadflieg as Romeo and Dorothea Mayer as Juliet, was such an enchanting performance that it was given no less than ten times between 26 May and 25 June before crowded houses. It was rather exceptional in that all the characters were impersonated by actors of talent. Geneva had the privilege of seeing the very first performance of *Timon* in French. Though that bitter and imperfect tragedy had been translated before, it had never been acted anywhere in French-speaking countries. The new translation, which unfortunately has not been published yet, is the work of Daniel Anet, a librarian at the University Library and a devoted student and lover of Shakespeare. He has scored a real success. His version is vigorous, natural, and eminently actable. In a short paper published in *Vie, Art, Cité*, a Lausanne review, in its January 1950 number, he explained his reasons for attempting a sort of compromise between the requirements of a modern and those of an Elizabethan stage. The compromise proved not only workable, but very satisfactory. Between 3 and 13 May, the play was given five times. It came as a revelation to many people. The audiences completely fell under the spell of Timon's unbridled violence. The company responsible for those performances, *La Société genevoise des Amis de l'Instruction*, composed of gifted amateurs and professionals, was fully equal to its task. At the end of August, the open-air Lausanne theatre (styled the *Théâtre du Château*, because its stage is on the stairs leading up to the terrace on the south of the medieval castle which is now the seat of the government), gave memorable performances of *La Nuit des Rois* (*Twelfth Night*) in a new adaptation by Paul Pasquier, the leading actor in the company. No scenery, but a ship's rigging—mast, half-curled sails, ropes—on the left, a double arch on the right, in the centre a simple throne under a dais, such was the stage from beginning to end, and it served its purpose perfectly well. With Aimé Clariond as Malvolio, the play could not fail. With Camille Fournier as Olivia, it could only be charming. Those two Paris stars were ably supported by the members of the company. The music was all Elizabethan airs, of Morley, Dowland, Campion, Byrd played on old instruments, and there was as much of it as was justifiable. The five performances could easily have been doubled, but Clariond had other engagements.

Obviously, Shakespeare is not losing his hold on Swiss audiences. This may be due partly to the importance given to his works in the education of our youth. In the summer, the Aarau Cantonal school produced *The Tempest* in German. The music was by Armin Schibler, specially composed for this performance. Neuchâtel had also its *Nuit des Rois* ably acted by a company of young amateurs.

GEORGES A. BONNARD

The U.S.A.

With Katharine Hepburn playing Rosalind and Olivia de Havilland appearing 'in person' as Juliet one might possibly discern a 'trend'—the return of movie stars to the theatre in the golden roles provided by the Bard. But Maurice Evans, ever faithful to the stage as well as to his favourite author, offered *Richard II* once again and Louis Calhern, a fine 'stage actor', even though a recent sojourner in Hollywood, boldly essayed *King Lear* during the current season, so that stage and screen actors shared the honours.

These four professional Broadway productions of Shakespeare, though they represent a hundred per cent increase over the number given the year before, can hardly be said to be an impressive output, but they do represent an enormous amount of energy, enthusiasm and financial outlay. With no professional repertory company such as the Old Vic or the Stratford Theatre, the American public must depend on individual producers and actors whose devotion to the art of the living theatre persuades them to launch forth on the precarious and often costly experiment of a Shakespearian offering. The Theatre Guild, which has to its credit a number of such enterprises, including Alfred Lunt and Lynn Fontanne in *The Taming of the Shrew* (1935–6), Helen Hayes and Maurice Evans in *Twelfth Night* (1940–1) and Paul Robeson in *Othello* (1943–4), gave Katharine Hepburn a gorgeous setting in a production of *As You Like It*, conceived and directed by England's Michael Benthall and designed by James Bailey. The visual effects provided by the enchanted forest and the enchanting Miss Hepburn, irresistible in classic tights, helped to make Shakespeare's lovely fantasy a nation-wide success. After a New York run of about five months (26 January to 3 June 1950) the production went on the road and has been received everywhere with enthusiasm.

In January of this year, Maurice Evans brought his familiar and much admired *King Richard II* to the New York City Centre where he has, for two consecutive winters, directed a season of drama for this civic enterprise. The New York City Centre of Music and Drama is a comparatively new venture which operates in a city-owned theatre on 55th Street, giving short seasons of opera, ballet and theatre at moderate prices in a valiant and successful effort to build a permanent, all-round repertory theatre for the city. The City Centre receives no municipal subsidy, but it does benefit by concessions in the matter of rent and maintenance and it is assisted by generous individuals and by performers willing to give time and energy to a public enterprise. Margaret Webster once more directed the production of *Richard II* as she did when Maurice Evans first played the role in New York in 1937, and the public responded warmly to the opportunity of seeing Evans again in this favourite role.

One of the most interesting offerings of the season was the production of *King Lear* staged by John Houseman. Louis Calhern, who played this great and taxing role, is associated in the public mind with a very different type of part. He was an admirable Colonel in *Jacobowsky and the Colonel*, an amusing Father Day in *Life with Father*. *The Magnificent Yankee*, which he played both on Broadway and on the screen, offered him in the part of Justice Oliver Wendell Holmes a fine opportunity for his authoritative and intelligent acting. To tackle Shakespeare at his most difficult required courage on the part of all concerned—the producers, Robert Joseph and Alexander Cohen, the director Houseman, and Calhern. Aided by Ralph Alswang as designer and Marc Blitzstein as composer, and abetted by a group of actors with varying degrees of experience in acting Shakespeare, this *King Lear* made a decided impression both on the critics and the public. It was warmly praised and played to eager audiences who welcomed the opportunity to see a great play done with intelligence, vigour and seriousness. Once again Shakespeare was discovered as a compelling playwright, but the problem here, as in so many cases of the kind, was the eternal one of costs. Only smash hits can survive on Broadway and though *King Lear* was cordially received and did what would normally be called good business, its running expenses were inevitably too high for its box office intake. It was, however, an eminently worth-while production and one that should have had a far longer life.

The latest Shakespearian opening was a much heralded production of *Romeo and Juliet* starring Olivia de Havilland. The production has been long in the making. Sponsored by Dwight Deere Wiman (who died before it reached New York), the project is one which Miss de Havilland has long had at heart. Miss de Havilland began her stage career as Hermia for Reinhardt in both the stage and screen productions of *A Midsummer Night's Dream* which the great German director launched in Hollywood in 1934. Since then this gifted and highly successful screen actress has been seen in thirty-four films, has won many awards and done some sensitive, effective acting in such roles as that of Melanie in *Gone With the Wind* and the heroines of *The Heiress*, *Hold Back The Dawn* and *The Snake Pit*. Miss de Havilland has come to Broadway in a production which is lovely to look at and full of movement and colour. Oliver Messel has set an authentically Renaissance stage and costumed it straight from the loveliest paintings of the period. Peter Glenville has directed a cast that brings some young American talents—particularly a handsome Romeo played by Douglas Watson—into contact with such seasoned Shakespearian veterans as Malcolm Keen and Jack Hawkins. A favourable press and the enthusiasm of Miss de Havilland's numerous admirers (not to mention the incredible beauty of Mr Shakespeare's poetry and the touching appeal of the story) promise well for a long run. The New York stage has at least been generous to the Bard in the quality of the physical investiture of his plays, even though it may not be able to compete in the quantity of productions with other more favoured countries.

Off Broadway, however, quantity can be counted on as well as—in many instances—quality. Shakespeare has always been and still remains a favourite—and quite rightly so—in the college and university theatres. A quick survey shows that *The Taming of the Shrew* was this year's most popular drama, with eight productions to its credit, including Margaret Webster's touring company production, and an arena style presentation in Washington, D.C., where the whole audience became the court of the Lord and Lady before whom the strolling players performed. *Much Ado About Nothing*, *Romeo and Juliet*, *Julius Caesar* and *The Merchant of Venice* (given in Margo Jones's Theatre-in-the-Round in Dallas, Texas), were next in order of popularity, with *Antony and Cleopatra*, *A Midsummer Night's Dream* and *King Lear* following hard upon. Single productions were recorded of *Macbeth*, *Othello*, *Love's Labour's Lost*, *As You Like It*, *Twelfth Night*, *Richard III*, *Henry IV* and *The Comedy of Errors*.

This is not a total accounting of all the productions throughout the United States, but it gives a good idea of how important a role Shakespeare plays in the theatre off Broadway. ROSAMOND GILDER

The U.S.S.R.

The year 1950 witnessed a number of new Shakespearian productions on the Soviet stage, with *Othello* still holding first place. The noble humanism of this tragedy strikes a highly responsive chord in the heart of our audience. As sung by Shakespeare, the love of Othello and Desdemona invariably evokes their deepest sympathies. In its interpretations of *Othello* the Soviet theatre stresses not the tragedy of jealousy, but the tragedy of trust deceived, thereby following in the footsteps of Pushkin—who said: "Othello is not jealous by nature; on the contrary, he is trustful."

The fervour of the Soviet playgoer's love for Othello and Desdemona is matched by the intensity of his hatred for Iago, that destroyer of human happiness. Many is the time I have felt an audience literally go cold with wrath when Lodovico speaks the words:

"O Spartan dog,
More fell than anguish, hunger, or the sea!
Look on the tragic loading of this bed;
This is thy work: the object poisons sight."

New productions of *Othello* were staged, in 1950, in Voronezh, Petrozavodsk, Tomsk, Tarnopol, Ufa (in Bashkirian), and Frunze (in the Kirghiz language).

In the spring of 1950 the Khamza Drama Theatre (Uzbekistan) revived its production of *Othello*, with the finest Uzbek actor, Abrar Khidoyatov, again appearing in the role of the Moor of Venice. His Othello leaves an indelible impression. He combines beauty and gentleness of movement, nobly restrained acting, with immense emotional power. A group of actors from a North Ossetian Drama Theatre recently toured Moscow, presenting a scene from *Othello* in the Moscow Actors' Club. The Ossetian actor Tkhapsayev plays Othello with a manly forcefulness set off by profound, moving lyricism. I must mention one more production of *Othello*, that staged in the Mossoviet Theatre by one of our best stage directors, Y. A. Zavadsky, a pupil of C. Stanislavsky and E. Vakhtangov. This production has been running for seven years already, yet every performance is fresh and effective.

Hardly less popular is *Romeo and Juliet*, especially among our youth, which always prizes faithfulness. The contrast between the fresh bright characters of Romeo and Juliet and such creatures as Tybalt, who thirst for bloodshed, cannot but impress audiences and evoke a lively response. Successful productions of *Romeo and Juliet* appeared in 1950 in Gorky, Novosibirsk, Irkutsk and Barnaul. At present it is in rehearsal in several other theatres as well; for example, in Sevastopol and Tashkent (in the Khamza Drama Theatre).

Such plays as *The Taming of the Shrew, Twelfth Night, Much Ado about Nothing* and *Merry Wives of Windsor*, which are particularly popular here, occupy their former prominent positions in the Shakespearian repertory of our theatres. The Moscow Theatre of Satire put on a colourful and gay production of *The Comedy of Errors* in 1950.

Shakespeare is also widely represented in the music theatres of the Soviet Union. New productions of Verdi's opera *Othello* scored hits in 1950 in Kuibyshev, Odessa and Tashkent (in the Navoi State Opera and Ballet Theatre).

Shakespeare's plays offer ample opportunity not only for actors but also for elocutionists. In a special recital Golubentsev told the story of *Romeo and Juliet*, stopping here and there to read passages from it. Glumov, another elocutionist, recites *Hamlet* in the same way. I must mention in passing that elocution is an independent field of art in the Soviet Union and many dramatic actors devote themselves exclusively to this genre.

In 1950 the State Literature Publishing House put out the eighth (and last) volume of its edition of the Complete Works of Shakespeare, edited by A. A. Smirnov, with generous annotations. Almost all the plays are presented in new versions, many of them made specially for this edition. T. L. Shchepkina-Kupernik, Soviet veteran translator, was one of the main contributors. Special mention should be made of *Measure for Measure*, rendered by the talented translator M. Zankevich. He has produced the best of all Russian translations of this play, which is noted as being one of the most difficult works to render into another language.

At present a volume of Shakespeare's tragedies as translated by Boris Pasternak, and edited and prefaced by the author of these lines, is being prepared for the press. In 1950 Pasternak made an excellent translation of *Macbeth*, which, while being deeply poetic, is remarkable for natural vitality of speech.

S. Marshak and the author of these lines have just completed a version of *The Merry Wives of Windsor*. We spent more than two years on it in an effort to convey the natural quality of Shakespearian speech, its great variety of intonations and the living breath of the Shakespearian text. Our translation is coming out as a separate volume and has been accepted for production by the Mossoviet Theatre.

It should be noted that the number of people who are reading Shakespeare in the original is steadily growing in the Soviet Union. To assist these readers, the Foreign

Languages Publishing House put out in 1950 separate editions of *King Lear* and *Othello* in English for which I compiled the glossaries and provided the annotations.

In 1950 the Soviet Union marked the 150th anniversary of the birth of the great Russian actor P. S. Mochalov. One of Mochalov's best roles was that of Hamlet. His performance in it has been described in detail in Belinsky's famous article '*Hamlet*, Shakespearian Drama, and Mochalov in the Role of Hamlet', an article which is a classic of Russian dramatic criticism. Thanks to Belinsky, we have a vivid picture of those days in 1837

when Shakespeare was first shown on the Russian stage in all his striking power. Since then Shakespeare's popularity in the country has grown immeasurably. In Soviet times the work of the great poet and playwright has become available to all Soviet people as part of their cultural heritage. This fact is one link in the chain of numerous other facts testifying how ardently the people of our country love and how deeply they value all the genuinely beautiful and genuinely human treasures produced by the culture of the English people.

M. MOROZOV

SHAKESPEARE PRODUCTIONS IN THE UNITED KINGDOM: 1950

A List compiled from its Records by the Shakespeare Memorial Library, Birmingham

JANUARY

23   *As You Like It:* Bristol Old Vic Company, at The Theatre Royal, Bristol. *Producer:* ALAN DAVIS.

     The Taming of the Shrew: The Playhouse, Nottingham. *Producer:* ANDRÉ VAN GYSEGHEM.

     Macbeth: The Playhouse, Sheffield. *Producer:* GEOFFREY OST.

30   *The Taming of the Shrew:* Salisbury Arts Theatre Company, at The Arts Theatre, Salisbury. *Producer:* DENIS CAREY.

FEBRUARY

2   *Hamlet:* Old Vic Theatre Company, at The New Theatre, London. *Producer:* HUGH HUNT.

8   *Richard the Second:* The Playhouse, Liverpool. *Producer:* MICHAEL MACOWAN.

28   *Othello:* Oxford University Dramatic Society, at The Playhouse, Oxford. *Producer:* ALAN COOKE.

MARCH

9   *Measure for Measure:* Shakespeare Memorial Theatre, Stratford-upon-Avon. *Producer:* PETER BROOK.

14   *King Henry the Fourth,* Part Two: Cambridge University, Marlowe Society and A.D.C., at The Arts Theatre, Cambridge. Producer and actors are anonymous.

20   *Twelfth Night:* The Overture Players, at The New Theatre, Bromley. *Producer:* GUY VERNEY.

20   *Hamlet:* Midland Theatre Company, at The College Theatre, Coventry. *Producer:* ANTHONY JOHN.

28   *King Henry the Eighth:* Shakespeare Memorial Theatre, Stratford-upon-Avon. *Producer:* TYRONE GUTHRIE.

APRIL

17   *The Merchant of Venice:* Citizen's Theatre, Glasgow. *Producer:* JOHN CASSON.

19   *Macbeth:* Adelphi Guild Theatre Co., at The Playhouse, Buxton. *Producer:* R. WARD.

25   *Julius Caesar:* Bristol Old Vic Company, at The Theatre Royal, Bristol. *Producer:* ALAN DAVIS.

MAY

2   *Julius Caesar:* Shakespeare Memorial Theatre, Stratford-upon-Avon. *Producers:* ANTHONY QUAYLE and MICHAEL LANGHAM.

13   *The Taming of the Shrew:* Tavistock Little Theatre. *Producer:* VINCENT PEARMAIN.

15   *As You Like It:* The Tuska Theatre Company, Henley-on-Thames. *Producer:* PIERRE ROUVE.

     Romeo and Juliet: Arts Theatre, Ipswich. *Producer:* WARREN JENKINS.

23   *A Midsummer Night's Dream:* The Renegade Company, at Ilford Town Hall. *Producer:* JAMES COOPER.

25   *The Winter's Tale:* Regent's Park Open Air Theatre, London. *Producer:* ROBERT ATKINS.

29   *Macbeth:* Arts Theatre, Cambridge; 8 June at The Arts Theatre Club, London. *Producer:* ALEC CLUNES.

JUNE

5   *Twelfth Night:* Harrow School, Harrow-on-the-Hill, Middlesex. *Producer:* RONALD WATKINS.

7   *A Midsummer Night's Dream:* Oxford University Dramatic Society, in New College Gardens, Oxford. *Producer:* ANTHONY BESCH.

8   *The Comedy of Errors:* Cambridge University Amateur Dramatic Club, at the A.D.C. Theatre. *Producer:* JOHN BARTON.

19   *The Merchant of Venice:* Regent's Park Open Air Theatre, London. *Producer:* ROBERT ATKINS.

28   *A Midsummer Night's Dream:* Pittville Gardens, Cheltenham. *Producer:* LESLIE FRENCH.

JULY

2   *Pericles:* The Under Thirty Theatre Group, at Rudolph Steiner Hall, London. *Producer:* JOHN HARRISON.

4   *Twelfth Night:* First Folio Theatre Company, at Walpole Park, Ealing. *Producer:* KENNETH McCLELLAN.

17   *The Taming of the Shrew:* Regent's Park Open Air Theatre, London. *Producer:* ROBERT ATKINS.

18   *King Lear:* Shakespeare Memorial Theatre, Stratford-upon-Avon. *Producer:* JOHN GIELGUD.

AUGUST

7   *All's Well That Ends Well:* Marlowe Society, at The Arts Theatre, Cambridge. *Producer:* DONALD BEVES.

SEPTEMBER

19   *Troilus and Cressida:* London Artists' Theatre Productions, at Toynbee Hall Theatre, London. *Producer:* PETER A. BUCKNELL.

25   *The Merchant of Venice:* Young Vic Company, at the Opera House, Cheltenham, afterwards on tour. *Producer:* GLEN BYAM SHAW.

26   *King Lear:* Salisbury Arts Theatre Company, at The Arts Theatre, Salisbury. *Producer:* PETER POTTER.

OCTOBER

16   *Julius Caesar:* Colchester Repertory Theatre. *Producer:* WALLACE EVENNETT.

17   *The Merry Wives of Windsor:* Bristol Old Vic Company, at The Theatre Royal, Bristol. *Producer:* DENNIS CAREY.

30   *The Merry Wives of Windsor:* The Playhouse, Nottingham. *Producer:* ANDRÉ VAN GYSEGHEM.

NOVEMBER

11   *The Winter's Tale:* Questors Theatre, London. *Producer:* ABRAHAM ASSEO.

14   *Twelfth Night:* Old Vic Theatre, London. *Producer:* HUGH HUNT.

23   *The Winter's Tale:* The Loft Theatre, Leamington Spa. *Producer:* VERNON FREAKLEY.

27   *Richard the Second:* Birmingham University Dramatic Society. *Producer:* DAVID TURNER.

DECEMBER

4   *Othello:* Colchester Repertory Theatre. *Producer:* WALLACE EVENNETT.

During the year Donald Wolfit has been on tour with a repertory of Shakespearian plays including: *The Merchant of Venice; As You Like It; Twelfth Night; The Taming of the Shrew; Macbeth;* and *King Lear.*

PLATE III

A. *Twelfth Night*, Old Vic, 1950. Production by HUGH HUNT;
Costumes and Settings by ROGER FURSE. THE OPENING SCENE

B. *Twelfth Night*. VIOLA'S EMBASSY TO OLIVIA

PLATE IV

Twelfth Night. THE MIDNIGHT CAROUSAL

PLATE V

The Merchant of Venice, Young Vic, 1951. Production by GLEN BYAM SHAW;
Settings by GAY DANGERFIELD. SHYLOCK DEBATES THE LOAN

PLATE VI

A. *Henry V*, Old Vic, 1951. Production by GLEN BYAM SHAW;
Costumes and Settings by MOTLEY. "ON THIS UNWORTHY SCAFFOLD"

B. *Henry V*. THE FRENCH COURT

SHAKESPEARE IN THE WATERLOO ROAD

BY

RICHARD DAVID

[*The plays selected this year by our reviewer for extended criticism are Twelfth Night, Merchant of Venice, and Henry V at the Old Vic Theatre, October 1950–March 1951*]

For some years before the war there was one theatre in England, and perhaps only one, which could be confidently relied upon to produce Shakespeare for Shakespeare's sake—the Old Vic in the Waterloo Road. When in 1941 the building was damaged by bombs, the company moved to another theatre, in London's west end; but though there were still individual productions of distinction and star performances of particular roles, something of the special glory of the Old Vic seemed to evaporate with the change of quarters. The post-war reorganization of the Memorial Theatre at Stratford, of old the double shrine of Ham and Whimsy, and the startling emergence there of a true Shakespearian style have since provided another stage on which authentic productions of Shakespeare's plays may be expected. Yet even with this second stronghold in being, there are many who have waited anxiously for the reopening of the theatre in the Waterloo Road, in the hope that with it might reappear the old qualities, of faithfulness to the text and to the spirit of the plays, of star turns subordinated to team-work, and of stage-craft inventive but never fanciful or perverse.

No one who, little more than a year before, saw the still derelict building, with sagging galleries and the cleared pit vast and dreary in its dilapidation, would have guessed that the reconstruction could be so quickly carried through, or that the result could be so charming. By some feat of the original designer the theatre, which holds 500 people on the ground floor alone, gives an impression of great intimacy. It seems to assume good relations between stage and auditorium. The new décor, of crimson furnishings and patterned crimson panels contrasting with the French grey of walls and balustrades, is at once festive and cosy. The audience settles immediately into a mood of cheerful expectancy. Here once more is at least a perfect setting for Shakespeare.

The season opened gloomily with a production of *Twelfth Night* by Hugh Hunt. The gloom was in one sense actual. Roger Furse's costumes and settings for the play were on the grand scale, but it was a decayed grandeur. The Illyrian streets (Plate III A) had the peeling and water-worn dignity of a side-canal in Venice, Olivia's garden (Plate III B) the evergreen frowsiness of some great mansion where the family is seldom in residence. The dresses were of rich and weighty stuffs, but their colours were blacks and russets and sombre browns, the dash of scarlet in Antonio's cloak (and Malvolio's garters) positively swearing with the subfusc of the general effect. All this for the gentry; when the "members of the commonwealth" appeared on the stage (and, as will be seen, they did so only too often) it was in the garb of convicts. Seldom can the most high-spirited of Shakespeare's comedies have been presented against so glum and portentous a background.

What was the point of this drabness? If we are charitable we may take it as a reflexion of the producer's belief (more cynical by ten years than Lytton Strachey's) that Shakespeare was bored with comedy by the time he came to *Twelfth Night*, and in it exchanged his youthful delight in excess for disillusioned satire, his comic verve for perfunctory horse-play. This would explain the mechanical slickness with which the more farcical scenes were thrown off and thrown away, the absence of any pleasure (save malicious pleasure) in the raillery, and two staggering instances of miscasting. Ursula Jeans, for all the accomplishment of her acting, and the fluency and control of her speaking of verse, could not give Olivia precisely that unworldliness without which she must appear (at least to a modern audience) a monstrous bundle of vanities and affectations; and Leo McKern delivered both the lines and the music of Feste in an offhand style that said plainly "there is nothing to be made of this stuff".

Now *Twelfth Night* is certainly a mature comedy by comparison with, say, *The Merchant of Venice* or *A Midsummer Night's Dream*, but it is a wry mind that finds in it either disillusion or distaste. The alternative title *What You Will* is surely a token rather of the author's benevolence than of his boredom. As for Feste, we happen to know precisely why his part is what it is. In 1599 William Kemp, who had created the more orthodox clown roles of Dogberry and Touchstone, resigned his connexion with Shakespeare's company to become a free-lance entertainer, and his place as comic lead was taken by Robert Armin. By comparison with Kemp, Armin was a lightweight and an intellectual (he himself wrote comedies) whose strong points were his singing and his "slipper tongue". It was for this reason that Shakespeare wrote in for Feste not only the songs but the patter and word-play that depend for their effect on an unusually smooth and glib delivery. Such a gallimaufry of puns and nonsense might still be brought off by a virtuoso speaker with immense vitality and self-confidence.

But perhaps it was not so much Shakespeare that was bored with *Twelfth Night* as the producer himself; and indeed we have all seen and read the play so often that there is some excuse for feeling it to be hackneyed—why then present it at all?—or so easy and straightforward that little trouble need be given to its presentation. In fact, however, though familiarity may disguise it from us, *Twelfth Night* is (as far as language goes) an extremely difficult play, full of current slang and topical allusions beyond Shakespeare's other comedies. As the most mature of his essays in this genre it is also his nearest approach to the colloquial plays of London life and character for which Jonson at the turn of the century was beginning to set the fashion. Line after line of the dialogue makes a topical point that can be grasped to-day only with the aid of an erudite note. Yet the general drift is always clear, and the types portrayed so striking and universal that we tend to set up in our minds a precise picture of Malvolio, Sir Toby, or Sir Andrew, without any very exact remembrance or perhaps understanding of the words out of which they are formed. Hunt's production made the most of this tendency. The 'characters' were writ large in make-up and action, while the words, when not omitted, edited, or misapplied, were allowed, nay, assisted to go hang. Thus Paul Rogers's Malvolio, impressive at his first appearance, degenerated with the donning of his yellow stockings into pure butt and buffoon. Roger Livesey, made up as the pop-eyed military man on the cover of *Lilliput*, played Sir Toby with the good-humour and engaging reasonableness of Colonel Chinstrap, and might have carried it off; but the scene of his midnight carousal (to mention only one) was obliterated beneath the antics of the two knights with a ladder brought on, for no plausible reason, by Sir Andrew (Plate IV). They were certainly funny, but if we want such fun the place to go for it is the circus, where ladders are longer, the clowns are trained to the job, and buckets of whitewash are provided extra; where, too, we are spared the uneasy feeling that somewhere in the background a play is proceeding, which, could we but catch a word of it, might be worth the hearing.

This buffoonery overflowed every scene of the play and even the gaps between them. The sets had been admirably designed for rapid change without lowering the curtain, but their over-elaboration of detail made the operation, though speedy, a complicated one and quite an effort of adjustment to the new environment was required each time of the audience. To cover the physical and mental break the producer brought on a crowd of Illyrian peasants who capered and roared in chorus before the dissolving background. The same horror of gaps presumably inspired in him another piece of invention, though it was frequently employed even where no shift was to be made. This was the introduction in one scene of a character from the next who linked the two together like a held note in music. Unfortunately these 'suspensions by anticipation' often produced an unpleasant discord in the earlier scene. Thus when Maria arrived to congratulate the eavesdroppers she brought with her (all ready for the subsequent encounter with Viola) Feste. This called attention in the most blatant manner possible to the oddity of the substitution of Fabian for Feste in the box-tree (probably due to Armin's being, as we have seen, unsuited to knockabout), and to cover this a great deal of unnecessary and distracting byplay—surprise, resentment, malignant satisfaction—was required of the two. Similarly Aguecheek was present all through Olivia's declaration of love to Viola, and though this may be defended in the light of his subsequent assertion that he himself had witnessed Olivia's favours to the page, the actual sight of his face poking out of the box-tree is a discordant interruption in a scene of poetry. In planning such ingenuities, such irruptions of supers, such elaborations of 'business' a producer must ask himself three questions. Are they required by Shakespeare's text? No. Are they nevertheless a part of the necessary machinery of production on a modern stage? No—for where, after an indoor scene, the 'chorus' could not plausibly be introduced, the shift was made quite happily without it. Are they required for the translation of Shakespeare's intention into modern terms? No. Then away with them.

From a generally disastrous production it is all too easy to collect examples of how Shakespeare's comic points were missed, or masked, or bungled; but it is time to turn to the other, by many held the more important, the romantic half of the play. In this the producer seemed equally at sea. The miscasting of Olivia has already been noted, and Alec Clunes, playing Orsino with a fine blend of genuineness and affectation, had some ado to live down a series of misrepresentations and indignities. An opening scene in which the music was presented not as Orsino's self-indulgence but as a serenade to Olivia (Plate III A) made an entirely false impression; and surely the Duke might have been allowed more than three attendants before he offered, as escort to Viola, "Some four or five...all, if you will." Hunt would have spared himself (and his Orsino) a titter if he had sent on a few of his redundant supers here instead of between the scenes. Yet all such faults were more than redeemed by the exquisitely moving performance of Peggy Ashcroft as Viola. How far she herself controlled her own part in the production cannot be guessed, but at least her presence on the stage seems to have influenced the producer and dissuaded him from the worst extravagances. Where some 'bright idea' for the reinterpretation of Viola was admitted, it was in keeping and effective. Such was the impulsive variety of her speech and movement in her first scene; or the taking of the cry "Olivia" (the climax of the "Make me a willow cabin" speech) as a hastily remembered substitution for the "Orsino" that possessed her own thoughts. This was a performance that brought out every subtlety of music as of meaning in the part, and but for this many more seats must have stood empty after the first interval.

A month or two after *Twelfth Night* was first presented, the theatre was given up to eight performances by the Young Vic company of another Shakespearian comedy. *The Merchant of Venice* as directed by Glen Byam Shaw was in almost every respect the exact opposite of Hunt's *Twelfth Night*. It opened oddly enough with Antonio and his friends listening, in fixed attitudes, to music 'off', so that for a moment one almost imagined that here at last was the *Twelfth Night* mislaid on the previous visit. This time of course the effect was wrong. The *Merchant* provides an authentic albeit a mild example of a style of opening highly characteristic of Shakespeare, in which the effect is gained by suddenly plunging the audience into the middle of a conversation between the characters, and to substitute a tableau is to weaken it. This first false step, however, was also the last. The producer was by no means lacking in invention and daring. To take but one instance, Portia's application of her line "the moon sleeps with Endymion" to the dusky Jessica lying entranced with Lorenzo on the moonlit bank, was pretty and apt, though purists may frown at it, and drew a cloak of tenderness and humanity over the matrimonial squabbles of the final scene. Yet the aim was straight-forwardness and simplicity above all. A pair of structures, either side of the stage, in which variously patterned doors representing different locations could be rapidly substituted one for another, and instantly interchangeable backcloths, ensured that the scene could be shifted in the twinkling of an eye. There was little business, save some foolish pranks on the part of Morocco's followers, that was not in the spirit of the play, nothing interposed between the audience and the text, nothing that could be a drag upon the lively conduct of the intrigue. The slashing cuts, even, though they may be deplored, had clearly been made with a shrewd eye to the speeding of the play and scrupulous examination of what could best be spared—classical allusions, Elizabethan topicalities, Shylock's philosophizing over Laban and usury, and much of the brasher fun, for example the French and Scottish suitors *in toto* and Gobbo's final decline, at Belmont, into bawdy quibbling.

And how infinitely these earlier comedies gain from actors who have youth, and spring, and vitality ! The freshness and gaiety, of the ladies especially, together with the producer's good sense and the imaginative simplicity of Gay Dangerfield's settings, provided one of the most enjoyable and exhilarating evenings I have spent in the theatre for some time. Of course these comparatively inexperienced players were not capable of Miss Ashcroft's subtlety. The praiseworthy attempt to give every word its meaning and every line its due weight resulted sometimes in a mere absence of light and shade. A really flamboyant image, such as that of Antonio's wrecked silks "enrobing" the waters, might go for little where the values of *all* words were heightened; while dramatic innuendos were often made too prominent. Portia carries off her suspiciously clear recollection of Bassanio's name with "as I think so was he called"; to highlight this subterfuge with gasps and blushes is to make the heroine more of a novice than she is. Naturally those scenes and speeches made most effect that call for no more than honest plain speaking. John Garley's matter-of-fact and pawky Gobbo was a case in point, and so was a good, straight Bassanio by Keith Michell, who managed to suggest something warmer than mere cupboard

PLATE VII

Henry V. KATHARINE'S ENGLISH LESSON

PLATE VIII

A. *Henry V.* THE ENGLISH FORCE EMBARKS

B. *Henry V.* "WE HAPPY FEW, WE BAND OF BROTHERS"

love for the friend and the wife whose resources he exploits. The markedly Eastern Shylock of Powys Thomas was impressive in his clamour for justice or when in his desolation he cried, like his compatriots at the Wailing Wall, "all sorrows are mine"; but his graspingness and the exaggerated guile of his asides (Plate V) were more fitted to the Jew of Malta, and the force of "Hath not a Jew eyes?" spent itself in monotonous ferocity.

The senior company, returning in a second Shakespearian production, redeemed the disaster of their first. *Henry V* has already been largely rescued in our time from the disgrace under which it has for so long lain, regarded as a piece of jingoism in which Shakespeare paid sycophantic tribute to the powers that be. Even so, recent productions both on stage and screen have generally continued to present it primarily as a vehicle for pageantry and rhetorical magnificence, as a fine flight of the poet's, indeed, but very far above the earth. All the more credit then to Glen Byam Shaw and the Old Vic players for bringing out the earthy side of it. If indeed the prologues to the acts are read over with this in mind, it is immediately clear that what the author feared of his Globe was not lack of pageantry—the Elizabethan actor, with the Queen's cast-off clothing bought up to swell his wardrobe, could sport cloth-of-gold with the best—but lack of realism. To strain the march of events into two hours, the armed forces of "two mighty monarchies" into the wooden 'O' of the theatre—it was this Shakespeare despaired of doing.

If to bridge the gulf between make-believe and historic fact was really Shakespeare's intention, no better interpreter of it could have been found than the Chorus of Roger Livesey. Here was no formal Prologue, but an actor, in undress and with the inadequate resources of his stage exposed behind him (Plate VI A), come to plead for the audience's co-operation in the reconstruction of history in its very form and pressure. From the start he won our complete sympathy and loyalty. We enjoyed the irony of his lame excuses, the homely jokes about sea-sickness and aldermen. When he cried to us "Work, work your minds" we could almost feel our imaginations creaking into action. It is true that the great purple passages appeared a little watered—the night-scene in particular, though its setting, with Chorus himself illuminated as by the soldiers' watchfires, was especially suggestive; the rombustious bravado of the fleet's sailing came over well enough. Where Chorus so brilliantly achieves his main object, of getting the audience to grapple with the play, he may well be forgiven some of his high notes.

The lead of Chorus was strongly followed in all the scenes of the play proper. The dandified French were of course allowed their frills and finery, their canopies and their gold plate (Plate VI B); but Motley's settings and costumes as a whole emphasized the sober and the practical. Of set-pieces there was practically nothing, and the bareness of the stage, broken only by a few banners fluttering down from tall poles, created a powerful and moving impression of space and air and impending action. The physical setting was touched in, firmly and economically, with a few significant properties most skilfully placed—the masthead lights of the fleet awaiting Henry's embarkation (Plate VIII A), a couple of cannon, battered and grimy from hard use, two or three lumbering provision wagons, above all the actual persons of the English soldiers, their clothes stained and torn, their hurts bound with dirty bandages, their weapons shabby though workmanlike. The direction and acting of this 'crowd' matched its appearance, never obtrusive but always ready simply and succinctly to reinforce a point when required. Above all at those moments when this background of the common life and the ordinary citizen overflows into the centre of the stage: when, over the campfire, Bates, Court and Williams typify the fatalism and the resentment, the cantankerousness mixed with plain sense of the Tom, Dick and Harry who find themselves (as we so often lately) playing grudging parts in a real 'History'; or when the ruffled Williams blurts to his Commanding Officer the excuses of every honest old sweat—the admirable bluntness and lack of exaggeration with which such scenes were played gave great solidity to the whole.

Such is the framework of the play; what of its centrepiece? Alec Clunes might well have seemed an unlikely choice for the King. In recent years he has often appeared a too studied actor whose naturally commanding voice is carefully modulated and directed, and whose movements are precise with mannerisms; an ideal Orsino, he could hardly be expected to loosen into Harry the Fifth. All such doubts were instantly routed by the compelling reality of his first set speech—the rejection of the Dauphin's tennis-balls. The combination of inflexibility and of compassion for those who must suffer by it was exactly calculated, and yet all sense of calculation was lost in the free outpouring of speech. This tension, this control, and at the same time this naturalness, this ease, were never absent.

True, the speech before Harfleur did not come off, but that was less the actor's fault than the producer's. He had not realized that "Once more unto the breach" falls into two sections, the first addressed to the nobility, the second to the yeomen, or that, like all Henry's exhortations, it seems to appeal as much to the reason as to the blind heroism of its hearers. To ignore the division makes nonsense of the speech and throws away the only chance of introducing variety into what must otherwise be monotonous rodomontade. To deliver the speech as an extended battle-cry in the heat of action is to strain our credulity as well as our nerves. Some pause, some retiring-ground must be found (above all in a production aiming at realism) in which Henry, searching out the mode of appeal that will best fire each man to action, may proceed in due order to rally his followers. In the other great speeches the exploratory quality of Henry's argument was given free scope. Just because it began so quietly, so informally, "We few, we happy few, we band of brothers" gathered irresistible power as it proceeded, so that the climax was overwhelming; and in the speech on Commodity Clunes carried us with him through each turn of the King's thought. We were thus brought close to a Harry who was very much more than a heroic figure in a painted cloth. For one thing he seemed to bear at his back his whole family history from the preceding plays; and, though such things partly miss their effect when the whole sequence is not played consecutively, the heartfelt agony of the prayer before Agincourt, the quick turn of the head as the execution of Bardolph was confirmed, added extra dimensions, the son of the usurper and the dissolute young prince, to Harry the Conqueror. For another, this King was as happy in the homely scenes as in the heroics, and the wooing of the French princess had rare charm and lightness. In this he was greatly helped by the dainty Katharine of Dorothy Tutin, who had earlier brought down the house with an English lesson played with enchanting delicacy and spirit (Plate VII).

The charm of this Harry received a more dubious reinforcement from the producer's hand. In his anxiety to present a sympathetic portrait of a hero, Byam Shaw had juggled unfairly with light and shade and risked a sentimental one. Everything suggesting the harder, the politic side of the King's nature was cut—no killing of his prisoners, so approved by the practical soldier in Fluellen. On the other side the unattractiveness of his opponents was exaggerated. The faults of Shakespeare's French are venial—a braggart cowardice and that very fatuity with which the Dauphin taunts King Harry, of believing that battles can be won with a nimble galliard and that war is a sport like tennis in which the knack of the adept (and his dazzling equipment) are bound to tell. Disappointed of their confident hopes they snatch a sop to their warlike reputation in the killing of the boys of the English baggage-train; but chivalry can overlook even this lapse and still exchange compliments in a final reconciliation. In order, however, to engage the audience's loyalties more firmly on Harry's side, Byam Shaw sought to lend these rather frivolous foes the colours of a more recent and more deadly enemy of England, and their foppery, like Goering's medals and flash uniforms, covered not so much a cowardly feebleness as real viciousness and degeneracy. Paul Rogers's brutal Dauphin was vigorous and compelling, though it required some violence to the text (such as the cutting of the second French scene, which shows them in tamer mood), and certain of his excesses broke the cohesion of the play—the tray overturned in a tantrum, the peasant girl running from his drunken pursuit. Still, the presentation as a whole was, for an audience to whom the troublesome French of the 1590's are so many centuries below the horizon, a powerful strengthening to the play's realism.

Some of this ingenuity, nevertheless, might better have been turned to animating those dreadful stage-dummies, the bishops, who are liable to do such early and such severe damage to our sympathy for Henry. Shakespeare's audience took bishops and their authority so much for granted, that he had little need to guard against a misapprehension that would see in Canterbury and Ely a pair of scheming churchmen and in Henry a vain fool gulled into embarking on a shady adventure. The bishops need all the sanctification that the poetry of Shakespeare can give them; yet for a modern audience, uninterested in problems of royal succession, they must be shortened. Here is a real producer's problem, and it cannot be said that Byam Shaw solved it. To strip the bishops of everything save the barest exposition of the plot, to deny them even the glory of "the singing masons building roofs of gold", as here, is to confirm them mere intriguers, and the stature of the King, as the victim of their intrigue, is immeasurably diminished. It says much for the authority of Clunes's performance that he disposed of this grave initial handicap at a blow.

The winning humanity of the King, however achieved or reinforced, was reflected from him in all the lesser characters with whom he came in contact. Mention has already been made of the three soldiers at the campfire. The little groups of nobles, too, as Henry gathered them about him with humorous reassurances (Plate VIII B), kindled from him into personalities. Mark Dignam's busy Exeter, hard-bitten and genuine, was only the most striking of a striking team. Beyond the nobles the King's steadying influence extended to the working officers, and it was a joy to find a Fluellen who was not wholly caricature. The ruthless cutting of his part, which did not even spare the salmons of Monmouth and Macedon, no doubt helped in keeping him strictly to business and allowing no opportunity for deviations; but great credit must also go to William Devlin for a performance that cleverly balanced humanity with oddity. Only once did he topple to the chance of scoring an easy laugh, when in urging Captain Gower, in the interest of good discipline, to keep his voice down, he raised his own to a shout. This is a cheap joke and uncharacteristic of Fluellen, whose point (as Gower himself is later to impress upon the discomfited Pistol) is that pure eccentricities of manner disguise sound good sense as well as a generous heart.

And so to the comics—another producer's problem. For if the finer points of the King's conduct are lost to those in the audience who cannot connect this play with the three that go before it, without this connexion the comics lose all point. Unless the name Falstaff brings to our mind a crowd of associations, we are not open to the full force of a stroke of genius that employs a malapropism for the supreme assault on our emotions. The Bardolph and the Quickly of this play are little more than allusions to their former selves. The best that can be done—as with Costard and Launce and Gobbo and Dogberry and the rest of Shakespeare's clowns—is to play the parts straightforwardly and trust them to make their mark. Thus the natural gaminerie of Brian Smith (which wrecked last season's Moth, a very different character) carried the Boy triumphantly home; and Leo McKern, so unhappy as Feste, made a superbly vital Nym. But then Nym can be found in any bus or pub or workshop, though his 'humour' no doubt employs to-day another and more modern catch-phrase. Pistol, alas, is extinct. Certainly Robert Eddison, playing the part as a sort of gutter Osric, was not he, and one would have thought that the last means to choose for reanimating a "roaring boy" would be this effeminate posturing, this mincing drawl that flattened all the fun out of the frantic "I eat I eat I swear" and should certainly have called down more blows from Fluellen's cudgel. Yet with the promise of the junior company, the real achievement of the senior in our memory, we may have some confidence that even Shakespeare's Dodos may one day come to life again at the Old Vic.[1]

---

[1] Since this was written, the Governors of the Old Vic have announced the resignation of the director responsible for the two productions praised in this review, and the imminent disbanding of the Young Vic company.

PLATE IX

A. *Romeo and Juliet*, New York, 1951. Direction by PETER GLENVILLE;
Costumes and Settings by OLIVER MESSEL

B. *Hamlet*, Royal Netherlands Theatre, Antwerp, 1945

THE YEAR'S CONTRIBUTIONS TO SHAKESPEARIAN STUDY

I. CRITICAL STUDIES

reviewed by J. I. M. STEWART

Only a small number of substantial critical studies has become available for review in the period here covered. It seems likely that the increasing difficulties of publishers on both sides of the Atlantic are in part the explanation of this, since it is clear from the quantity of work appearing in journals that the race of Shakespearian commentators is in no danger of dying out. Nor do the commentators appear in any danger of running short of material, since they enjoy a constantly increasing scope in the discussion of one another's views. If, as is probable, the journals are soon constrained to further economies in point of space, these writers will do well to sacrifice, in the first place, the element of elaborate debate which is at present fashionable among them. Critical essays now frequently take the form of a progress through veritable thickets of contemporary opinion, so that the total effect is of little more than a babel of voices. A laudable sense of academic courtesy is one factor predisposing to this, as is also, perhaps, an influence from techniques of investigation that have proved notably successful in the natural sciences. But to read extensively in interpretative studies conducted in this manner is to experience a mild intellectual claustrophobia—or even a feeling that one is missing a good deal of the play as a result of the earnest, if not always lively, conference being conducted in the stalls. Many of those who write about Shakespeare might with great advantage—at least to themselves—write more directly. The hard fact is that when the impulse to do so is in abeyance the likelihood of interesting communication is small.

The year's most readable book on Shakespeare is an eccentric one. Why do we speak of stolen literary property as pirated? Surely, D. S. Savage supposes,[1] because of an extravagant joke which Shakespeare built into *Hamlet* in his first authorized text of the play, the Good Quarto of 1604. In the surreptitious text of 1603 there are no pirates for Hamlet to encounter; he has to make do with a storm at sea. In subsequently showing his prince as captured by pirates, therefore, the dramatist is providing an amusing exposure of the 'pirates' who captured his play. But this is not all. The capture of the prince was a put-up job; he had arranged it in advance—probably with a group of friends in the Danish navy. Was the pirating of the play, then, also a put-up job, and is Shakespeare in his additions amusingly giving himself away? Savage is sure of it. And he makes other notable discoveries of the same order. "As Hamlet personifies the Good Quarto", he gravely writes, "so Laertes would seem to be put forward as a personification of the Bad". This is Shakespearian investigation as the late Heath Robinson might have given it to us, or such as Mr Emett might evolve when not absorbed with the Oyster Creek and Far Tottering Railway. Sir Walter Raleigh once remarked that if he couldn't have his poetry good he liked it rum. Something of the same consideration may be applied in the present field.

---

[1] D. S. Savage, *Hamlet and the Pirates. An Exercise in Literary Detection* (Eyre and Spottiswoode, 1950).

We may now turn to more serious endeavour. Willard Farnham, whose *Medieval Heritage of Elizabethan Tragedy* is widely known as a distinguished contribution to historical criticism, has written a study, more strictly interpretative in kind, of the later development of Shakespearian tragedy.[1] He is chiefly concerned with four heroes: Timon, Macbeth, Antony and Coriolanus. These—"deeply flawed but noble-spirited tragic figures"—evidence in Shakespeare a pursuit of moral paradox having many parallels in the literature of the opening years of the seventeenth century. Earlier, in Brutus, Shakespeare had been the first English playwright to rediscover the Aristotelian conception of the noble hero with a tragic flaw, and had thus "made it possible for English tragedy to reach a greatness hitherto attained only by Greek tragedy". Brutus is, of course, essentially noble, and a hero entirely in consonance with the principles of the *Poetics*. So, too, are the protagonists who immediately succeed him; with all their faults they are nothing if not admirable characters. Over against these stand the heroes of the final tragedies—rare spirits so deeply tainted that the taint is apparently inseparable from their heroic greatness. And with them we come, as it were, to the frontier of Shakespeare's tragic art, for in these plays he is exploring territory "in which defects of human nature, including viciousness ...can take on dignity through a quality in their very being". This, if correctly phrased, is certainly mysterious, as Farnham acknowledges on his first page. His subsequent analysis of his chosen heroes—from Timon, "most capable of winning admiration when he might seem to be least deserving of it", to Coriolanus, "a man who is supremely guilty of pride the vice and at the same time supremely noble in pride the virtue"—is full of interest, and is made in the light of a wide knowledge of the history of ethical theory and persuasion. It would be an unreasonable expectation, no doubt, that the 'mystery' here forthrightly and learnedly tackled should be entirely dissipated at the close of the book.

Another writer concerned to consider individual plays in the light of a general conception of tragedy is Clifford Leech.[2] He accepts I. A. Richards's thesis that the tragic effect resides in an equilibrium of opposing forces; rejects Una Ellis-Fermor's suggestion that the balance is between the view that the world is controlled by an alien and hostile destiny and the view that somehow this apparent evil may be explained in terms of good; and goes on to maintain that the true tension of tragedy lies between our terror before a "revelation of evil methodized" and our pride in man's ability to withstand with fortitude the operation of a 'justice' that is at best utterly inhuman and remote. Leech concludes that the tragic picture is incompatible with the Christian faith, or with any form of religious belief that assumes the existence of a personal and kindly God. This view, which runs sharply counter to one increasingly important current interpretation of Shakespearian drama, must be admitted to have cogency. Nevertheless, it is a view before which difficulties arise. There is no evidence that devout persons find themselves excluded from, or offended by, the experience of tragedy, or that the kind flourishes best upon a desuetude of the religious response to life. Tragedy may indeed be characteristically a product of the encroachment of scepticism upon a traditional and still powerfully felt religious faith, as appears to have been the case with Thomas Hardy. Leech's book is both widely-ranging and

---

[1] Willard Farnham, *Shakespeare's Tragic Frontier* (University of California Press; Cambridge University Press, 1950).

[2] Clifford Leech, *Shakespeare's Tragedies and Other Studies in Seventeenth-Century Drama* (Chatto and Windus, 1950).

stimulating, and around his central contention he has disposed much felicitous and illuminating comment, particularly on the later plays.

S. C. Sen Gupta has written a book[1] of somewhat the same scope in the field of comedy, and he, too, begins with an investigation of the nature of the literary kind with which he has to deal. From this he proceeds through an account of the rise and development of English comedy in general to a consideration of the cardinal principles of Shakespearian comedy and thence to an examination of the individual plays and their interrelations. Comedy, Sen Gupta holds, always exploits deviations from truth or reality. The comedy of criticism is concerned with the pretence and absurdity inherent in individual departures from what is felt as the true role of man in society. The comedy of escape affords a holiday from the difficult business of seeing and maintaining life as a serious and sensible business. It is characteristic of the greater writers, such as Cervantes, Shakespeare, Molière and Shaw, that in their work the two kinds are perpetually in a quickening interchange. In the light of this broad controlling conception Sen Gupta reviews not only the romantic comedies proper but also the dark comedies, the comic element in the tragedies, and the final plays. A concluding chapter on Falstaff takes exception to Quiller-Couch's statement that the character is "built on the old Morality structure imported through the Interlude", and argues that what is here striking about Shakespeare's greatest comic creation is his fundamental difference from the Vice of the medieval Moralities. This is a thoroughly well-informed and at the same time pleasingly independent work.

A scholarly work of more specialized interest comes from Italy.[2] Anna Maria Crinò surveys the rise and growth there of an interest in Shakespeare, and proceeds to a literary study of a number of eighteenth-century translations of individual plays, including some translations still unpublished. She records the curious fact that Hamlet's story was first dramatized in Italy in 1705 by a playwright unaware of the existence of Shakespeare's tragedy, but with Saxo Grammaticus as his ultimate source. This small but entirely adequate book adds an important chapter to the history of the plays on the Continent. It must be warmly welcomed both for its own merits and as representative of learned concern with Shakespeare in the country from which so much of his inspiration was drawn.

Again of specialized interest—but of a very different sort—are certain chapters dealing with Shakespeare in a volume of posthumously published papers by the late Ella Freeman Sharpe. At the time of her death, it appears, the writer was preparing an extended study of the plays in the light of the principles of Freudian psycho-analysis, and of this material certain parts were sufficiently far advanced to be published.[3] One paper, accepting Ernest Jones's well-known work as making clear "the unresolved Œdipus conflict which is the fundamental problem" of *Hamlet*, proceeds "to gather from the play the lighting-up of the regressive movement of the libido due to the retreat from the central Œdipus difficulty", and to conclude from this—by arguments not altogether lucid to a lay reader—that *Hamlet* is a tragedy not of procrastination but of impatience. A longer paper entitled 'From *King Lear* to *The Tempest*' makes these plays

[1] S. C. Sen Gupta, *Shakespearian Comedy* (Calcutta: Oxford University Press, 1950).

[2] Anna Maria Crinò, *Le Traduzioni di Shakespeare in Italia nel Settecento* (Rome: Edizioni di Storia e Letteratura, 1950).

[3] Ella Freeman Sharpe, *Collected Papers on Psycho-analysis* (The International Psycho-Analytical Library, no. 36; Hogarth Press, 1950).

an occasion for discussing the role of regression in manic-depression. In the course of it we read: "I realized that three hundred years after the creation of this play, even for a partial understanding...one needs an inner conviction of psycho-analytical facts and the methods of ascertaining them". But it may be doubted whether, upon consideration, the broad conclusions arrived at here would be found very unfamiliar to literary students. A further, and unfinished, paper on *Hamlet* proceeds upon the assumption that "the play, both as a whole and in its parts, [is] more likely to yield understanding of its creator than is obtainable by concentration on the individual character of Hamlet as identifiable with the poet". The grammar of this is confused, but the sense is clear, and again the literary reader will scarcely quarrel with it. These papers are perhaps a little inclined to lose sight of the very special sense in which they afford an 'understanding' of their subject, and they scarcely do justice to their writer's talent. Of much greater importance to the critic is an inquiry into the psychology of metaphor and figurative language. But this, being virtually unconcerned with Shakespeare, is outside our present interest.

Esoteric in quite another fashion is Beryl Pogson's interpretation of some of the plays.[1] As not infrequently in writing of this kind, one is aware of a rather baffling mingling of sensitive response and strained argument. That the most lamentable comedy of Pyramus and Thisbe is designed to promote in us "a vision of the illusions of this mortal life", or that the passion of Antony and Cleopatra is a representation of Divine Union having a near analogue in the Song of Songs, or again that the "strange invisible perfume" floating from the barge on Cydnus is related to the Holy Spirit that "cometh up like a pillar of smoke, perfumed with myrrh and frankincense", is not a proposition to which all readers will very certainly assent. But on the whole the writer avoids the excesses of subjective interpretation, and her search for an allegorical continuum running through the plays is often thoughtful and suggestive.

If Pogson is remote from Sharpe, so is F. S. Boas from either in a volume of essays brought together under the title *Queen Elizabeth in Drama*.[2] Nothing here is offered by way of interpretation, and the suggestion of the book is rather that of a formal visitation to a familiar library. A wide field of literary history is checked over and found to be still in place. The process is a little time-consuming, but we nevertheless know ourselves to be fortunate in the learning and urbanity of our guide. In "Joan of Arc in Shakespeare, Schiller, and Shaw" the same writer has printed elsewhere a straightforward comparative study leading to the conclusion that the Joan of 1 *Henry VI*, although inconsistently and—at the close—repellently portrayed, is studied more for her own sake, and less in terms of one or another ideology, than in Schiller or Shaw.[3]

Hamlet, almost inevitably, is the play which has received most attention in the journals. J. J. Lawlor addresses himself to a familiar question: Why does Hamlet delay his revenge?[4] There is a clue in Tourneur's *Atheist's Tragedy* and Chapman's *Revenge of Bussy D'Ambois*, both plays demonstrably influenced by *Hamlet*, in which "the duty of revenge is called into question throughout". This major variation upon the primitive revenge play, "the debating the issue

---

[1] Beryl Pogson, *In the East My Pleasure Lies. An Esoteric Interpretation of some Plays of Shakespeare* (Stuart and Richards, 1950).

[2] F. S. Boas, *Queen Elizabeth in Drama and Related Studies* (Allen and Unwin, 1950).

[3] *Shakespeare Quarterly*, II (January 1951), 35–45.

[4] 'The Tragic Conflict in *Hamlet*', *Review of English Studies*, n.s., 1 (April 1950), 97–113.

Revenge versus Justice, following as it does on Shakespeare's *Hamlet* and owing much in incidental matter and phrase to *Hamlet*, may demonstrate what Shakespeare's immediate audience and his fellow dramatists apprehended in *Hamlet*—a reluctance to act which springs from a scruple about the justice of Revenge". But why does Shakespeare not make this explicit? Because, Lawlor thinks, "in the presentation it is of the highest importance that the hero shall not *openly* call in question the ethics or the efficacy of Revenge. Do that, and the thematic unity is broken; we pass from tragic intensity to controversial ardour". The tragic conflict in the play is that between Revenge and Justice. But not only does Hamlet not admit this; it is unknown to him. "Shakespeare's triumph is to make the hero fail to understand himself...Hamlet delays his revenge on Claudius because of an aversion from the deed of vengeance, an aversion whose true nature remains hidden from him, but is apprehended by the Elizabethan audience as a deep-seated scruple about the justice of Revenge." Lawlor does not go on to consider what the Elizabethan audience made of Hamlet's unawareness of the ethical struggle within himself. Modern critics have been lavish in the provision of furniture for Hamlet's unconscious mind. Here is an accession. J. V. Cunningham, however, contends that criticism of this sort falsifies the Elizabethan conception of tragic conflict.[1] Analysing the twenty-four passages in which *tragedy* or one of its derivatives occurs in Shakespeare's works, he concludes that for the dramatist the distinguishing mark of tragedy is violent death; the tragic attitude, the attitude toward death; the tragic effects, those appropriate to violent death—as fear, sorrow and wonder. It follows that "the effect of tragedy is...not infinitely subtle but quite obvious". "Many of the notions which we associate with tragedy are not to be found in Shakespeare....The tragedy of *Hamlet* is the holocaust which concludes it, and the tragedy of Hamlet himself is his death." Marco Mincoff, examining the structure of the tragedies, finds "a fairly definite pattern" which is followed more strictly in *Hamlet* than in the other plays.[2] "Every structural feature of that tragedy can be matched in the majority of the remaining ones, while each deviation from the pattern of *Hamlet* stands alone and can easily be explained through the special circumstances of the play in question." John Paterson finds in *Hamlet*[3] an "intensely critical, almost disillusionist, attitude...towards language"; traces through the play "an explicit hostility to language as speech divorced from thought and real motive"; and relates this to the central principle of the tragedy, "the confusion of appearance with reality". D. R. Godfrey has been thinking along somewhat similar lines. In 'The Player's Speech in *Hamlet*: A New Approach' he considers the purpose and significance of what may appear a mere excrescence upon the play.[4] To maintain simply that Shakespeare wrote the speech to outdo or burlesque Marlowe and Nashe convicts the dramatist of halting the action of his tragedy for personal and inartistic motives. Is there some other explanation? The substance of the speech, Godfrey believes, is a forceful and imaginative reproduction of Hamlet's own story, and its bombastic form has dramatic point because Hamlet's spiritual transformation in the course of the play may be viewed in terms of a changing attitude to rant. "Rant at Elsinore is atavistic, outmoded like the Players who still declaim it, a sign, in particular in

[1] '"Tragedy" in Shakespeare', *ELH*, XVII (March 1950), 36–46.
[2] 'The Structural Pattern of Shakespeare's Tragedies', *Shakespeare Survey*, 3 (1950), 58–65.
[3] 'The Word in *Hamlet*', *Shakespeare Quarterly*, II (January 1951), 47–55.
[4] *Neophilologus*, XXXIV (July 1950), 162–9.

Laertes, of arrested development." To the unending debate on this play there have been yet further contributions which can receive only bare mention: Ernst Weigelin's 'Hamlets Selbstbetrug',[1] K. Smidt's 'Notes on *Hamlet*',[2] Edward Duncan's 'Unsubstantial Father: A Study of the *Hamlet* Symbolism in Joyce's *Ulysses*',[3] and John R. Moore's 'A Spanish Hamlet'.[4] Elsinore remains, moreover, a happy hunting-ground for purely fanciful writers, as is evidenced by Michael Innes and Rayner Heppenstall in a series of entertainments originally broadcast in the B.B.C's Third Programme.[5]

There has been some interesting writing on other of the major tragedies. Most notable, here, perhaps, are two papers by Kenneth Muir. These admirably exemplify the exciting rewards in criticism that may succeed upon "the dull duty of an editor". In 'The Uncomic Pun'[6] Muir prosecutes a close analysis of numerous puns, quibbles and ambiguities in *Macbeth* in an endeavour to determine their dramatic function, and concludes that the serious pun serves four main purposes in dramatic poetry. It provides an illogical reinforcement of the logical sequence of thought. It often links together unrelated imagery and acts as a solvent for mixed metaphors. It makes the listener aware of a complex of ideas which enrich the total statement. And it promotes a use of language which seems "to shoot out roots in all directions, so that the poetry is firmly based on reality". The banishing of the pun from the Restoration stage except for comic purposes was the symbol of a radical defect, a turning away from the genius of the language. "Great drama went out with the serious pun because by its use Shakespeare and other Jacobean dramatists were able to bring into their plays a much wider range of experience." Muir's judgement here may appear a little to overstate a case. But his essay is admirably considered—not least so in wisely avoiding the cloudy theme of the psychology of wit—and is based upon material much of which is new, and important for the close study both of *Macbeth* and of a general linguistic problem. In 'Samuel Harsnett and *King Lear*'[7] Muir works from the same close scrutiny of a text. He shows that Shakespeare's indebtedness to *A Declaration of Egregious Popish Impostures* is more extensive than the vigilance of editors has hitherto remarked. But this essay does much more than add some new footnotes to *King Lear*. It is an accession to our knowledge of the manner in which Shakespeare's mind played upon literary material. Of *King Lear* itself two further studies may here be mentioned. J. C. Maxwell is concerned with the tragedy as "a Christian play about a pagan world" and with the effects achieved by Shakespeare through this duality.[8] Examining the various modes of invocation employed, he finds that "self-confident paganism fades out as Lear's mind changes....We are witnessing the break-up of a religious outlook that based itself naively on the pagan pantheon". In 'The Poetry of the Storm in *King Lear*' George W. Williams presents an able and elaborate linguistic analysis of the lines opening the second scene in Act III.[9]

[1] *Shakespeare-Jahrbuch*, LXXXII–LXXXIII (1948), 99–102.
[2] *English Studies*, XXXI (August 1950), 136–41.
[3] *University of Toronto Quarterly*, XIX (January 1950), 126–40.
[4] *Modern Language Review*, XLV (October 1950), 512.
[5] *Three Tales of Hamlet* (Gollancz, 1950).
[6] *The Cambridge Journal*, III (May 1950), 472–85.
[7] *Review of English Studies*, n.s. II (January 1951), 11–21.
[8] 'The Technique of Invocation in King Lear', *Modern Language Review*, XLV (April 1950), 142–7.
[9] *Shakespeare Quarterly*, II (January 1951), 57–71.

Of *Othello* there have been substantial studies by Hoover H. Jordan[1] and Frank Prentice Rand[2], while Derek Traversi[3] has explored with some subtlety the implications of the view that Othello and Iago are "beneath the obvious division, complementary figures in a coherent poetic mood". In 'The Imagery of *Romeo and Juliet*'[4] E. C. Pettet examines "the note of Fate and premonition, affecting characters and audience alike, with which Shakespeare invests every major development of his story". In particular, from the moment of the hasty, secret marriage of the lovers, "the atmosphere grows heavy and portentous with doom...at every important juncture in the rest of the play the lips of the lovers are touched with premonition". Bertrand Evans has also contributed to the study of this play, writing a long essay on 'The Brevity of Friar Laurence'.[5] This year the Roman plays do not come prominently under notice. Mention must, however, be made of Marvin Felheim's 'The Problem of Time in *Julius Caesar*'.[6] In the face of much "mystifying exegesis" by previous students of time-analysis, the writer endeavours to show that "time in this tragedy need raise no problem at all if the reader pays attention to what Shakespeare has to say". What attention Shakespeare himself paid to the clues thus entered upon may to some appear a little uncertain. The English history plays, too, have been less popular than usual: nevertheless, several studies call for notice. Robert Adger Law examines 'Deviations from Holinshed in *Richard II*'.[7] In 'Bolingbroke's "Decision"' Brents Stirling[8] considers the element of political doctrine in the same play, and its revelation integrally with progressive growth of plot and of characterization. The inner mind of Bolingbroke becomes clear when we realize that he is the living symbol of opportunism, and that opportunism is essentially a tacit vice. He is aware in a sense of the ends to which his means commit him, but he relies upon events to clarify his purposes. His portrayal presents at once a subtle study in psychological realism and a moral judgement upon a code of political behaviour. In 'The Courtship Scene in *Henry V*',[9] Paul A. Jorgensen contrasts the condemnations of literary critics with E. E. Stoll's "practical observation that 'the wooing scene itself...must have been enough to float the play'"; goes on to show how Shakespeare relied for his success upon popular appreciation of the plain soldier as a literary convention; and proceeds to a widely ranging comparative study of the type as evidenced in both the dramatic and the non-dramatic writing of the time.

The romantic comedies are apparently out of favour—perhaps because it becomes steadily more apparent that they are apt to elude the weighty approaches of the learned. The problem comedies, however, continue to be vigorously debated. In 'Virtue is the True Nobility'[10] M. C. Bradbrook presents an able and characteristic study of *All's Well that Ends Well*. The play fails, she declares, "because Shakespeare was trying to write a moral play" with characters having "a symbolic and extra-personal significance" and Shakespeare "was not happy when he

[1] 'Dramatic Illusion in *Othello*', *Shakespeare Quarterly*, I (July 1950), 146-52.
[2] 'The Over Garrulous Iago', *ibid.* pp. 155-61.
[3] 'Othello', *The Wind and the Rain*, VI (Spring 1950), 248-69.
[4] *English*, VIII (Autumn 1950), 121-6.   [5] *PMLA*, LXV (September 1950), 841-65.
[6] *Huntington Library Quarterly*, XIII (August 1950), 399-405.
[7] *University of Texas Studies in English*, XXIX (1950), 91-101.
[8] *Shakespeare Quarterly*, II (January 1951), 27-34.
[9] *Modern Language Quarterly*, XI (June 1950), 180-8.
[10] *Review of English Studies*, n.s., I (October 1950), 289-301.

was theorizing". One suspects that the writer is here not wholly unconscious of a little trailing her gown. But the essay has many admirable perceptions. "The juxtaposition of the social problem of high birth versus native merit and the human problem of unrequited love recall the story of the Sonnets; the speeches of Helena contain echoes from the Sonnets, but the story to which her great speeches are loosely tied does not suit their dramatic expression." *Measure for Measure* continues to be among the most discussed of Shakespeare's plays. Robert M. Smith takes occasion of the Stratford production to exhibit and discuss the bewildering diversity of interpretations attempted in recent years.[1] Willie Sypher[2] examines the element of casuistry in the play. Clifford Leech, a volume of whose essays has already been noticed, has also given us an essay entitled 'The "Meaning" of *Measure for Measure*'.[3] Its burden is the hazardousness of extracting any simple thesis from a work in which an almost baffling complexity of meanings is the predominant feature. *The Winter's Tale* is the last play to attract the interest of several critics. Paul N. Siegel considers Leontes in the light of the Elizabethan concept of the tyrant as a monarch who—like Richard III and Macbeth—fails to maintain in himself a right subjugation of passion to reason.[4] F. D. Hoeniger attempts[5] "a revaluation based on a new and revolutionary interpretation of the play's meaning...especially at variance with the still prevailing view first formulated by Lytton Strachey". Only if we approach *The Winter's Tale* as an allegory can we do justice to its greatness. "Such passages as the famous discussion on art and nature in Act IV can be integrated into the whole meaning of the play only if we go beyond the literal level of interpretation". By doing so we shall find that the symbolism of the play "revolves around the life-death-life pattern of nature and of human existence". Four themes are suggested alike by the fable and the imagery: identity between parents and children; summer, winter and the rebirth of nature; youth, age, death and resurrection; art or the creative imagination, and its relation to nature. Richard Wincor[6] considers both *The Winter's Tale* and the other final plays in their relationship to traditional 'festival Drama'—by which he means drama growing out of seasonal rites and worship. This is an interesting essay upon a theme not easily exhausted. Most of the plays, in fact, might be commented in terms of it.

Of numerous papers on miscellaneous topics several particularly deserve mention. T. Walter Herbert has had the excellent idea of examining the structure and movement of Shakespeare's verse in passages preluding the entries of the various ghosts in the plays.[7] He shows how the tempo, texture and syntax are regularly modified for the purposes of achieving an effective introduction of the supernatural. In 'Words Out of a Hat? Alliteration and Assonance in Shakespeare's *Sonnets*',[8] Ulrich K. Goldsmith supports E. E. Stoll, as against B. F. Skinner, in the view that conscious art directs Shakespeare's alliterative practice. Goldsmith first considers the poet's alliterative technique against the historical background of English versification

[1] 'Interpretations of *Measure for Measure*', *Shakespeare Quarterly*, I (October 1950), 208–18.
[2] 'Shakespeare as Casuist: *Measure for Measure*', *Sewanee Review*, LVIII (Spring 1950), 262–80.
[3] *Shakespeare Survey*, 3 (1950), 66–73.
[4] 'Leontes a Jealous Tyrant', *Review of English Studies*, n.s., I (October 1950), 302–7.
[5] 'The Meaning of *The Winter's Tale*', *University of Toronto Quarterly*, XX (October 1950), 11–26.
[6] 'Shakespeare's Festival Plays', *Shakespeare Quarterly*, I (October 1950), 219–40.
[7] 'Shakespeare Announces a Ghost', *Shakespeare Quarterly*, I (October 1950), 247–54.
[8] *J.E.G.P.* XLIX (January 1950), 33–48.

in the sixteenth century, passes to a particular examination of a number of sonnets and sonnet lines, and concludes with a searching study of the interrelation of alliteration and assonance. M. Willson Disher has written a short series of papers entitled—somewhat ambitiously—'The Trend of Shakespeare's Thought'.[1] Attempting in the first place to measure Sir Philip Sidney's influence over Shakespeare, he concludes that the latter's "discipleship to Sidney was fanatical". Shakespeare wholeheartedly accepted the "creed of virtue set forth in *Arcadia*" and, above all, its "ideal of friendship as the only true love". Disher then proceeds to consider "new ideas caused by the reinstatement of Mary Fytton". The autobiographical character of the plays, he believes, "can no longer be denied" in the light of what we can confidently conjecture of Shakespeare's involvement in her story. It is in fact possible to spy out enough of his personal history to explain "consistently and coherently the whole trend of [his] thought down to the mental collapse over *Timon*". It seems likely that the impact of Disher's ideas will not be in the main upon the literary criticism of Shakespeare.

Finally, it must be noted that to *Shakespeare Survey*, 3, F. P. Wilson contributes a paper[2] which may be called, strictly, a model in its kind, since it adds to knowledge unobtrusively and gracefully, and with a Shakespearian understanding of where to stop off. Do you find it hard not to trumpet discoveries and labour points? Read these seven pages.

2. SHAKESPEARE'S LIFE, TIMES AND STAGE

reviewed by CLIFFORD LEECH

In further illustration of Shakespeare as a "learned grammarian" T. W. Baldwin has turned to the non-dramatic poems and has explored in characteristic detail his debt to Ovid and the Renascence commentators.[3] But in addition, by considering together passages from the poems and the plays where Shakespeare uses the same image, Baldwin tries to arrange them in chronological order on the assumption that the simpler form of the image and the less condensed expression will "almost certainly" be the earlier. Thus in *Venus and Adonis* the young man is anxious to keep "a false sound" from entering "the quiet closure of my breast", which he calls the "bedchamber" of his heart; in *Richard III* Rivers, invoking Pomfret Castle, refers to the murder of Richard II "Within the guilty closure of thy walls"; in Sonnet 48 "the gentle closure of my breast" is a prison, as in *Richard III*, in which the loved one can come and go at will. Although the verbal resemblance is greatest between *Venus and Adonis* and Sonnet 48, Baldwin believes that the *Richard III* passage intervened, introducing into the image the notion of a prison. Evidence is thus produced for the dating of the *Sonnets* and the early plays. The *Sonnets* are shown to have been written during the years 1593-9, and to have comprised six approximately equal series of some twenty-five sonnets each: each series would fill a quire of paper, and would be accompanied by one or more dedicatory sonnets. Baldwin accepts Southampton as the patron, but rejects the notion that the poet's personal history is recorded.

[1] *Times Literary Supplement*, 20 October, 27 October and 3 November 1950.
[2] 'Shakespeare's Reading', pp. 14–21.
[3] *On the Literary Genetics of Shakspere's Poems and Sonnets* (Urbana: University of Illinois Press, 1950).

The Dark Lady is "a literary paradox", close companion to Rosaline and Phoebe. It is perhaps significant that he has little to say on Sonnet 129.

By taking the *Sonnets* as literary exercises Baldwin is saved from the profitless speculation into which so many have fallen, but that there is an alternative snare is made evident by his use of the word 'genetics'. He assumes that Shakespeare will know every line of the poems as well as Baldwin himself does, that his poetic practice is akin to that of the scientist who can proceed from experiment to experiment because each step has been carefully recorded in a note-book. Especially in a dramatic context, an image may be introduced incidentally and may not fully recall to the poet any previous use he has made of it. In the examples given above, it would surely be possible for 'closure' to be used simply for a prison, as in *Richard III*, even though Shakespeare had earlier elaborated the prison-motive in Sonnet 48. This would apply also to sonnets written some time apart. Though we are greatly in Baldwin's debt for the light he has thrown on Renascence learning and its availability, we may question his picture of a poet at work.

The *Sonnets* have also been discussed by way of further comment on Leslie Hotson's *Shakespeare's Sonnets Dated*. Hotson has brought forward additional references to the Armada's crescent-shape, made immediately after the defeat,[1] but opinion seems to be hardening against *c.* 1589 as the date of composition: Alfred Harbage[2] finds it impossible to believe that Shakespeare could have achieved maturity of style in some of the sonnets, only to lose it again in the narrative poems and the early plays; Edward Hubler[3] suggests that Hotson too readily assumes that the quality and character of writing is wholly dependent on the person or public addressed; F. W. Bateson[4] argues cogently that, in order that the parallelism between the first and second quatrains of Sonnet 107 may be preserved, "the mortall Moone" must be an object threatened (the public analogue of "my true love") and not the threat itself. The date 1603, preferred by Harbage[5] and F. S. Boas[6], may seem late for Sonnet 107 but is by no means so difficult to accept as 1589. Bateson joins with Arthur J. Perrett[7] and G. Wilson Knight[8] in insisting that Cleopatra, and not Antony's fleet, is "our terrene moone".

Another series of conjectures began with the publication of three articles by M. Willson Disher,[9] among whose fancies we may list a denial that the Dark Lady was truly dark, a deduction that after all she may have been Mary Fytton, a suggestion that the first seventeen sonnets were addressed to Southampton and the following ones to Pembroke, an implication that the period of sonnet-writing came to an end just before the composition of the Last Plays, and an identification of the Rival Poet with Spenser, his "affable familiar ghost" being Harvey.

[1] 'The Date of Shakespeare's Sonnets', *Times Literary Supplement*, 2 June 1950.

[2] 'Dating Shakespeare's Sonnets', *Shakespeare Quarterly*, 1 (April 1950), 57–63.

[3] Review of *Shakespeare's Sonnets Dated*, *Shakespeare Quarterly*, 1 (April 1950), 78–83.

[4] 'Elementary, My Dear Hotson! A Caveat for Literary Detectives', *Essays in Criticism*, 1 (January 1951), 81–8.

[5] Harbage suggests that the pyramids of Sonnet 123 could be the pyramidal structures erected in London to welcome James.

[6] *Times Literary Supplement*, 7 July 1950. Boas cites a parallel between Sonnet 107 and Joseph Hall's *The King's Prophecie* (1603).

[7] *Ibid.* 16 June 1950.

[8] *Ibid.* 14 July 1950.

[9] 'The Trend of Shakespeare's Thought', *Times Literary Supplement*, 20 October, 27 October, 3 November 1950.

Correspondents of the *Times Literary Supplement* proceeded to remind us that the Rival Poet could be Chapman or Marlowe, provoking Lawrence Durrell[1] to suggest that the claims of Kyd and Greene had been overlooked.

We tread on altogether firmer ground when reading Levi Fox's account of the recent discovery of a seventeenth-century copy of Shakespeare's will,[2] and J. Dover Wilson's persuasive argument (which will doubtless have its sequel in the New Cambridge *Henry VI*) that in the *Groatsworth of Wit* Greene was attacking Shakespeare as a plagiary.[3] F. S. Boas's recent collection of papers[4] includes 'Queen Elizabeth, the Revels Office and Edmund Tilney', 'Aspects of Shakespeare's Reading', and 'Ovid and the Elizabethans'. We may correct the statement that the Phaeton legend is mentioned by Shakespeare only in *Romeo and Juliet*, and the reference to the two titles of Marston's *Sophonisba* as constituting two plays. Boas's interpretation of the concluding reference to Mercury in *Love's Labour's Lost* may be doubted, and in mentioning the Calyphas incident in *Tamburlaine* he seems to overlook its ironic implications. But these things do not hinder one's enjoyment of the book's freshness and enthusiasm.

The year has seen the appearance of two straightforward biographies. Miss Marcette Chute[5] has given the general reader a thoroughly acceptable book, wisely reserving the sonnets for an appendix. Her picture is slightly rose-tinted, and she is in no way concerned with the climate of Elizabethan thought. A few of her statements might be questioned, as that the author's manuscript was used as a prompt-copy, or that the name 'Oldcastle' was changed before the writing of 2 *Henry IV*, and one might wish that she had not rigorously avoided reference to her sources. But the writing has been sensibly done. D. Waldo Clarke's book[6] is intended mainly for foreign students and gives a workmanlike sketch of Shakespeare's life and career. A few corrections are needed: the publication-date of *Campaspe* is given as 1579, Greene and Peele are described as writing only for private stages, and we are told that prose is only occasional in the tragedies, "usually for moments of comic relief". Not every reader will agree that the Last Plays "show no sense of strain".[7]

---

[1] *Times Literary Supplement*, 5 January 1951. In *Notes and Queries*, CXCV (18 March, 13 May, 2 September 1950), 114–15, 205–6, 385–6, H. A. Shield has put forward some further 'Links with Shakespeare': he identifies the poet with Houghton's Shakeshaft, and has a William Hughes for 'Mr W. H.' He has a theory for Shakespeare's access to Alan Keen's copy of Hall. Cecil G. Gray, *ibid.* (23 December 1950), 558–9, has his own notion on this last matter, making Shakespeare the tutor of Lord Herbert of Cherbury.

[2] 'An Early Copy of Shakespeare's Will', *Shakespeare Survey*, 4 (1951), 69–77.

[3] 'Malone and the Upstart Crow', *Shakespeare Survey*, 4 (1951), 56–68.

[4] *Queen Elizabeth in Drama and Related Studies* (Allen and Unwin, 1950). Further suggestions concerning Shakespeare's reading are made by A. D., '"Henry IV" Part Two and the Homily against Drunkenness', *Notes and Queries*, CXCV (15 April 1950), 160–2, and by Murray Abend, 'Some Biblical Influences in Shakespeare's Plays', *ibid.* (23 December 1950), 554–8.

[5] *Shakespeare of London* (New York: Dutton, 1949; London: Secker and Warburg, 1950).

[6] *William Shakespeare* (Longmans, Green; Essential English Library, 1950).

[7] William Bliss has published *Yorick's Crib to the Examination Paper on Shakespeare in 'The Real Shakespeare'* (Sidgwick and Jackson, 1949), an innocent codicil to his fanciful account of Shakespeare, reviewed in *Shakespeare Survey*, 1. W. J. Fraser Hutcheson in *Shakespeare's Other Anne* (Maclellan, 1950) asserts that 'Anne Whateley', a nun, was Drayton's Idea, Spenser's Rosalind, Daniel's Delia, and author or part-author of *Amoretti*, *The Faerie Queene*, *Love's Labour's Lost*, *The Arte of English Poesie*, and Shakespeare's *Sonnets*, and is to be traced wherever a poem was printed over the signature 'Ignoto': the book is not so entertaining as it sounds.

Old subjects of contention have momentarily lifted their heads. H. David Gray and Percy Simpson[1] have disputed concerning Gray's identification of Shakespeare with Aesop in *Poetaster*:[2] Simpson appears to have weakened Gray's case that Aesop was Shakespeare, Gray to have weakened Simpson's case that Aesop was Heminge. Louis Marder[3] and John Robert Moore[4] have poured much cold water on John H. Long's suggestion[5] that Shakespeare used Thomas Morley's *Plaine and Easie Introduction* (1597) when writing *The Taming of the Shrew*: their most telling arguments are that Shakespeare could have learned the nature of the gamut from many other sources and that 1597 is too late for the composition of the play: nevertheless, Shakespeare may have needed a work of reference for the scene, and we cannot be entirely sure of the play's date. Edward S. Le Comte[6] has suggested that the Essex affair was in Shakespeare's mind in *Hamlet*, particularly in the last scene, the Prince representing Essex and Fortinbras James VI: the suggestion is put forward with much caution, and leaves one ready to admit the possibility that, in writing this play in which we are made to feel intimate observers at the Danish court, Shakespeare may have been reminded of the recently disturbed court that was close at hand. E. A. B. Barnard[7] has reported the recent discovery of documents at Northwick Park, Blockley, recording a grant of the manor of Tredington, and of a share in the manor of Blockley, to Roderigo Lopez in 1586: Tredington, he tells us, is twelve miles from Stratford, Blockley a few miles further. Howard Parsons,[8] replying to Abraham Feldman's argument that Chettle was not referring to Shakespeare in *Kind-Harts Dreame*,[9] makes the unwarranted assumption that it was the three 'playmakers' who had protested on Shakespeare's behalf: J. C. Maxwell[10] points out that it is specifically to one of the complainants that Chettle apologizes.

Among recent contributions to our knowledge of Shakespeare's age, the long-delayed English publication of *The Enchanted Glass*[11] stands pre-eminent. No brief indication can be given of the scope of its learning, but in its wisdom of judgement it should serve as a continual corrective to rash generalization. Hardin Craig can explore the broad seams and the crannies of Renascence thought, but never assumes that his charting can do more than lay down general principles for an understanding of Shakespeare and his contemporaries. He sees that in Shakespeare there is no straightforward following of a single line of thought: the Renascence was an age of debate, and drama the art of debate: Shylock the usurer and Bolingbroke the usurper have, in Shakespeare, a case. Sometimes, indeed, Craig seems to differentiate too sharply between Shakespeare and his contemporaries, overlooking perhaps an ambivalence in Chapman's presentation of Bussy. He refers to the cruelties of the age as characteristic of its 'cocksure

[1] 'Shakespeare or Heminge? A Rejoinder and a Surrejoinder', *Modern Language Review*, XLV (April 1950), 148–52.

[2] Noted in *Shakespeare Survey*, 2 (1949).

[3] 'Shakespeare's Musical Background', *Modern Language Notes*, LXV (November 1950), 501–3.

[4] 'Shakespeare and Morley Again', *Modern Language Notes*, LXV (November 1950), 504–5.

[5] Noted in *Shakespeare Survey*, 4 (1951).

[6] 'The Ending of *Hamlet* as a Farewell to Essex', *ELH*, XVII (June 1950), 87–114.

[7] 'Shakespeare and Shylock', *Times Literary Supplement*, 12 May 1950.

[8] 'Shakespeare and the Scholars', *Notes and Queries*, CXCV (24 June 1950), 283–4.

[9] Noted in *Shakespeare Survey*, 4 (1951).

[10] 'Shakespeare and the Scholars', *Notes and Queries*, CXCV (5 August 1950), 349.

[11] *The Enchanted Glass: The Elizabethan Mind in Literature* (Blackwell, 1950).

mentality', yet excesses may have come not through over-confidence but through an awareness of tension.

In two recent articles[1] Craig has considered the relations between the morality play and Elizabethan tragedy. He warns us against regarding any use of allegorical figures as constituting a morality, which is a play concerned with a conflict between good and evil forces for the possession of a central figure representing man in general or a class of men. We are reminded that Marlowe's or Shakespeare's heroes may represent man subject to temptation. *Faustus* and *Macbeth* have the morality pattern except for "the element of intercession". But we may wonder whether this is not crucial in determining the nature of the play: the very inexplicitness of Elizabethan tragedies prevents them from being wholly moral plays. H. B. Parkes[2] has usefully commented on the 'double vision' of the Elizabethans, suggesting that from Marlowe onwards they found it increasingly difficult to reconcile the traditional view that the frame of things was good with their awareness of irredeemable evil in man himself. In the seventeenth century, he says, the dramatists moved either, with Fulke Greville, towards Calvinism or, with Fletcher, towards make-believe. He seems to be on less firm ground in considering that Shakespeare from *Macbeth* to the Last Plays shows a return to full acceptance of the traditional view: this may give an over-simplified picture, especially of the later Roman tragedies. J. C. Maxwell[3] has made an illuminating study of the differing ways of addressing and referring to the gods in *Lear*. He shows that the Christian attitude is more noticeable towards the end of the drama. Yet his concluding remark, "a Christian outlook is both presupposed and expressed", may go too far. Shakespeare inevitably makes his characters use Christian terms when they approach a reconciliation with the nature of things, yet the play surely leaves us with the feeling that no religious framework can easily hold the sum of things presented: there remains a tension between the 'presupposed' scheme and the implications of the fable. Davis P. Harding,[4] in order to elucidate the situation in *Measure for Measure*, has shown by detailed reference to legal writings that *sponsalia de praesenti* constituted a valid marriage but that consummation before the Church ceremony, though frequently practised, was held a sin. In Shakespeare's play "the ideal and the real exist side by side until, in the bed-trick business, Shakespeare is obliged to dispense with the former altogether". So Isabella blames her brother for consummating with Juliet, yet later acquiesces in the Mariana affair. Harding notes the Duke's anxiety to get the union of Angelo and Mariana blessed by the Church. He does not, however, observe the contrast between the Duke's elaborate suggestion of the scheme and Isabella's ready agreement. Ralph M. Sargent[5] argues that Shakespeare in *The Two Gentlemen* made use of the story of Titus and Gisippus in *The Gouernour*: he puts a reasonable case for this, but is less happy in his defence of Shakespeare's management of the story: referring to *The Old Wives' Tale*, he does not note that Peele's use of the love-and-friendship theme is far more adult than Shakespeare's.

[1] 'Morality Plays and Elizabethan Drama', *Shakespeare Quarterly*, I (April 1950), 64–72; 'Motivation in Shakespeare's Choice of Materials', *Shakespeare Survey*, 4 (1951), 26–34.

[2] 'Nature's Diverse Laws: The Double Vision of the Elizabethans', *Sewanee Review*, LVIII (Summer 1950), 402–18.

[3] 'The Technique of Invocation in "King Lear"', *Modern Language Review*, XLV (April 1950), 142–7.

[4] 'Elizabethan Betrothals and *Measure for Measure*', *Journal of English and Germanic Philology*, XLIX (April 1950), 139–58.

[5] 'Sir Thomas Elyot and the Integrity of *The Two Gentlemen of Verona*', *PMLA*, XLV (December 1950), 1166–80.

L. A. Cormican, in an article full of strange matter,[1] tells us that around 1600 Shakespeare turned away from fashionable literary modes to the language of the people and the religious beliefs commonly expressed in it: he was "a great administrator", "a competitive business man", who in this way stole a march on his contemporaries: he had the good fortune to die before orthodox belief was shaken.

This year's most valuable comparison of Shakespeare with a contemporary has been made by W. B. C. Watkins, who relates the characteristic methods and attitudes of Shakespeare and Spenser.[2] Shakespearian complexities are well brought out, and in particular Watkins's account of *Antony and Cleopatra* is to be admired. The comparison with Spenser, with his "positive commitment to Christianity", renders the interpretation less partisan than some recently encountered, and at the same time makes us realize more fully the allegorical element in Shakespeare's drama. Minor contemporaries of Shakespeare are the concern of William Peery,[3] W. J. Olive[4] and Geoffrey Ashe.[5] Peery throws doubt on Nathan Field's ever acting with the King's Men during Shakespeare's lifetime, and adduces some admittedly doubtful parallels between Field's plays and Shakespeare's. Olive lists a number of resemblances between *The City-Night-Cap* and various Shakespeare plays: there is no doubt that Davenport used situations from *Pericles* and *Measure for Measure*, but few of the verbal parallels carry conviction. Ashe notes verbal echoes in *Lear* and *Timon* of William Strachey's poem printed before *Sejanus*: he suggests that Strachey was Jonson's collaborator in *Sejanus*, and became personally known to Shakespeare as a result.

The employment of Elizabethan psychological notions has produced strange results in John W. Draper's study of *Twelfth Night*.[6] Not only are we given the humour and the astral complexion of almost every character in the play, but we are made to understand that this is no air-borne romance but a realistic comedy, in fact "Shakespeare's play of social security". It is a serious study of a group of people concerned with their establishment in society, and Olivia is a sovereign ruler, "a counterpart of Queen Elizabeth". Orsino is "genuinely ill with a mild case of a serious disease", Malvolio is dangerously ambitious, and Sir Andrew is a usurer's son. Draper gives a great deal of attention to what will happen to the characters after the play is over: he does not, of course, see anything ludicrous in Olivia's final situation.

As Draper recognizes, the Elizabethans associated certain traits with particular professions, and Paul A. Jorgensen[7] has considered Shakespeare's soldiers as exemplifying the characteristic traits of their different ranks within the profession. He notes that Falstaff reflects current criticisms of the behaviour of army captains, and that the relationship of Iago and Cassio can be more fully understood in the light of Elizabethan comments on the closely associated ranks of Ancient and Lieutenant. Jorgensen concludes that Shakespeare must have acquired from books some of his knowledge of the military profession.

[1] 'Medieval Idiom in Shakespeare: (1) Shakespeare and the Liturgy', *Scrutiny*, XVII (Autumn 1950), 186–202.

[2] *Shakespeare and Spenser* (Princeton University Press; London: Cumberlege, 1950).

[3] 'Shakespeare and Nathan Field', *Neophilologus*, XXXIV (October 1950), 238–45.

[4] 'Davenport's Debt to Shakespeare in *The City-Night-Cap*', *Journal of English and Germanic Philology*, XLIX (July 1950), 333–44.

[5] 'William Strachey', *Notes and Queries*, CXCV (25 November 1950), 508–11.

[6] *The Twelfth Night of Shakespeare's Audience* (Stanford University Press; London: Cumberlege, 1950).

[7] 'Military Rank in Shakespeare', *Huntington Library Quarterly*, XIV (November 1950), 17–41.

Ronald Watkins, who has the advantage of considerable experience with schoolboy-actors and a platform-stage, makes a strong plea for the production of Shakespeare in a rebuilt Globe.[1] His book is attractively written and illustrated, and it leaves us in no doubt that his productions in the imagined theatre would be agreeable. But when he argues that a reconstructed Elizabethan playhouse might be used for the acting of new plays as well as Shakespeare's, he seems to overlook that a living theatre can never remain fixed in its production-methods and equipment. A rebuilt Globe would be an interesting place for 'research': it would not be a living theatre: for its audiences it would necessarily have an antiquarian character. This is an entirely different matter from incorporating into a modern, and developing, theatre certain features of the Elizabethan stage which seem profitable in themselves.

But the difficulty of reconstruction seems also to be underestimated in this book. Watkins has accepted as a whole the conclusions of John Cranford Adams concerning the playhouse[2] (though he does on one occasion join issue on the frequency of the use of the 'study' and the 'chamber'), and of T. W. Baldwin concerning the 'lines' followed by individual members of the King's Men (which he suggests should be borne in mind when recruiting a modern Shakespeare company). That our knowledge of these matters is yet far from complete has been brought out in recent articles by George F. Reynolds[3] and C. Walter Hodges.[4] Reynolds notes the paucity of evidence for the existence of a 'tarras' in front of a 'chamber', and argues that Elizabethan drama depended greatly on intimacy of effect, which would be impaired by a too frequent use of the upper stage. Hodges usefully indicates a number of our remaining uncertainties, and in particular reminds us that De Witt shows no inner stage. He deduces that, if there was one at the Swan, it cannot have been much used on that day: "I therefore find it evident that the use of such a feature in the form that we have been accustomed to picture it was neither a permanent nor an indispensable part of Elizabethan public stage practice." Warren Smith[5] further suggests that the Elizabethan stage may have used an acting-level above that of the platform but lower than the 'tarras': he takes examples from *Richard II*, *Troilus* and *Julius Caesar* to show an insufficiency of time for descent from the upper stage. His suggestion is that the base of the 'state' was used in these cases and for Cleopatra's monument, but we may note the underlining in the text of the difficulty of raising Antony's body. Smith's argument does not carry complete conviction, but it leaves us feeling less assured.

That we have still much to ascertain concerning the nature of Elizabethan acting is evident from a book by B. L. Joseph[6] and an article by S. L. Bethell.[7] Watkins has noted the frequency of passages where an actor's facial expression is fully described by another actor: in the absence of theatrical lighting, this gives an approximation to the effect of a cinema 'close-up'. His assumption is, evidently, that Elizabethan acting was not basically different from, but simply

---

[1] *On Producing Shakespeare* (Michael Joseph, 1950).

[2] Useful summaries of Adams's ideas have recently been given in two articles: John Cranford Adams, '"That Virtuous Fabrick"', *Shakespeare Quarterly*, II (January 1951), 3–11; Irwin Smith, 'Notes on the Construction of the Globe Model', *ibid*. pp. 13–18.

[3] 'Was there a "Tarras" in Shakespeare's Globe?', *Shakespeare Survey*, 4 (1951), 97–100.

[4] 'De Witt Again', *Theatre Notebook*, V (January–March 1951), 32–4.

[5] 'Evidence of Scaffolding on Shakespeare's Stage', *Review of English Studies*, n.s., II (January 1951), 22–9.

[6] *Elizabethan Acting* (Oxford English Monographs, Oxford University Press, 1951).

[7] 'Shakespeare's Actors', *Review of English Studies*, n.s., I (July 1950), 193–205.

less visible than, modern acting. Joseph, however, has argued that in the seventeenth century an actor's gestures were strictly formalized and were identical with those practised by the orator. That there was an element of formality, and that in certain sections of a play (e.g. in direct address to the audience) it was the orator's formality, are propositions likely to command assent. But that the increasing use of intimate scenes in Jacobean and Caroline drama did not lead to an acting-style of a more 'naturalistic' kind is indeed difficult to credit. Bethell's conclusion, that Elizabethan acting was a blend of formal and naturalistic elements, seems eminently reasonable, but even he does not seem to recognize that acting, along with all other theatrical arts, cannot have remained stationary during the years 1576–1642.[1]

3. TEXTUAL STUDIES

reviewed by JAMES G. McMANAWAY

Though it is customary to speak of Nicholas Rowe as the first editor of Shakespeare, the editing began at least as early as the First Folio. Evidence is not wanting that those responsible for this volume were at some pains to publish better texts than had been available previously. *King Lear* is a case in point, a play printed in the Folio from a copy of the 'Pied Bull' Quarto that had been elaborately corrected by reference to the playhouse manuscript. Somewhat the same thing was done with *Troilus and Cressida*, a play of which the slightly longer Folio text differs repeatedly from that of the Quarto. Final proof of this fact is presented by Philip Williams,[2] who is thus able to dismiss once and for all the rival hypothesis that the printer of the First Folio used an independent manuscript. In the 1609 Quarto of *Troilus*, the printer followed certain conventions in the use of roman and italic types; so did the printer of the Folio, though the conventions were not necessarily the same. The Quarto was set by two compositors with easily recognizable habits of spelling and treatment of speech-headings; so was the Folio text of *Troilus*, as Edwin E. Willoughby demonstrated twenty years ago. Now Williams reports the discovery of so many cases in which the Folio agrees—abnormally—with the Quarto in the use of italic and roman types, in the abbreviation of speech-headings, and in idiosyncratic spellings, that one, and only one, explanation will suffice: a marked copy of the Quarto served as printer's copy for the Folio.

Unaware of Williams's paper, which had not yet come from press, Miss Alice Walker

---

[1] Martin Holmes, 'An Unrecorded Portrait of Edward Alleyn', *Theatre Notebook*, v (October–December 1950), 11–13, suggests that the portrait of Tamerlane in Richard Knolles's *Generall Historie of the Turkes* (1603) is a portrait of Alleyn in the part of Tamburlaine. Among recent accounts of Shakespeare on the modern stage the following may be noted: Bertram Shuttleworth, 'Irving's Macbeth', *Theatre Notebook*, v (January–March 1951), 28–31, describes the underlinings and annotations made by Irving in a copy of *Macbeth*, now in the University of Pennsylvania Library, for his performance in 1875; Richard David, 'Shakespeare's Comedies and the Modern Stage', *Shakespeare Survey*, 4 (1951), 129–38, commenting on the Old Vic *Love's Labour's Lost* and the Stratford *Measure for Measure*, makes valuable observations on the principles underlying recent productions in this country; Ján Šimko, 'Shakespeare in Slovakia', *ibid.* pp. 109–16, and Vladeta Popović, 'Shakespeare in Post-War Yugoslavia', *ibid.* pp. 117–22, indicate the trend of producers' interpretations elsewhere.

[2] 'Shakespeare's *Troilus and Cressida*: The Relationship of Quarto and Folio', in *Studies in Bibliography* (Charlottesville, Virginia: Bibliographical Society of the University of Virginia, 1950), III, 131–43.

published a study[1] of a different aspect of the textual problem of *Troilus*. It has long been known that Jaggard encountered some obstacle to the printing of *Troilus*, which was intended to follow *Romeo and Juliet* in the Folio. After three pages of text had been put in type (leaves gg 3ᵛ–4ᵛ), the play was laid aside. The last page of *Romeo*, which had occupied gg 3ʳ, was re-set on the first recto of a new quire, Gg, with *Timon of Athens* following on the verso. When it was possible to resume printing *Troilus*, the economical Jaggard salvaged leaf gg 4, containing the second and third pages of *Troilus*, but he had to cancel leaf gg 3. A hitherto unprinted Prologue to *Troilus* was used to fill the recto formerly occupied by the concluding lines of *Romeo*, and on the verso of the cancel Jaggard put a resetting of the first page of *Troilus*. The cancelled leaf (gg 3) survives in five copies of the Folio. A few unimportant variants have been found by Miss Walker between the first and the second settings of the first three pages of *Troilus* in the Folio; between the Quarto text and the first setting in the Folio the variants are likewise few and unimportant. But beginning with the fourth page of the Folio text she finds a great many substantive differences between Quarto and Folio. She concludes that in the interval while Jaggard was working out a solution of the difficulty which had interrupted work on *Troilus* he had been supplied (presumably by John Heminges and Henry Condell) with a copy of the Quarto into which someone had copied the superior readings, the corrected speech-headings, the more adequate stage directions, and the new passages of text which differentiate the Folio from the Quarto. But for the delay, she guesses, the Folio would have preserved merely an uncorrected reprint of the Quarto text. Another possibility, which she does not suggest, is that Heminges and Condell interrupted Jaggard's work on *Troilus* so that they might have time to collate the Quarto with a manuscript and thus provide a superior text.

Not all the variants introduced into the Folio text are superior; so Miss Walker offers the hazardous conjecture that a different hand had supplied these in the marked copy Jaggard used, beginning with the fourth page of the Folio. This may be correct, but it complicates the problem by introducing an otherwise unknown agent, and it is hardly susceptible of proof. Perhaps Williams, or someone else, will be able to account for the inferior variants as the work of a copyist or of the Folio compositors.

Sir Walter Greg's latest contribution to editorial theory will prove of the utmost value to future editors, as it will dismay most of those who have hitherto done editorial work in this period. In a closely reasoned and amply illustrated essay[2] read at the English Institute in New York in 1949, he gives a new definition to the term, copy-text, and prescribes new methods of procedure for editors. The heart of the essay is contained in the following passage:

It is therefore the modern editorial practice [in dealing with English Renaissance printed texts] to choose whatever extant text may be supposed to represent most nearly what the author wrote and to follow it with the least possible alteration. But here we need to draw a distinction between the significant, or as I shall call them 'substantive', readings of the text, those namely that affect the author's meaning or the essence of his expression, and others, such in general as spelling, punctuation, word-division, and the like, affecting mainly its formal presentation, which may be regarded as the accidents, or as I shall call them 'accidentals', of the text.

---

[1] 'The Textual Problem of *Troilus and Cressida*', *Modern Language Review*, XLV (October 1950), 459–64.
[2] 'The Rationale of Copy-Text', *Studies in Bibliography*, III, 19–36.

This distinction, as he points out, is not arbitrary or theoretical, for scribes and compositors of the period tended to react differently to the two categories: they attempted to reproduce the 'substantives', but the 'accidentals' were regarded as within their own power. This is sound but revolutionary doctrine. It means, for example, that the editors of the Variorum *Faerie Queene* erred in selecting the 1596 edition of *The First Three Books*, even though Spenser altered single words, supplied missing phrases and lines, and wrote new stanzas to alter the concluding incident of Book Three. It can be demonstrated that Spenser did not supply Richard Field with a new manuscript of the poem for the 1596 edition; instead he revised a copy of John Wolfe's edition of 1590, introducing such new readings as he desired but ignoring many of the typographical and other errors in 1590, including those in the errata list. Since the authoritative text is that which most nearly reproduces the manuscript of the author, the quarto of 1590 should have been used as the copy-text. Spenser's substantive changes in 1596 should have been inserted. In this, as in all other reprinted texts, there are many doubtful readings, possibly introduced by the printer, which require the exercise of editorial intelligence and taste, for as Greg warns, the editing of a text cannot be reduced to a fool-proof mechanical procedure: "No juggling with copy-text will relieve the editor of the duty and necessity of exercising his own judgement." This pithy essay should be read by everyone seriously concerned about the purity of Shakespeare's text.

In a manner as gay as it is earnest, Peter Alexander discusses the punctuation of Shakespeare's text.[1] Editors are frequently called upon, as in the case of *Hamlet*, to decide between the punctuation of a good Quarto and that of the Folio. Which should be accepted? Or does the punctuation lie within the power of the editor? After a swift review of editorial attitudes towards Shakespeare's text, and particularly its punctuation, Alexander advances the proposition that the editors of the First Folio tried, at least in some plays, to impose upon the copy-text a punctuation that would make the plays easy reading. In the plays that were printed from Shakespeare's own manuscripts, however, such as the good Second Quarto of *Romeo* and of *Hamlet* and the Folio text of *Coriolanus*, there is observable a different style of punctuation, lighter, more fluent perhaps, but, if its principles might be discovered, no less adequate than the other and perhaps more authoritative. Some of the principles governing this other style (Shakespeare's own, Alexander suggests) were discovered inductively by Alfred E. Thiselton, but generally the subject has been neglected, despite Percy Simpson's investigation in 1911, and desultory studies by others of more recent date. It is not easy to formulate Shakespeare's habits of punctuation, because printing-houses were even then attempting to secure a measure of uniformity in punctuation as in spelling. Alexander's challenge is one that should no longer be declined.

In somewhat the same vein as Alexander's discussion of punctuation, Kenneth Muir offers 'A Test for Shakespearian Variants'[2] to be applied in the choice between verbal variants. Four lines from *Lear* (II, i, 76ff.) serve as an example:

and thou must make a dullard of the world, if they not thought the profits of my death, were very pregnant and potentiall spurres to make thee seeke it.

(Quarto)

---

[1] 'Shakespeare's Punctuation' (Annual Shakespeare Lecture), *Proceedings of the British Academy*, 1945 (for the British Academy by the Oxford University Press, 1950), pp. 61–84.

[2] *Notes and Queries*, CXCV (25 November 1950), 513–14.

> And thou must make a dullard of the world,
> If they not thought the profits of my death
> Were very pregnant and potentiall spirits
> To make thee seeke it. (Folio)

Nearly all editors, including Duthie, read *spurres* because of the sense, though they mention the *ductus literarum*. Muir presents the claims of *spirits*, because he finds that in eight of the twenty-one other passages in which Shakespeare uses *potent* and *potential* he also uses *spirits* or an equivalent. Moreover, in three of the fourteen passages in which Shakespeare uses *pregnant*, the word *spirits* (or an equivalent) will be found. His conclusion is that there is ample evidence of a close association in Shakespeare's mind between *spirits* and both *potent* and *pregnant*; and he finds no such association for *spurs*. If *spirits* means 'evil spirits' or 'incitements', as it may in *Macbeth*, I, v, 27, "That I may pour my spirits in his ear", the Folio reading may be correct. Muir admits that the application of this test is limited. He might have added that it is in harmony with Housman's dictum which Alexander quotes with approval in his discussion of punctuation: "The merits essential to a correction are those without which it cannot be true, and closeness to the manuscripts is not one of them; the indispensable things are fitness to the context and propriety to the genius of the author."

One of the imponderables in editing Shakespearian texts is the proof-reading of the original editions. It may be assumed, I think, that Shakespeare read the proofs of *Venus and Adonis* and *Lucrece*, but the conditions of dramatic composition and publication were such that it is improbable he had the opportunity to read the proofs of any of his plays published in quarto before 1616. Naturally he did not see proofs of the First Folio; but did anyone else read its proofs? And, if so, how carefully were they read? The only two pages of Folio proof known until recently have been described by E. E. Willoughby and Charlton Hinman; now Hinman has discovered a third page of Folio proof, again in the course of collating the text of *Othello* in the Folger Library First Folios with the mechanical device of his own invention. In the account[1] of his discovery, Hinman points out that again only one page in the forme, p. 292 in *King Lear*, bears the proof-reader's marks; that in the three pages of proof only one error marked for correction would require the reader to consult the copy from which the text had been set; and that the corrector of the press seems to have been concerned, in all three pages, with the niceties of typography and elimination of obvious typographical errors rather than with the intention of the author. Hinman's account should be read at length, but two other points may be mentioned here. One is that in the conjugate page, 281, which bears no corrector's marks, one press correction was, nevertheless, made: two types that were riding high and taking too much ink were adjusted at the same time that the five corrections were made on page 282 pursuant to the marked instructions of the proof-reader. The second is that the uncorrected states of the two pages of which Hinman has discovered marked proof are found in Folger Folios nos. 15, 31, 47, 48 and 69, and in the Chatsworth copy, used by Sir Sidney Lee for his facsimile, and in no others. This fact suggests that Jaggard's shop had a method of segregating corrected from uncorrected states of the formes of the First Folio, a thing hitherto unsuspected. Much remains to be learned of Renaissance methods of proofing.

[1] 'Mark III: New Light on the Proof-Reading for the First Folio', *Studies in Bibliography*, III, 145–53.

Representative of the editions of Shakespeare in English now being produced, the following four may be mentioned. *Antony and Cleopatra*, edited by J. Dover Wilson,[1] is the twenty-fourth volume of the New Shakespeare. The play causes little textual difficulty for the editor, for, as is generally agreed, the author's fair copy was used in printing the First Folio, the only early edition. Wilson makes his usual changes in the punctuation and attempts to normalize the lineation, which is frequently hypermetrical because Shakespeare appears to have tried to economize space by running on half-lines.

The Arden Shakespeare has for many years been highly esteemed for its conservative texts and scholarly introductions, though the volumes differed somewhat in excellence. Most of them appeared before the editing of Shakespeare was revolutionized by the discoveries of the analytical bibliographers and the textual critics; so the publishers have begun to issue a new series of revised and re-edited volumes under the general editorship of Miss Una Ellis-Fermor. The first title to appear is *Macbeth*, edited by Kenneth Muir.[2] Muir's edition is avowedly based on that of Henry Cunningham, but it is largely free of the disintegrating tendencies that were so strong in his predecessor's. In a brief tabulation, Muir accepts as genuine all the scenes previous critics have attributed to another hand than Shakespeare's except the Hecate passages of III, v and IV, i, but he thinks "it has been too easily assumed that the interpolator was Middleton". He does not attempt to explain how the text of songs from Middleton's *Witch* was available in 1673 when Davenant's operatic version was performed, though if we had the answer to this question we should know a great deal more than now we do about what happened to the dramatic library of the King's Men at the closing of the theatres in 1642. In most things Muir is conservative; I wish that he had been more zealous to preserve the dramatic lineation of the Folio.

For nearly fifty years, it seems, there has been no publication in England of Shakespeare's works in one volume with an independently revised text. The Tudor Shakespeare,[3] edited by Peter Alexander, is designed to provide readers with a convenient volume, printed in small but clear type, which gives a straightforward text with modern spelling and modern punctuation. Collation of sample passages of text indicates that Alexander is aware of the best and the latest discussions of textual problems and that at all doubtful points he shares with the reader the fruit of his learning.[4]

An Explanatory Introduction to Thorpe's Edition of Shakespeare's Sonnets with Text Transcription,[5] a handsomely printed book, restates the Countess de Chambrun's beliefs about the *Sonnets*: they written between about 1592 and 1604, addressed for the most part to the Earl of Southampton, and made available to Thomas Thorpe by the Earl's stepfather, William Hervey, in a deliberately confused order so that the uninitiated would not penetrate too deeply into their private meaning.

The controversy about the date of Shakespeare's *Sonnets*, started by the publication of Leslie Hotson's book by that name, continues unabated, with attention focused primarily on

---

[1] Cambridge University Press, 1950.   [2] Methuen, 1951.

[3] *William Shakespeare: The Complete Works*, Collins, 1951.

[4] An attractively printed edition of *Romeo and Juliet* has a good introduction for the general reader by Nevill Coghill. The Folio Society, 1950.

[5] Aldington, Kent: The Hand and Flower Press, 1950.

Sonnet 107. Hotson has published two replies to his critics. In the first,[1] he cites several immediately contemporary manuscript references to the Armada's half-moon shape and repeats his arguments that Sonnet 107 refers to a recent, not a distant, event. In a more recent utterance,[2] he continues his defence along the same lines and then returns to the offensive by mentioning several other sonnets which he interprets as alluding to specific contemporary events: Sonnet 66, "Tired with all these, for restful death I cry", is, he believes, an outburst against Elizabethan control of the stage that was particularly severe from 1586 to 1593; Sonnet 25, "Let those who are in favour with their stars", is a commentary on the shameful treatment accorded Sir Francis Drake. Hotson reminds us that youth is the time for sonneteering and that the pose of assumed age is characteristic of youth; so Shakespeare's references in the *Sonnets* to his advanced age are really a sign of his youth, for who is more worldly-wise than twenty-two when counselling nineteen? The Rival Poet, according to Hotson, is indubitably Christopher Marlowe, and Shakespeare's description of *Venus and Adonis* as the first heir of his invention means (as of course it need not!) that the poem was literally the first work from Shakespeare's pen.

I. A. Shapiro cites evidence that the moon-shaped formation of the Armada was better known, or more frequently referred to, in Jacobean than in Elizabethan times, the only "certainly independent reference" of immediately contemporary date being J[ames] L[ea]'s *Birth, Purpose and morall Wound of the Romish holie League* (1589, cited by Hotson, pp. 7–9). The others are derivative, tracing through Ubaldini (1590) to Stow (1592), Speed (1611), Stow (1615), and Camden (1615). Shapiro gives two new late references (1621, 1624). As the Armada literature increased, then, popular references to the shape of its formation in the Channel became more numerous; but Michael Lewis, Professor of History at the Royal Naval College, Greenwich, reminds us of the grave doubts of naval historians that the Armada sailed in a crescent formation. F. S. Boas directs attention to Joseph Hall's *The King's Prophecie* (1603), which describes the poet's dread of evil when Elizabeth should die and his joy "beyond all mortall feare, Beyond all mortall hopes", now that James is safely upon the throne. "False starres and falser wizards" are rebuked for their vain predictions of evil. Boas considers this a close parallel to Sonnet 107. G. Wilson Knight adds one more commentary upon "terrene moon" of *Antony and Cleopatra*, III, xiii, 153, and its possible bearing on the meaning of Sonnet 107. His point is that not only have Antony's good "stars" left their "orbs" but his terrene moon (Cleopatra) is eclipsed. Hence the passage has no relation to Sonnet 107.[3]

It has often been observed that some of the lines of the "To be or not to be" soliloquy are inapplicable to Hamlet's circumstances and contrary to his experience. What does he know of

> The oppressor's wrong, the proud man's contumely,
> The pangs of disprized [sic] love, the law's delay,
> The insolence of office, and the spurns
> That patient merit of the unworthy takes...

[1] *Times Literary Supplement*, 2 June 1950, p. 348. See also the following contributions: I. A. Shapiro, 21 April 1950, p. 245; Michael Lewis, 23 June, p. 389; F. S. Boas, 7 July, p. 421; and G. Wilson Knight, 14 July, p. 437.

[2] 'More Light on Shakespeare's Sonnets', *Shakespeare Quarterly*, II (April 1951), 111–18.

[3] Putting aside the controversies about topical allusions, F. W. Bateson writes a beautiful analysis of Sonnet 107, in 'Elementary, My dear Hotson! A Caveat for Literary Detectives', *Essays in Criticism*, I (January, 1951) 81–8.

"the pangs of disprized [sic] love" only excepted? Kristian Smidt believes[1] that certain lines of the soliloquy constitute "a personal lyric of Shakespeare's, written independently of the play, and then, by a stroke of genius, interpolated in it at the point where Hamlet may suitably rise above his own particular troubles to become the spokesman of all mankind". He points out that if two of the lines which are "out of character" be slightly rearranged, the passage becomes two 'blank verse' sonnets. The passage in question begins, "Whether 'tis nobler in the mind", and concludes, "Than fly to others". The mood and sentiment are, as Smidt comments, in close harmony with those of Sonnet 66, "Tired with all these, for restful death I cry", but there is nothing in the record to show that Shakespeare ever suffered such mythical sorrows as are mentioned by Hamlet or was accustomed to using his dramatis personae as mouthpieces.

The Bad Quarto of Romeo and Juliet by Harry R. Hoppe, which was reviewed in these pages in an earlier volume, continues to receive praise from the reviewers, though these do not always agree among themselves. G. I. Duthie agrees[2] with Hoppe that the reporters had performed in a shortened version but were also familiar with the full text and attempted to reproduce the latter. Miss Madeleine Doran disagrees[3] that Hoppe has found evidence of the reporters' familiarity with both a long and a short version of the play. Shakespeare's text, she thinks, may well have been cut in preparing the prompt-book; and the reporters, if use of their manuscript by an acting company were contemplated, may have made cuts on their own responsibility. "There is no way, however," she continues, "to tell at just what stage these lines were cut out, or indeed whether they were deliberately cut at all and not just forgotten by the reporters at the right place and remembered at the wrong one." Both reviewers find Hoppe's identification of the reporters (Bird, Shaw and Spencer) plausible; and Duthie holds to the opinion that the use of italic type in printing the Nurse's lines at I, iii, 1–36 is proof that they had "an authentic document" at their disposal.

The minute examination of *Henry V*, begun by Dover Wilson and Duthie in the New Shakespeare and contributed to independently by J. H. Walter (in *Modern Language Review*, XLI (July 1946), 237–45), is carried forward by Allan Wilkinson,[4] who argues logically that if IV, i, 35–305 is an interpolation, so also must be IV, vii, 123–viii, 77, which concludes the episode between Hal and Williams.

In discussing the authorship of attributed plays and those in which the presence of more than one author is suspected, it is dangerous to rely upon subjective judgements and always desirable to find, if possible, objective tests which will help to confirm or disprove attributions. In the course of testing Dover Wilson's thesis that Act I of *Titus Andronicus* is by George Peele and the rest of the play largely by Shakespeare, J. C. Maxwell[5] finds a grammatical construction which appears frequently in Peele's late play, *David and Bethsabe*, and his poems, and also in Act I of *Titus* but rarely in Acts II–V. The construction consists in the use of a possessive (A) adjective or (B) pronoun as the antecedent of a relative clause, e.g.

---

[1] 'Notes on *Hamlet*', *English Studies*, XXXI (August 1950), 136–41; see particularly pp. 138–41.

[2] *Modern Language Review*, XLV (July 1950), 375–7.

[3] *Journal of English and Germanic Philology*, XLIX (January 1950), 112–14.

[4] 'A Note on *Henry V* Act IV', *Review of English Studies*, n.s., I (October 1950), 345–6.

[5] 'Peele and Shakespeare: A Stylometric Test', *Journal of English and Germanic Philology*, XLIX (October 1950), 557–61.

(A) *Titus Andronicus*, I, i, 5–6.

> I am his first-born son, that was the last
> That ware the imperial diadem of Rome;

(B) *Titus Andronicus*, I, i, 306–7:

> Agree these deeds with that proud brag of thine,
> That saidst, I begged the empire at thy hands.

Ignoring doubtful constructions (which he takes into account in a special way), Maxwell finds that *Titus* I (495 lines) has six (4 A + 2 B) instances, as compared with *Titus* II–V (2026 lines), with four A examples, a ratio of six or seven to one. A comparison of the figures for Peele's poems and Shakespeare's narrative verse discloses that here, too, the construction is about six times as common in Peele as in Shakespeare. Maxwell has applied the same test to other works of Peele and Shakespeare and to other plays of the period with varying results, none of which seems to invalidate his assertion that "a strikingly high frequency is found, among a tolerably large number of works, only in Peele's poems, in his one reasonably well preserved late play, and in the first act of *Titus Andronicus*".

Incidental to the preparation of his critical edition of *King Lear*, G. I. Duthie made an exhaustive study of the systems of shorthand used in England before 1607, when the First Quarto of that play was published. His findings are given in a book[1] whose importance is out of all proportion to its size. Timothy Bright's *Characterie* and Peter Bales's *Brachygraphie* are shown to be too crude and cumbersome for use by a pirate of a play. John Willis's *Stenographie* was a better system, but not even its inventor claimed more for it than that with it a man "well practiced in this Art, may write *Verbatim*, as fast as a man can treateably [i.e., deliberately, distinctly, intelligibly] speake". Whereas,

if the speaker from whose mouth we note, be very swift of deliverie, so that he transporteth our imagination beyonde the indevour of our handes; it shall not be amisse to write only the Verbes & Substantives, and other Words essential to the speech delivered, reserving a space for the rest which are of lighter circumstance, to be supplyed with Penne immediately after the speech is ended.

The difficulties of a stenographic reporter in the playhouse can be readily imagined: swift speech, rapid action, entrances and exits, and much that is calculated to transport the imagination beyond the endeavour of the hands. In a word, there was no adequate method of reporting plays by shorthand in Shakespeare's day—certainly the text of the First Quarto of *Lear* was not so reported.

The Elizabethan systems of shorthand were not supple enough for the pirating of plays. How then were texts of *Romeo and Juliet* and *Hamlet* stolen? Modern scholars are in agreement that the bad quartos of these and certain other plays were written down from memory by actors who had taken part in performances of them. Accepting H. D. Gray's proposal that the minor actor who played Marcellus and Luciano was the pirate of *Hamlet*, J. M. Nosworthy contributes additional proofs,[2] suggests that the actor also played the part of an Attendant Lord,

---

[1] *Elizabethan Shorthand and the First Quarto of 'King Lear'*, Oxford: Blackwell, 1949.
[2] '*Hamlet* and the Player Who Could Not Keep Counsel', *Shakespeare Survey*, 3 (1950), 74–82.

and points out that uniformly good reporting is not to be expected in the circumstances. The reporter will remember his own lines with reasonable accuracy; the lines spoken just before he enters or exits, cues for stage business in which he participates, and passages of text which grip his attention either because of their content or of their association with violent action, not quite so well. At times, his attention may wander, and once he leaves the stage for a long interval he may have only the haziest recollection of the text. Incidentally, Nosworthy makes several shrewd guesses about readings in the First Quarto which appear superior to those of the Second Quarto and the Folio.

The great figures in Shakespearian scholarship are often too remote geographically or academically to be more than names to their contemporaries. The opportunity to know two of these men better, one dead, the other living, is afforded by J. Dover Wilson's revelation of the private character as well as the intellectual stature of the late Alfred W. Pollard,[1] and the lively and entertaining introduction by an unnamed admirer to the more-than-octogenarian Percy Simpson.[2] Both sketches should be read, as much for their literary quality as for the portraits they paint.

[1] In *Proceedings of the British Academy*, 1945, pp. 257–306. In this same volume are tributes to J. W. Mackail (pp. 245–55) and Oliver Elton (pp. 317–44).
[2] *A List of the Published Writings of Percy Simpson*. Oxford: Clarendon Press, 1950.

BOOKS RECEIVED

BALDWIN, T. W. *On the Literary Genetics of Shakspere's Poems and Sonnets* (Urbana: University of Illinois Press, 1950).

BLISS, WILLIAM. *Yorick's Crib to the Examination Paper on Shakespeare in 'The Real Shakespeare'* (London: Sidgwick and Jackson, 1949).

BOAS, FREDERICK S. *Queen Elizabeth in Drama and Related Studies* (London: Allen and Unwin, 1950).

CHUTE, MARCETTE. *Shakespeare of London.* With a Preface by Sir Ralph Richardson (London: Secker and Warburg, 1951).

CRAIG, HARDIN. *The Enchanted Glass: The Elizabethan Mind In Literature* (Oxford: Blackwell, 1950).

DONNER, H. W. *Svenska Översättningar av Shakespeare's Macbeth.* I. *Schillers Inflytande på Geijers Översättning.* Acta Academiae Aboensis Humaniora, xx, i (Åbo: Åbo Akademi, 1950).

DRAPER, JOHN W. *The Twelfth Night of Shakespeare's Audience* (Stanford, California: Stanford University Press; London: Cumberlege, Oxford University Press, 1950).

DUTHIE, GEORGE IAN. *Elizabethan Shorthand and the First Quarto of 'King Lear'* (Oxford: Blackwell, 1949).

FARNHAM, WILLARD. *Shakespeare's Tragic Frontier: The World of His Final Tragedies* (Berkeley and Los Angeles: University of California Press, 1950).

GARDE, AXEL. *Hamlet i Generationernes Spejl. Et Essay* (Copenhagen: Gyldendal, 1946).

HEPPENSTALL, RAYNER and INNES, MICHAEL. *Three Tales of Hamlet* (London: Gollancz, 1950).

HUTCHESON, W. J. FRASER. *Shakespeare's Other Anne* (Glasgow: Maclellan, 1950).

LEECH, CLIFFORD. *Shakespeare's Tragedies and Other Studies in Seventeenth Century Drama* (London: Chatto and Windus, 1950).

List of the Published Writings of Percy Simpson, A (Oxford: At the Clarendon Press, 1950).

POGSON, BERYL. *In the East My Pleasure Lies. An Esoteric Interpretation of Some Plays of Shakespeare* (London: Stuart and Richards, 1950).

Proceedings of the British Academy, 1945 (Published for the British Academy by Geoffrey Cumberlege, Oxford University Press).

RUBOW, PAUL V. *Shakespeare og hans Samtidige. En Række Kritiske Studier* (Copenhagen: Gyldendal, 1948).

SEN GUPTA, S. C. *Shakespearian Comedy* (London: Cumberlege, Oxford University Press, 1950).

Shakespeare Quarterly, vol. I (New York: Shakespeare Association of America, 1950).

SHAKESPEARE, WILLIAM. *Antony and Cleopatra.* The New Shakespeare. Edited by John Dover Wilson (Cambridge University Press, 1950).

SHAKESPEARE, WILLIAM. *Macbeth.* The Arden Edition of the Works of William Shakespeare. Edited by Kenneth Muir. Based on the Edition of Henry Cunningham (London: Methuen, 1951).

SHAKESPEARE, WILLIAM. *Romeo and Juliet.* Second Quarto, 1599. Shakespeare Quarto Facsimiles No. 6 (London: The Shakespeare Association and Sidgwick and Jackson, 1949).

SHAKESPEARE, WILLIAM. *The Complete Works.* A new Edition, edited with an introduction and glossary by Peter Alexander (London and Glasgow: Collins, 1951).

SHAKESPEARE, WILLIAM. *The Living Shakespeare: Twenty-two Plays and the Sonnets.* Edited by Oscar James Campbell (New York: Macmillan, 1949).

SHAKESPEARE, WILLIAM. *The Tragedy of Romeo and Juliet*. Introduction by Nevill Coghill. Designs by Jean Hugo (London: The Folio Society, 1950).

SHARPE, ELLA FREEMAN. *Collected Papers on Psycho-Analysis*. Edited by Marjorie Brierley with a Preface by Ernest Jones. The International Psycho-Analytical Library, no. 36 (London: The Hogarth Press and The Institute of Psycho-Analysis, 1950).

WATKINS, RONALD. *On Producing Shakespeare*. With drawings by Maurice Percival (London: Michael Joseph, 1950).

WATKINS, W. B. C. *Shakespeare and Spenser* (Princeton University Press; London: Cumberlege, 1950).

Year's Work in English Studies, The, vol. XXIX, 1948. Edited for the English Association by Frederick S. Boas (London: Cumberlege, Oxford University Press, 1950).

INDEX

Abend, Murray, 139 n.

Acting, Elizabethan, 143–4 and n.

Adams, John Cranford, 143

Adams, Joseph Quincy, 25

Aimerito, Lella, 113

Albertini, Edda, 113

Alexander, Peter, 45, 146, 148

Alfieri, Vittorio, 10, 94

Alleyn, Edward, 144 n.

Alswang, Ralph, 116

Alterman, Nathan, 112

Altick, R. D., 86, 88

Andreoni, Maria A., 113

Anet, Daniel, 115

Ardens, N. N., 105 n.

Aristotle, 86

    Poetics, 130

Armada, The Spanish (1588), allusion to it in Shakespeare's *Sonnets*, 138, 149

Armin, Robert, 122, 123

Armstrong, E. A., 88

Ashcroft, Peggy, 123–4

Ashe, Geoffrey, 142

Asseo, Abraham, 120

Atkins, Robert, 119, 120

Austria, report on Shakespeare in, 111

Authorship problems in Shakespeare's plays, *see under* Shakespeare

Avinoam, Reuben, 113

Backer, Fr. de, 109

Bailey, James, 115

Baldwin, T. W., 143

    On the Literary Genetics of Shakspere's Poems and Sonnets reviewed, 137–8

Bales, Peter, *Brachygraphie*, 151

Balfoort, M., 108

Barnard, E. A. B., 140

Barnard, Sir John, 56

Bartlett, Henrietta C., 53

Bartlett, John, *Concordance to Shakespeare*, 86

Barton, John, 120

Bateson, F. W., 138, 149 n.

Beaumont, Francis and Fletcher, John, *Knight of the Burning Pestle*, 4

Belgium, Shakespeare and:

    recent productions, 111

    traditions of acting on the Flemish stage, 106–10

Belinsky, V. G., 118

Belleforest, F. de, *The hystorie of Hamblet*, 53

Benassi, Memo, 113

Benckendorf, Count A. von, 99

Benthall, Michael, 115

Bentley, R., seventeenth-century publisher, 51

Bentley, Richard, 2

Berger, André, 111

Bergman, Ingemar, 114

Besch, Anthony, 120

Bethell, S. L., 85, 143–4

Beves, Donald, 120

Bible, The (*see also* Theological significance in Shakespeare's plays), 54, 63, 73, 87

Biography of Shakespeare, *see under* Shakespeare

Bizzarri, Carla, 113

Blanc, Anne Marie, 114

Bliss, William, 92 n., 139 n.

Blitzstein, Marc, 116

Blount, Edward, Elizabethan publisher, 26

Boas, F. S., 132, 138, 139, 149

Bodkin, Maud, 91 n.

Boileau, Nicolas, 98

Bonjour, Adrien, 114

Bradbrook, M. C., 135–6

Bradley, A. C., 75

Brewster, E., seventeenth-century publisher, 51

Bright, Timothy, *Characterie*, 151

British Museum, 50, 55, 57 n.

Brook, Peter, 119

Brooks, Cleanth, 85, 86, 87

Brown, S. J., 91 n.

Brunelli, Bruno, 113

Bucknell, Peter A., 120

Bulgakov, A. Y., 100

Burgersdyk, L. J., 109

Butter, N., Elizabethan publisher, 52

Byrd, William, 115

Byron, John, 58

Byron, Lord George Gordon, 93–4, 98, 100, 104

    Mazeppa, 93

    The Corsair, 105 n.

Caimi, Gino, 113

Calderón de la Barca, Pedro, 94

Calhern, Louis, 115, 116

Calvinism, 141

Cambridge (*see also* Trinity College Library), 50–4

INDEX

Cambridge (*cont.*)
Catharine Hall, 50
Editions of Shakespeare in College libraries (Emmanuel, King's, Pembroke), 54
Editions in Fitzwilliam Museum, 54
Camden, William, 149
Campion, Thomas, 115
Cane, Gigi, 113
Capell, Edward, 7, 19, 53
collection in Trinity College library, Cambridge, 50–1, 52, 53
Capocci, Valentina, 113
Carey, Dennis, 119, 120
Casson, John, 119
Caxton, William, *Troy Book*, 53
Cervantes Saavedra, Miguel de, 131
Chambers, Sir E. K., 25, 57 n.
Chambrun, Countess C. L. de, 148
Chapman, George, 139, 140
Revenge of Bussy D'Ambois, 132
Chaucer, Geoffrey, 50, 54
Cherix, Pierre, 114
Chettle, Henry, *Kind-Heart's Dream*, 140
Christian religion, *see* Theological significance in Shakespeare's plays
Chute, Marcette, 139
Cinthio, Giraldi, 71, 72
Clariond, Aimé, 111, 115
Clark, W. G. and Wright, W. Aldis, editors of The Cambridge Shakespeare, 2, 3, 25, 51
Clarke, D. Waldo, 139
Clemen, W. H., 81, 92 n., 112
Clopton, Sir Hugh, 55, 56
Clunes, Alec, 119, 123, 126, 127
Coertze, L. I., 113–14
Coghill, Nevill, 148
Cohen, Alexander, 116
Collier, John Payne, 2, 25, 46 n.
Comedy, Shakespeare's concept of, 131, 135–6, 141
Companies of actors, Elizabethan, *see under* Theatre, Elizabethan
Comte, Edward S. Le, *see* Le Comte
Condell, Henry, 145
Contention betwixt Yorke and Lancaster, The first part of the, 52; *The Whole contention between the two famous houses Lancaster and York*, 52
Cooke, Alan, 119
Coomb, John a, 55
Coomb, Judith, 55
Coomb, William, 55
Cooper, James, 119

Coopman, Hendrick, 110 n.
Cormican, L. A., 142
Corneille, Pierre, 111
Cornwall, Barry (B. W. Procter), 101
Coryate, Thomas, *Crudities*, 72
Craig, Hardin, 43, 44, 140–1
Crinò, Anna Maria, 131
Croce, Benedetto, 113
Cunningham, Henry, 148
Cunningham, J. V., 133
Czechoslovakia, report on Shakespeare in, 111–12

D., A., 139 n.
Damirale, M. N., 51
Dangerfield, Gay, 124
Daniel, Samuel, 139 n.
Davenant, Sir William, 53, 148
Davenport, Robert, *The City-Night-Cap*, 142
David, Richard W., 144 n.
Davis, Alan, 119
Debucourt, Jean, 111
Delius, Nicolaus, 39
Deloney, Thomas, *The Gentle Craft*, 80 n.
Delvig, Baron Anton A., 99
Deutschbein, Max, 112, 114
Devlin, William, 127
De Witt, Johannes, Swan Theatre drawing, 143
Dickens, Charles, *David Copperfield*, 44
Diels, Joris, 108
Dignam, Mark, 127
Dilis, Jan, 107, 108
Disher, M. Willson, 137, 138
Doeselaer, Frans Van, 107
Donne, John, 89
Doran, Madeleine, 150
Dorlandus, Petrus, *Den Spieghel der Salichiet van Elckerlyck* (1495), 107
Dostoievsky, Feodor, 61, 103, 114
Dowland, John, 115
Drake, Sir Francis, 149
Dramatic Unities, 94, 98
Draper, John W., 142
Drayton, Michael, 139 n.
Driessens, Victor, 107
Dryden, John, 25, 52, 53
Duncan, Edward, 134
Durrell, Lawrence, 139
Duthie, G. I., 37, 147, 150
Elizabethan Shorthand and the First Quarto of King Lear reviewed, 151
Dyce, Alexander, 27

Economidis, D., 112
Eddison, Robert, 128
Editing Shakespeare for continental readers, 10–15
Editions of Shakespeare's Works, *see under* Shakespeare
Eliot, T. S., 80 n., 87
　Family Reunion, 79
Elizabeth, Queen, 132, 139, 142, 149
Elliott, G. R., 78
Ellis-Fermor, Una, 81, 84, 88–9, 90, 130, 148
Elton, Oliver, 152
Elyot, Sir Thomas, *The Governour*, 79, 141
Emendation of texts (*see also under* Shakespeare, William, textual problems), 1–9, 16–17
Emett, Rowland, 129
Esmoreit (medieval Flemish play) 107
Essex, Robert Devereux, Earl of, 140
Etienne, Claude, 111
Euripides, 53
Evans, Bertrand, 135
Evans, Maurice, 115, 116
Evennett, Wallace, 120
Everyman, 107

Farnham, Willard, *Shakespeare's Tragic Frontier* reviewed, 130
Faure, Renée, 111
Feldman, Abraham, 140
Felheim, Marvin, 135
Field, Nathan, 142
Field, Richard, Elizabethan printer, 146
Finkel, Simon, 112
First Part of the Contention betwixt...Yorke and Lancaster see *Contention betwixt...Yorke and Lancaster*
Fisher, T., Elizabethan publisher, 52
Flatter, Richard, 7
Flemish stage, Shakespearian productions on, 106–10
Fletcher, John (*see also* Beaumont, Francis), 141
Folger Shakespeare Library, *see under* Libraries
Fontanne, Lynn, 115
Fournier, Camille, 115
Fox, Levi, 57 n., 139
Francis, F. C., 53
Francke, A., 114
Freakley, Vernon, 120
French, Leslie, 120
Fricker, Robert, 114
Furse, Roger, 121
Fuseli, J. H., 113
Fytton, Mary, 137, 138

Gambino, Ercole A., 113
Garley, John, 124
Garrick, David, 51
Gassmann, Vittorio, 113
Gellner, Julius, 112
Germany, report on Shakespeare in, 112
Gesta Romanorum, 39
Gevers, Jos, 108–9
Gielgud, John, 120
Gigli, Lorenzo, 113
Gilhuys, Charles, 108
Ginsberg, Ernst, 114
Giorgi, Elsa De', 113
Glenville, Peter, 116
Globe Theatre, *see* Theatre, Elizabethan
Gloriant (medieval Flemish play), 107
Glumov, —, 117
Gnedich, Nicolai I., 105 n.
Godfrey, D. R., 133–4
Gold, Käthe, 114
Goldsmith, Ulrich K., 136
Golubentsev, —, 117
Googe, Barnaby, *Eglogs*, 53
Gosson, Henry, Elizabethan printer, 26
　his quarto of *Pericles*, 26–38
Grace, W. G., 2
Granville-Barker, Harley, 87
Gray, Cecil G., 139 n.
Gray, H. D., 140, 151
Gray, Thomas, 59
Grécourt, Jean B. de, 93
Greece, report on Shakespeare in, 112
Green, Henry, 27
Green, Rev. Joseph, 57
Green, Robert, 139
　Groatsworth of Wit, 139
Greg, Sir W. W., 3, 20, 24, 25, 46 n., 51, 52, 54, 145–6
Gregor, Joseph, 110 n.
Grein, W. T., 108, 109
Greville, Fulke, 141
Gruyter, J. O. de, 108
Grylls, William, 50–1
Guizot, F., 105 n.
Günther, Alfred, 114
Guthrie, Tyrone, 119
Gyseghem, André van, 119, 120

Halkin, S., 113
Hall, Edward, 104, 139 n.
Hall, John, 57
Hall, Joseph, *The King's Prophecie* (1603), 138 n., 149

INDEX

Halliwell-Phillipps, J. O., 46 n., 57 n.

Handwriting as a source of textual corruption, 5, 34–5.

Hanmer, Sir Thomas, 51

Harbage, Alfred, 138

Harbord (Harbert), Thomas, 55

Harding, Davis P., 141

Hardy, Thomas, 130

Harrison, John, 120

Harsnett, Samuel, *A Declaration of Egregious Popish Impostures*, 134

Hart, Elizabeth (née Shakespeare), 56

Hart, George, 56

Hart, H. C., 19, 20, 80 n.

Hart, Shakespeare, 56–7

Hart, Thomas, 57

Harvey, Gabriel, 138

Hastings, W. T., 91 n.

Havilland, Olivia de, 115, 116

Havrevold, —, 113

Hawkins, Jack, 116

Hayes, A., 105 n.

Hayes, Helen, 115

Hazlitt, William, 98, 105 n.

Heilman, R. B., 85, 87, 88

Heminges, John, 140, 145

Hepburn, Katharine, 115

Heppenstall, Rayner, 134

Herbert of Cherbury, Lord, 139 n.

Herbert, T. Walter, 136

Herford, C. H., 105 n.

Herringman, H., seventeenth-century publisher, 51, 52

Hervey, William, 148

Heuer, Hermann, 112

Heyningen, Miss C. van, 113–14

Hill, C. J., 5

Hilpert, Heinz, 112

Hinman, Charlton, 47, 147

Hodges, C. Walter, 143

Hoeniger, F. D., 136

Holinshed, Raphael, 66–8, 87, 104, 135

Holmes, Elizabeth, 81

Holmes, Martin, 144 n.

Homer, 53

Hoppe, Harry R., 46 n., 47, 150

Hornstein, L. H., 91 n.

Hotson, Leslie, 138, 148–9

Houghton, Alexander, 139 n.

Houseman, John, 116

Housman, A. E., 2, 5, 147

Hubler, Edward, 138

Hughes, William, as the 'W. H.' of the *Sonnets*, 139 n.

Hunt, Hugh, 119, 120, 121, 122, 124

Hutcheson, W. J. Fraser, 139 n.

Imagery in Shakespeare's plays, *see under* Shakespeare

Innes, Michael, 134

Ireland, Samuel, 57 n.

Irving, Sir Henry, 107, 144 n.

Israel, report on Shakespeare in, 112–13

Italy, report on Shakespeare in, 113

Jaggard, William, printer of the First Folio, 21, 22, 23, 24 n., 145, 147

James I, King (James VI of Scotland) 68, 138 n., 140, 149
  Basilicon Doron, 68

James, D. G., 83

Jeans, Ursula, 122

Jenkins, Warren, 119

John, Anthony, 119

Johnson, Dr Samuel, 1, 51, 105 n.

Jones, Ernest, 131

Jones, Margo, 116

Jonson, Ben, 53
  Poetaster, 140
  Sejanus, 142

Jordan, Hoover H., 135

Jorgensen, Paul A., 135, 142

Joseph, B. L., 143–4

Joseph, Robert, 116

Joseph, Sister Miriam, 82

Joyce, James, *Ulysses*, 134

Kamashev, I. S., 105 n.

Karamzin, Nicolai M., 95, 98

Karthaios, K., 112

Keats, John, 1

Keen, Alan, 139 n.

Keen, Malcolm, 116

Kellner, Leon, 6

Kemp, William, 122

Kendrick (Kenwrick), Rev. Edward, 55

Khidoyatov, Abrar, 117

King's Men, *see* Theatre, Elizabethan

Kireevsky, Ivan V., 100–1

Kirschbaum, Leo, 25

Knight, G. Wilson, 62, 66, 81, 83, 85, 88, 138, 149

Knights, L. C., 71, 81

Knolles, Richard, *Generall Historie of the Turkes*, 144 n.

Kolbe, F. C., 91 n.

Krauss, Werner, 112

Kyd, Thomas, 139

Kyte, Sir William, 56

158

INDEX

Lanc, Emile, 111

Lancelot van Denemarken (medieval Flemish play) 107

Langham, Michael, 111, 119

Law, Robert Adger, 135

Lawlor, J. J., 132-3

L[ea], J[ames], 149

Leake, W., seventeenth-century publisher, 52

Le Comte, Edward S., 140

Lee, Sir Sidney, 147

Leech, Clifford, 136

  Shakespeare's Tragedies reviewed, 130-1

Letourneur, P., 105 n.

Lewis, Cecil Day, 88

Lewis, Michael, 149

Libraries (*see also under* British Museum; Cambridge;

  Trinity College Library)

  Folger Shakespeare Library, 51, 147

  Stadtbibliothek, Zurich, 46 n.

  University of Pennsylvania Library, 144 n.

Lirondelle, A., 105 n.

Livesey, Roger, 122, 125

Logeman, Henri, 110 n.

London (*see also* British Museum; Old Vic Theatre;

  Theatre, Elizabethan), 55

  Temple, the, 50

Long, John H., 140

Lopez, Roderigo, 140

Lucretius, 2

Lüdeke, H., 114

Lunt, Alfred, 115

Lyly, John, *Campaspe*, 139

McClellan, Kenneth, 120

Machiavelli, Niccolo, 72, 73

McIlwraith, A. K., 47

Mackail, J. W., 152

McKern, Leo, 122, 128

McKerrow, R. B., 10, 11, 12, 47, 54

Macowan, Michael, 119

Malone, Edmond, 19, 20, 25, 57 n.

Marder, Louis, 140

Marlowe, Christopher, 133, 139, 149

  Dr Faustus, 141

  Tamburlaine, 139, 144 n.

Marshak, S., 117

Marston, John, *Sophonisba*, 139

Martin, T., 53

Maxwell, J. C., 91 n., 134, 140, 141, 150-1

Mayer, Dorothea, 115

Menetto, Carlo A., 113

Meskin, Aharon, 112

Messel, Oliver, 116

Michell, Keith, 124

Middleton, Thomas, 148

  The Witch, 148

Milani, Luciana, 113

Milton, John, 50, 51

  Hermes, or, a guide to the elements, &c., 53

  Paradise Lost, 53, 75

Mincoff, Marco, 133

Miracle plays in Belgium, 106-7

Mochalov, P. S., 118

Modzalevsky, B. L. and L. B., 104

Molière (J. B. Poquelin), 101, 102, 131

Mommsen, T., 25

Mont, Pol de, 107

Monteyne, Lode, 110 n.

Moore, John R., 134, 140

Morality plays, 107, 141

Morley, Thomas, 115

  A Plaine and Easie Introduction to Practicall Musicke, 140

Morozov, M. M., 88

Moussorgsky, M. P., 100

Muir, Kenneth, 46 n., 92 n., 134, 146-7

  Arden *Macbeth* reviewed, 148

Murry, J. M., 91 n.

Mystery plays in Belgium, 106-7

Nashe, Thomas, 133

Neilson, W. A., 5

Neoplatonism, 72, 73, 80 n.

Neri, Nicoletta, 113

Neveux, Georges, 111

New Place, *see under* Stratford-upon-Avon

Newton, Sir Isaac, 53

Nicholas I, Tsar of Russia, 99-100

Nicoll, Allardyce, 92 n.

Ninchi, Annibale, 113

Norway, report on Shakespeare in, 113

Nosworthy, J. M., 151-2

Obey, André, 111

O'Connor, Frank, 92 n.

Oehlenschläger, A., 52

Okes, Nicholas, Jacobean printer, 22

Old Vic Company, 115, 119, 120

  production of *Henry V*, 125-8

  production of *Twelfth Night*, 121-4

Old Vic Theatre, 115, 120, 121

Olive, W. J., 142

O'Loughlin, S., 92 n.

Onions, C. T., 20

INDEX

Ossian (James MacPherson), 93
Ost, Geoffrey, 119
Ovid, 137, 139
Oxford, Earl of (Edward Harley, 1689–1741), 55, 56
Oxford English Dictionary, The, 20, 24 n.

Pagnani, —, 113
Pallin, Ingemar, 114
Parkes, H. B., 141
Parny, Viscount de (1753–1814), 93
Parsons, Howard, 140
Pasquier, Paul, 115
Pasternak, Boris, 117
Pastore, Annibale, 113
Paterson, John, 133
Pearmain, Vincent, 119
Peele, George, 139, 150–1
    David and Bethsabe, 150
    The Old Wives' Tale, 141
Peery, William, 142
Pembroke, William Herbert, Earl of, 138
Perrett, A. J., 138
Pettet, E. C., 135
Pilgrim Trust, 53
'Piracy' of Shakespearian texts, 35–8, 129, 151–2
Plaksin, V., 105 n.
Plautus, 53
Pogodin, M. P., 100
Pogson, Beryl, 132
Polevoy, N. A., 100
Policardi, Silvio, 113
Pollard, A. W., 3, 25, 50, 51, 152
    with Redgrave, G. R., *Short-Title Catalogue*; reference
    numbers to books in Trinity College Library, Cam-
    bridge, 51–4
Pope, Alexander, 15 n., 19, 20, 50, 51
    The Dunciad, 1
Popović, Vladeta, 144 n.
Porson, Richard, 2
Portland Papers in the British Museum, 55, 57 n.
Potter, Peter, 120
Printing, Elizabethan methods of, 5–7, 18, 21–2, 24
    and n., 28–35, 144–5, 146, 147, 150
    distinguishing marks of compositors of *Pericles*, 47–9
Prior, Moody, 88, 92 n.
Proclemer, Anna, 113
Productions of Shakespeare's plays:
    in the United Kingdom during 1950, 119–20
    Old and Young Vic productions reviewed, 121–8
    recent performances abroad, 108–9, 111–18
Psychological interpretation of Shakespeare's plays, 131–2

Psychology, Elizabethan, 142
Punctuation of Shakespeare's plays, 3–4, 47–9, 146
Pushkin, Alexander, 117
    Shakespeare's influence on, 93–104
    Boris Godunov, 93, 94–8, 99–100, 101, 102–3, 104, 105 n.
    Evgeny Onegin, 93–4
    Little Tragedies, 101–2, 103, 105 n.
    Poltava, 93
    The Captain's Daughter, 104
    The Gypsies, 94
    The Stone Guest, 105 n.

Quadflieg, Will, 115
Quayle, Anthony, 119
Quiller-Couch, Sir A. T., 131

Racine, Jean, 10, 93, 111
Raevsky, N. N., 94, 105 n.
Raleigh, Sir Walter (1861–1922), 129
Rand, Frank P., 135
Randone, Salvo, 113
Ravid, Shoshanna, 112
Redgrave, G. R., *see* Pollard, A. W.
Reed, Isaac, 105 n.
Reinhardt, Max, 116
Religious thought in Shakespeare's plays, *see* Theological
    significance
'Reporting' of Shakespeare's plays, 17, 22–4, 26–8, 35–8,
    40, 41, 45, 150–2
Reynolds, George F., 143
Richards, I. A., 83, 91 n., 130
Richter, Walter, 114
Roberts, James, Elizabethan printer, 52
Robeson, Paul, 115
Robinson, Heath, 129
Rogers, Paul, 122, 127
Ronde, Th. de, 110 n.
Rondiris, D., 112
Rossi, Ernesto, 107
Rotas, V., 112
Rouve, Pierre, 119
Rovina, Hannah, 112
Rowe, Nicholas, 2, 25, 50, 51, 144
Royal Netherlands Theatre, Antwerp, 107–8, 109
Rylands, G. H. W., 87

Sabbe, Maurits, 110 n.
Sackton, A. H., 81
Sanderson, Cobden, 51
Sanvic, Romain, 111
Sargent, Ralph M., 141

INDEX

Savage, D. S., *Hamlet and the Pirates* reviewed, 129
Saxe-Meiningen, Duke of, 107
Saxo Grammaticus, 131
Schibler, Armin, 115
Schiller, J. C. F. von, 10, 132
  Schlegel-Tieck translation of Shakespeare, 111
Schmitt, Saladin, 112
Schröder, Rudolf A., 112
Schubert, Franz, 112
Schücking, Levin L., 114
Scott, Sir Walter, 94, 99, 100, 103, 104
Sen Gupta, S. C., *Shakespearian Comedy* reviewed, 131
Sewell, George, 51
Shaaber, M. A., 15 n.
Shakeshaft, William, as identifiable with Shakespeare, 139 n.
Shakespeare, William:
  authorship problems: in *Pericles*, 25, 45; in *Titus Andronicus*, 150–1
  biographical studies of, 139–40
  biographical suggestions about, 53, 55–6, 129, 137–9, 142, 149–50
  concept of comedy, 131, 135–6, 141
  concept of tragedy, 66–9, 130–1, 133
  earlier editions of, 1–2, 19–21, 25, 51
  editing for continental readers, 10–15
  family, 56–7
  handwriting, 5, 34–5
  imagery, 132,134,135,136,138; nature and functions of, 62–5, 81–92; use in *Othello*, 66–80; in *Macbeth*, 66–8
  influence on Pushkin, 93–105
  New Place, 55–7
  'piracy' of texts, 35–8, 129, 151–2
  printing methods in early texts, 5–7, 18, 21–2, 24 and n., 28–35, 47–9, 144–5, 146, 147, 150
  psychological interpretation of plays, 131–2
  punctuation in early texts, 3–4, 47–9, 146
  recent performances: in England, 119–20, 121–8; abroad, 108–9, 111–18
  'reporting' of plays, 17, 22–4, 26–8, 35–8, 40, 41, 45, 150–2
  textual problems: in general, 1–9, 16–17, 144–8, 150–2; in *Othello*, 18–24, 80 n.; in *Pericles*, 25–49
  theological significance in plays, 66–80, 87, 141
  tomb in Stratford Church, 55, 56–7
  topical references in *Sonnets*, 137–8, 148–9
  traditions of acting his plays in Belgium, 106–10
  translations: in Afrikaans, 113–14; in European languages, 50, 51, 52, 111, 112, 113, 115, 117–18; in Hebrew, 52

  use of source material, 66, 71, 134, 135, 137, 140, 141, 142
  versification, 136–7
  will; copy at Shakespeare's Birthplace, 56, 57
  works relating to in Trinity College Library, Cambridge, 50–4
  Plays:
    All's Well, 3, 109, 120, 135–6
    Antony and Cleopatra, 8, 26, 51, 64–5, 68, 89, 91 n., 113, 116, 130, 132, 138, 142, 143, 148, 149
    As You Like It, 13, 15 n., 109, 112, 114, 115, 116, 119, 120
    Comedy of Errors, 116, 117, 120
    Coriolanus, 97, 113, 130, 146
    Cymbeline, 109
    Hamlet, 4, 21, 26, 37, 41, 51, 72, 78, 84, 86, 89, 91 n., 98, 107, 108, 109, 111, 112, 113, 114, 115, 117, 118, 119, 129, 131, 140, 146, 149–50, 151–2; notes on acting, 58–61; current criticism of, 132–4
    Henry IV (2 parts), 51, 95, 119, 139; influence on Pushkin's *Boris Godunov*, 96–7
    Henry V, 21, 51, 54, 97, 135, 150; Old Vic production reviewed, 125–8
    Henry VI (3 parts), 7, 52, 132, 139
    Henry VIII, 119
    John, 112, 114
    Julius Caesar, 24 n., 97, 107, 109, 112, 113, 116, 119, 120, 130, 135, 143
    Lear, 52, 63, 68, 70, 71, 72, 85, 87, 90, 96, 109, 111, 112, 115, 116, 118, 120, 131–2, 134, 141, 142, 144, 146–7, 151
    Love's Labours Lost, 4, 52, 116, 139, 144 n.
    Macbeth, 52, 63, 64, 71–2, 73, 75, 76, 86, 87, 89–90, 92 n., 95–6, 109, 111, 112, 113, 114, 116, 117, 119, 120, 130, 134, 136, 141, 144 n., 147, 148; theological significances in, 66–8, 78–9; imagery in, 82, 83–5
    Measure for Measure, 8, 43, 44, 68, 102, 108, 109, 117, 119, 136, 141, 142, 144 n.
    Merchant of Venice, 5, 24 n., 52, 101, 107, 108, 109, 113, 115, 116, 119, 120, 122; Young Vic production reviewed, 124–5
    Merry Wives, 3, 52, 108, 109, 111, 112, 117, 120
    Midsummer Night's Dream, 21, 52, 108, 109, 111, 112, 116, 119, 120, 122, 132
    Much Ado, 52, 109, 112, 113, 114, 116, 117
    Othello, 5, 6–7, 41, 52, 54, 63, 64, 89, 107, 108, 109, 111, 112, 113, 115, 116, 118, 119, 120, 135, 147; diabolic imagery in, 66–80; popularity in U.S.S.R., 117; relation of 1622 Quarto to First Folio text, 16–24

Shakespeare, William (*cont.*)

    Pericles, 52, 120, 142; textual corruption in, 25–8; distribution of verse and prose, 28–34; 1609 Quarto a reported text, 35–8; relationship to G. Wilkins's *The Painfull Aduentures of Pericles Prince of Tyre*, 39–45; evidence relating to compositors, 47–9

    Richard II, 52, 86, 95, 96, 115, 119, 120, 135, 143

    Richard III, 23, 24 n., 52, 95, 97, 102, 108, 109, 111, 114, 136; parallels with *Sonnets* and *Venus and Adonis*, 137–8

    Romeo and Juliet, 25, 26, 52, 54, 105 n., 107, 108, 109, 111, 112, 113, 115, 116, 117, 119, 135, 139, 145, 146, 151

    Taming of the Shrew, 52, 108, 109, 111, 112, 114, 115, 116, 117, 119, 120, 140

    Tempest, 3, 52, 78, 112, 113, 115, 131–2

    Timon of Athens, 2, 83, 89, 115, 130, 137, 142, 145

    Titus Andronicus, 4, 53; authorship question, 150–1

    Troilus and Cressida, 5, 53, 89, 120, 144, 145

    Twelfth Night, 65, 107, 108, 109, 111, 112, 113, 115, 116, 117, 119, 120, 142; Old Vic production reviewed, 121–4

    Two Gentlemen, 113, 141

    Winter's Tale, 63, 64, 65, 79, 107, 108, 109, 112, 114–5, 119, 120, 136

  Poems:

    Lucrece, 33, 147

    Passionate Pilgrim, 50, 53

    Sonnets, 53, 136–7, 139; evidence for dating, 137–8, 148–9

    Venus and Adonis, 50, 53, 137, 147, 149

  Editions:

    Arden, 80 n., 148

    Bad Quartos, 7–8, 23, 25–6, 28, 31, 37, 39, 150–1

    Cambridge edition (1863), 25, 50, 51, 54

    Early Quartos, 4, 5–7, 11–12, 16–24, 51–3, 54, 144–5, 146, 150–2

    First Folio, 2, 3, 4, 5–9, 12–13, 15 n., 25, 50, 54, 80 n., 144, 145, 146, 147, 151; text of *Othello* in relation to the 1622 Quarto, 16–24

    Second, Third and Fourth Folios, 9, 50–4

    Globe edition, 2, 3, 33, 46 n., 68, 79 n.

    New Cambridge edition, 4, 139, 148, 150

    Poems (1640), 53, 54

    Proposals for an edition for continental readers, 10–15

    Recent editions reviewed, 148–9

  Translations: into Afrikaans, 113–14; into European languages, 50, 51, 52, 111, 112, 113, 115, 117–18; into Hebrew, 52

  Eighteenth-century editions, 13; in Trinity College Library, Cambridge, 50–4

Shakespeare Association, 46 n.

Shakespeare Memorial Theatre, Stratford-upon-Avon, 58, 115, 119, 120, 121

Shapiro, I. A., 149

Sharpe, Ella Freeman, 131–2

Shaw, George Bernard, 131, 132

Shaw, Glen Byam, 120, 124, 125, 126–7

Shchepkina-Kupernik, T. L., 117

Shield, H. A., 139 n.

Shorthand, Elizabethan, its use for 'reporting' plays, 151

Shute, Anne, 53

Shuttleworth, Bertram, 144 n.

Sidney, Sir Philip, 137

  Arcadia, 137

Siegel, Paul N., 136

Šimko, Ján, 144 n.

Simmons, E. J., 105 n.

Simpson, Percy, 2–3, 4, 140, 146, 152

Singer, S. W., 19

Sisson, C. J., 46 n.

Sitwell, Edith, 73

Skinner, B. F., 136

Skouloudis, M., 112

Smidt, K., 134, 150

Smirnov, A. A., 117

Smith, Brian, 128

Smith, Irwin, 143

Smith, R. M., 51, 136

Smith, Warren, 143

Solomos, A., 112

Sources, Shakespeare's use of, 66, 71, 134, 135, 137, 140, 141, 142

South Africa, report on Shakespeare in, 113–14

Southampton, Henry Wriothesley, Earl of, 137, 148

Speed, John, 149

Spenser, Edmund, 50, 89, 138, 139 n., 142

  Faerie Queene, 146

  Hymne in Honour of Beautie, 80 n.

Spielmann, M. H., 57 n.

Spurgeon, Caroline F. E., 62, 81, 82–3, 84–5, 86, 87, 88, 91 n., 92 n.

Stadtbibliothek, Zürich, *see under* Libraries

Staging of Shakespeare's plays, *see under* Theatre, Elizabethan; Theatres; Productions of Shakespeare's plays

Stamm, Rudolf, 112

Stanislavsky, Konstantin, 117

Stanton, Thomas, 55

Stationers' Register, entries in, 26

Stauffer, D. A., 92 n.

INDEX

Steevens, George, 105 n.

Stirling, Brents, 135

Stoll, E. E., 114, 135, 136

Stow, John, 149

Strachey, Lytton, 122, 136

Strachey, William, 142

Stratford-upon-Avon (*see also* Shakespeare Memorial Theatre), 55–7, 140

New Place, 55–7

Shakespeare's birthplace, 57

Shakespeare's tomb, 55, 56–7

Sugden, Edward H., 80 n.

Swan Theatre, *see* Theatre, Elizabethan

Sweden, report on Shakespeare in, 114

Switzerland, report on Shakespeare in, 114–15

Sypher, Willie, 136

Terence, 53

Textual problems, *see under* Shakespeare; Emendation of texts

Theatre, Elizabethan, 103, 151; private stages, 139; problems of staging and acting, 143–4; public stages, 143

Company: King's Men, 142, 143, 148

Theatres: Globe, 143; Swan, 143

Theatres, *see* Old Vic Theatre; Royal Netherlands Theatre, Antwerp; Shakespeare Memorial Theatre

See also under Belgium; Czechoslovakia; Germany; Israel; Italy; Norway; South Africa; Sweden; Switzerland; U.S.A.; U.S.S.R.; Productions of Shakespeare's plays; Shakespeare, William, recent performances

Theobald, Lewis, 1–2, 16, 20, 21, 50, 51, 52, 80 n.

Theological significance in Shakespeare's plays, 66–80, 87, 141–2

Thiselton, Alfred, 3, 8–9, 146

Thomas, Powys, 125

Thomas, Sir Henry, 46 n.

Thorpe, Thomas, 148

Tieck, Ludwig, *see* Schlegel, August W. von

Tilney, Edmund, 139

Tkhapsayev, —, 117

Tolstoy, Count Alexis, 104

Topical references in the *Sonnets*, *see under* Shakespeare

Torsslow, —, 114

Tourneur, Cyril, *The Atheist's Tragedy*, 66, 69–70, 132

Tourneur, P. le. *see* Letourneur, P.

Traditions of acting his plays in Belgium, *see under* Shakespeare

Tragedy, Shakespeare's concept of, 66–9, 130–1, 133

Translations of Shakespeare's plays, *see* under Shakespeare

Traversi, Derek, 135

Trinity College Library, Cambridge; Shakespeare collection described, 50–4

Tsyavlovsky, M. A., 104 n., 105 n.

Turner, David, 120

Tutin, Dorothy, 126

Tuve, Rosemond, 83, 86, 91 n.

Twine, Laurence, *The Patterne of Painefull Adventures*, 39

Ubaldini, P., 149

Unities, Dramatic, *see* Dramatic Unities

University of Pennsylvania Library, *see under* Libraries

U.S.A., report on Shakespeare in, 115–16

U.S.S.R., report on Shakespeare in, 117–18

Vakhtangov, E., 117

Valentine, C. W., 92 n.

Vandermeulen, Gaston, 108

Vega, Lope de, 94

Verdi, Giuseppi, 117

Verney, Guy, 119

Versification, Shakespeare's, 136–7

Vertue, George, account of New Place, 55–7

Virgil, 53

Vocht, Henry de, 110 n.

Voltaire (François Marie Arouet), 93

Vyazemsky, Prince Peter A., 105 n.

Walker, Alice, 10, 144–5

Walker, Roy, 87

Walpole, Horace, 55

Walpole Society, 57 n.

Walter, J. H., 150

Warburton, John, 51

Ward, R., 119

Watkins, Ronald, 120

On Producing Shakespeare reviewed, 143

Watkins, W. B. C., 142

Watson, Douglas, 116

Webster, Margaret, 116

Weigelin, Ernst, 134

Wells, H. W., 81, 83, 86, 89

West, Hon. James, 57

Whateley, Anne, 139 n.

Whole Contention between…Lancaster and York, see *Contention betwixt…Yorke and Lancaster*

Wilkins, George, 39

The Painfull Aduentures of Pericles Prince of Tyre, 26, 39–45

Wilkinson, Allan, 150

INDEX

Williams, George W., 134

Williams, Philip, 144, 145

Willis, John, *Stenographie*, 151

Willoughby, E. E., 47, 144, 147

Wilson, F. P., 137

Wilson, John Dover, 4–5, 61, 139, 148, 150, 152

Wiman, Dwight D., 116

Wincor, Richard, 136

Witt, Johannes de, *see* De Witt, Johannes

Wolfe, John, Elizabethan printer, 146

Wolfit, Donald, 120

Wright, J., Elizabethan bookseller, 53

Wright, W. Aldis (*see also* Clark, W. G.), 50, 54

Yarmolinsky, A., 105 n.

Young Vic Company, production of *Merchant of Venice* reviewed, 120, 124–5

Zalkinson, Isaac E., 113

Zankevich, M., 117

Zavadsky, Y. A., 117

Zelinsky, V. A., 104 n.

Zellwecker, Edwin, 111

Zhukovsky, V. A., 99